# ESSENTIAL POEMS AND WRITINGS
## of
# ROBERT DESNOS

Desnos and the journalist Jesus Ortega à la terrasse des Deux Magots en 1929. (Archives Éditions Gallimard)

# ESSENTIAL POEMS AND WRITINGS

## OF

# ROBERT DESNOS

EDITED
WITH AN INTRODUCTION & ESSAY
by
MARY ANN CAWS

Translated by
MARY ANN CAWS, TERRY HALE, MARTIN SORRELL,
JONATHAN EBURNE, BILL ZAVATSKY, KATHARINE CONLEY,
PATRICIA TERRY, STEPHEN ROMER, TIMOTHY ADÈS,
PAUL AUSTER &  KENNETH REXROTH

BLACK
WIDOW
PRESS

BOSTON, MASS.

ESSENTIAL POEMS AND WRITINGS OF ROBERT DESNOS

Black Widow Press edition, December 2007

French texts from: *Destinée Arbitraire* © Editions Gallimard, 1975,
*Rayons et ombres*, © Editions Gallimard, 1992, *Domaine public*, © Editions Gallimard,
1953, *Corps et biens*, © Editions Gallimard, 1953, *Fortunes*, © Editions Gallimard 1945,
*Deuil pour Deuil*, © 1962, Editions Gallimard, *Oeuvres*, ed. M-C Dumas, © Editions
Gallimard, 1999. All French texts with permission of Editions Gallimard, Paris.

English language excerpts from *Mourning for Mourning (Deuil Pour Deuil)* and from
*Liberty or Love! (La Liberte ou L'amour!)* translated by Terry Hale are reprinted by
arrangement with BCM Atlas Press, UK. (www.atlaspress.co.uk). For both titles the
English language translations © Atlas Press (1994 & 1993). BWP thanks Atlas Press
for allowing us to include these passages in this anthology. All other English language
translations: All rights reserved by individual translators. All reprinted by permission. All
© 2007.

Special thanks to Marie-Claire Dumas and Jacques Fraenkel for their advice and help.

Introduction, arrangement, and essays © 2007 Mary Ann Caws

cover photo: Robert Desnos, 1929 (courtesy of Archives Éditions Gallimard)

Black Widow Press is an imprint of Commonwealth Books, Inc., Boston.
Joseph S. Phillips, Publisher.

All Black Widow Press books are printed on acid-free paper and put into sewn and
glued bindings. Black Widow Press is a registered trademark of Commonwealth Books,
Inc.

Black Widow Press
www.blackwidowpress.com

ISBN-13: 978-0-9768449-9-0
ISBN-10: 0-9768449-9-0

Library of Congress Cataloging-in-Publication Data
available at the Library of Congress: www.loc.gov

Prepress production by Windhaven Press (www.windhaven.com)
Printed by Thomson-Shore
Printed in the United States

10  9  8  7  6  5  4  3  2  1

# CONTENTS

NB: Translations without a translator noted are all by Mary Ann Caws.

Page numbers when not otherwise ascribed refer to the *Quarto Edition*, ed. Marie-Claire Dumas, Gallimard, 1999

DA       *Destinée arbitraire*, ed. Marie-Claire Dumas, Poésie/Gallimard, 1975
RO       *Les Rayons et les ombres*, ed.  M-C Dumas, Gallimard, 1992, 2006
DP       *Domaine public*, Gallimard 1953

Il a levé l'ancre pour toujours. Il
vogue. Son sillage enserre le monde.
Les éléments, les frontières et les
hommes ne peuvent rien contre lui, et
son étrave immaterielle est des celles
qui brisent les recifs les plus aigus.
(«Le Cuirassé Potemkine,» *Cinéma*)


(He has raised anchor forever. He is at
sail. His wake includes the world.
Elements, limits, and men are powerless
against him, and his immaterial
bowsprit is able to shatter the most
difficult shoals.)

# Introduction:
# The Poet-Adventurer

Surrealist poetry allows us, by its own tenets, no safe spot from which to look on; this is a cardinal point of surrealist poetics. But Desnos is unlike his fellow surrealists Breton, Péret, Eluard, and Aragon, none of whom force such a frequent awareness of the page as page, of the obsession as obsession. For that reason, Desnos' writing, close to contemporary sensibility in its self-consciousness, finds forms of irony and tragedy sufficiently complicated to retain our interest even after much close reading, even as they occur with a rare predictability. In the reader's place, which an author like Desnos would seem to invade, we may be forced to concur in the presence and the distance at which Desnos places himself in regard to his work, in the self-reflective or meta-texts where he becomes, and outspokenly, his own reader.

What has fascinated so many readers of Desnos over the years since his death of typhoid fever in the concentration camp of Terezina at 45, is his variousness and the feeling of his very present presentness, even now, years later. His writings could be broken down by theme, by style, and by image, but he maintained that all of them are part of one poem, the fragments of a great work of the subconscious. What is essential is the continuity, throughout the various styles and themes and images, of his poetic voice, in his poems, novels, and essays. And that, despite the difference in tone and subject, is the unifying feature, unmistakable from beginning to end. It has often been remarked upon: "The epoch departing with the swiftness of dream singles itself out, shaping in our memory fabulous contours where

1

there is inscribed, where there resounds the voice of Robert Desnos, this breathy, sustained and staccato voice which, even then, always seemed to hail us from a great distance."[1]

The most familiar works are those that date from 1922 to 1929. After 1930, he might be seen to turn aside from what I have been calling the language of poetic adventure and toward the more traditional forms which had always interested him, and a more popular vein. The obsessions so appealing in his major works give way to an attitude which might be called humanistic or journalistic (see the remarks of André Breton in 1930 after Desnos' separation from the surrealists), but it is in any case entirely different, determining a different style.

And yet in general, this great poet's work can be seen—in all its periods—as structured around the typical surrealist oppositions of dream and reality, nocturnal and diurnal vision, presence and absence. These are the poetic parallels, as I read them, to the everpresent vision of the daily, nightly, and ubiquitous surrealist marvelous. At the center of the work are the elements of movement, myth, and voyage, all intimately connected—whatever their component of dream or of reality—to the parallel concepts of language and of love. They are, in his view, inseparable. His very being, as a poet, is involved in his being as lover, and that is lifelong. His early fascination with the singer Yvonne George, an attraction that was unreciprocated, inspired the poems of *A la Mystérieuse* and *Les Ténèbres*. At her early death, from drugs and tuberculosis, he turned to a beloved friend Youki, the wife of the painter Foujita, who so named her, with the Japanese term for "pink snow," and who left her, knowing Desnos would take care of her, as he did. "I who am Robert Desnos/ To love you," as he was always to say of his loves, early and late.

Desnos's work moves from verbal games and grammatical deformations toward a more complex poetry and poetic prose, in which however, the language is as self-reflective as in the earliest poems, and subsequently outward to a more public domain, epitomized by his essays on imagery,

---

[1]   Georges Neveux, "Robert Desnos," *Confluences*, no. 7, Sept 1945, p. 680.

poetic revolution, and on the importance of cinema, as by his involvement with publicity and radio transmissions. Seen in another light, it moves from a youthful stress of word play and verbal mobility, in his poetic experiments, through the development of an interest in the power of communication and public expression, to a more formally structured work.

The early novels excerpted here: *Mourning for Mourning* and *Liberty or Love!* both construct and simultaneously destroy their own myth so brilliantly elaborated in a manner identical with that of Desnos' greatest poems. In an apparently conscious projection, epic adventure appears always to be juxtaposed with and perhaps even absorbed by the mockery of that adventure. For it is evident that the building up and the tearing down of emotion, the creation and undoing of myth, the development and destruction of adventure, apply also to our reading.

Our own involvement is increased and then parodied as the poet stresses, and then mocks his own emotions, attacking the pathetic repetitions of love, the sameness of myth, the melodrama of adventure, as well as the conventions of literature. "Banalité! Banalité!", Desnos will say of his own writing: it is both a desert, or a deserted beach where we might wander in the guise of an explorer (as in his novel *Liberty or Love!*) or as a madman, at the mercy of the wind. Our own self-reflections, summoned by his, seem to me the highest tribute we can pay to the voice of Robert Desnos, and the most faithful witness to its appeal. For the appeal is certainly not to any lovely landscape, or any easily-won construction. No, the work is marked by cadavers, ice floes for the stranding of vessels, and shards of broken bottles. The constructions are as desolate as the geography and the landscape: the deserted corridors of a palace, the bare stretches of a desert, or an endless beach where the figure of a mermaid forsakes the shore forever, or a path where all the foliage is withered. In an obsessed and obsessive universe, amid all the images of desolation, the problem of the reader's attitude poses itself with insistency. This intermingling of the personal reading in the text itself is in large part responsible for the presence of this eternally young poet of adventure.

—M.A.C.

# I. Novels

# Novels

It is in his lyric novels that Desnos writes his most characteristic and involved prose poetry: the narrative often seems secondary to the style, for which it serves as a mere prop. The details of structure within *Deuil pour deuil* and *La Liberté ou l'amour!* such as the repetitive or litanic form, the play of dualities, and the extended catalogue, are simple in appearance and vastly complicated in inner variations. Of course *Deuil pour deuil* and *La Liberté ou l'amour!* are also written in the form of novels, a form they undermine by the easy predominance of their images and their odd lyricism over any pretence at plot. All questions about occurrences or development of situation or psychological characterization would be as pointless as a demand to know what happens next after the encounter between the sewing machine and the umbrella on Lautréamont's dissection table. It all happens at once, like surrealist's convulsive beauty, or it happens not at all.

As for the essential scenery and figuration in the Desnos novels, which are in reality long narrative poems in prose, the meetings or associations between a light blue jacket, a skeleton, and a blonde virgin, or between a white-helmeted explorer, a pirate, and a woman clothed only in a leopard-skin coat are signs of the marvelous, encounters whose importance will be magnified by all the resources of surrealist genius until they assume the proportions of myth. The background of deserted and sunny squares pervaded by ennui remind us not only of the early de Chirico, but also of Breton's meditation on ennui in "Poisson soluble" and of his "mysterious road where fear lurks at every step"; the evocation of human loneliness by the presence of ruins and deserts, of hotel rooms and vast expanses of sea, is a successful surrealist and post-symbolist technique. Furthermore, the transformation of coffee into tea, of wine first into a dove and then into a crown, and of the wineglass into an hourglass and finally into a glass eye can be taken as perfect illustrations of Breton's remarks on openness and fusion.

Desnos' novels are linked to those of the other surrealists by a whole range of similarities, including imagery, scenery, and general statement. To take only one example, both in *La Liberté ou l'amour!* and in Louis Aragon's *Le Paysan de Paris,* there are to be found, in juxtaposition, extensive catalogues of varieties of sponges on the one hand and of city streets on the other, two objects which one might see as complementary, the former absorbing and the latter offering for exhibition. Compare, in this light, the passage in Desnos' novel which describes Bébé Cadum and the bath (soap and sponge) and that in Aragon's describing the barbershop (lather, soap, and sponge); or the description of the place de la Concorde in the former, and that of the passage de l'Opéra in the latter. So much for the apparently trivial: both novels make, specifically and by their entire implication, the point that ideas can be concrete only, never abstract, which in itself explains the intense interest of specific images and scenes. In both, the latter are far more striking than the hero's wanderings which serve as their pretext. One might make a case for each as a latter-day picaresque novel, with Paris as the overall scene for the peregrinations, whose stopping points are each the source of a lyric construction.

But Desnos always makes a point of denying any element of the marvelous to be found within writing itself. He repeatedly asserts the value of life against the sterility of the word, far more frequently than the other surrealists: many aspects of his style can be seen as directly related to that attitude.

The encounters, that take place on the page—all the supposed witnesses to a marvelous chance, to an intimate link between outer circumstances and inner desire—are vain ones for him. The surrealist hope of a writing so efficacious that the paper will reflect, like a mirror, all the poet's perceptions is illusory. Each mention of the marvelous is subsequently mocked. Juxtaposed with his celebrated creed: "I still believe in the marvelous when it concerns love, I believe in the reality of dreams" (LA, 48) is an ironic paragraph, beginning "Banalité! Banalité!", where Desnos pokes fun at the "sensual" style and the flowing prose in which writers usually, he says, speak of love, and commands his own style to be absurd, insufficient, and paltry, in a deliberate contrast to the vivacity of the action. His novels are marked by his tragic perception of the separation between the poet's voice or his letter on the one hand and the surrealities of life or love on the other: it is just these stylistic witnesses to his vision which gives to the novels their peculiarly poetic finality.

Bibliothèque Littéraire Jacques-Doucet © Man Ray Trust/ARS

1924
# extracts from *Deuil pour Deuil (Mourning for Mourning)*
### translated by Terry Hale[1]


THESE RUINS ARE SITUATED ON THE BANKS OF A WINDING river. The town must have been quite sizeable at some time in history. A few large buildings, a network of underground galleries, and a number of towers of bizarre construction are still to be seen. In these sunny, and deserted squares fear takes hold of us. But despite our fear, nobody, absolutely nobody, approaches us. The ruins are uninhabited. To the south-west, a tall edifice of some kind, open-sided and made of metal, has been erected, the purpose of which remains uncertain. It looks as if it is on the brink of toppling over, for it leans out at an angle above the river:

"Strange diseases, curious customs—where is the bell's clapper of love leading me? Amongst these stones I can find no vestige of that for which I am searching. The imperturbable and ever-changing mirror reveals to me only myself. Is the deserted town, a Sahara, the place where our magnificent encounter must necessarily occur? I watched from afar the arrival of beautiful millionairesses with their caravans of camels brocaded in gold. I waited for them, tormented and unmoved. Before they reached me they turned into shrivelled old women coated in dust, their drivers transformed into dotards. I have become accustomed to bursting into laughter at these funeral rites which serve me for a landscape. I have lived whole eternities in dark tunnels deep in the mines. I have fought with marble-white vampires but despite my clever words I was really always all alone in the padded cell where I tried my best to give birth to fire through the impact of my hard brain against the incredibly soft walls and to recall the memory of imaginary hips.

"That which I did not know, I invented better than any eighteen-carat America, than the cross or a wheel-barrow. Love! Love! I will summon you no more to describe the humming attributes of aircraft engines. I will speak of you tritely, for the commonplace is better calculated to set off the extraordinary adventure which I have been planning since my earliest words of whatever gender. As is fitting, I have taught old men to respect my black hair, and women to adore my limbs, but with respect to the latter I have always conserved my extensive yellow dominion where I ceaselessly confront the metallic vestiges of the high, inexplicable, pyramid-shaped construction in the distance. Love, would you condemn me to make of these ruins a ball of clay in which to carve my own likeness, or should I draw it forth as a weapon from my own eyes? In that case, which eye should I employ for this purpose and would it not be more advantageous for me to use both in order to fashion a pair of lovers that I can blindly rape, a new Homer standing on the Pont des Arts whose sinister arches I should gropingly undermine, at the risk of being abandoned, incapable of directing my steps towards the great yellow expanses teaming with sunshine where muskets stand guard over dead sentries. Love, would you condemn me to become the guardian spirit of these ruins and shall I live henceforth forever young amidst the little the white ruins allow me to glimpse of the moon?"

It was at this moment that they appeared. Pilotless planes weaving rings of smoke round enormous immobile air-borne light-houses perched on cliffs of ever-changing shapes, fanned out like an apotheosis. It was at this moment that they appeared:

The first wore a three-cornered hat, black tails and a white waistcoat; the second leg-of-mutton sleeves and a ruff; and the third a low-cut black silk chemisette that slipped from left to right and from right to left to reveal alternately, as far as the first hint of her breasts, two white but slightly swarthy shoulders.

I possess in high degree the arrogance of my sex. The humiliation of a man before a woman will either render me feverish and taciturn for days at a time or produce a white rage within me that I can only assuage by studied cruelties inflicted upon certain animals or objects; nonetheless, I seek out these inflammatory sights which occasionally force me to block my ears and shut my eyes.

I do not believe in God, but I have a sense of the infinite. No one has a more religious nature than I. I run up against unanswerable questions all the time. The questions that I acknowledge to myself are all unanswerable. Others would only be posed by people lacking in imagination and do not interest me.

These ruins are situated on the banks of a winding river. There is nothing special about the climate here. To the south-west, a tall edifice of some kind, open-sided and made of metal, has been erected, the purpose of which remains uncertain.

"KILL HIM! KILL HIM!" SCREAM THE AUDIENCE. I COULD SEE nothing of the tragic spectacle. Half-naked girls, strong men, young lads— they came and they went. But the monotonous, disturbing procession of people motivated by the same fears and the same desires does not produce drama. That resides in the fate of a shutter half-torn from its hinges which the lugubrious winter winds repeatedly shook as they laboured to rip it off completely in order, no doubt, to install it in some unknown window in the sky, probably the very same one at which every day at ten or three o'clock a beautiful blonde, stripped to the waist, silently waters a pot of geraniums while mentally comparing the blueness of her own eyes with the until then incomparable blueness of the sky deeper than a sea plied by the largest vessels whose cruel bows cut deep into the waves and remind the sleeping sharks amongst the coral that they have long since eaten all the fish to be found in these oceanic regions and that they are still hungry. The splash of tails then transforms the calm surface on which Gauguin's islands lie dream- ing and the women, dream-like stars bent over their own reflections at the portholes, the red eyes of the steamer, ask themselves what tremendous passion suddenly stirs these tarnished silver underbellies, those fearsome quadruple jaws with their soft red palates and dorsal fins whose colour recalls the peaceful sofas of fashionable smoking-rooms without it ever occurring to them that this very construction specially assembled to transport them to distant places was alone responsible for awakening those aquatic monsters, making their fins ring with the urge to travel and endowing their healthy frames with the unexpected agility required for them to head for temperate zones, whether arctic or tropical, to seek new prey, and steeling them for the dishonourable slaughter of myriads of pink shrimps in shallow waters.

In the end, the wind carried off the shutter. The sun made use of it to flay with alternate stripes of sunshine and shadow the crowd clamouring: "Kill him! Kill him!" in the street in which I vainly stand on tiptoe to discover the cause of so much hatred, while still following out of "THE CORNER OF MY EYE" the baroque flight of the shutter being supernaturally borne away by the wind towards, without any doubt whatsoever, the mysterious window. My double vigil was not in vain. The shutter slipped on to the invisible hinges of a window at which a gorgeous brunette with limpid eyes appeared at the very moment when, naked except for blindfolded breasts, she triumphantly escaped the reach of the crowd—who were still cowardly clamouring for an execution—before they even managed to place their little fingers on the white shoulders and majestic neck of she who, from the window high in the sky, studied their useless antics. Eventually she noticed me and said: "I know who you are but yet I am unable to say who we are. The ridiculous conjugal convention of the verb separates and unites us. I have marvellous eyes and enough jewellery to damn me. Look at my arms and my neck. An indescribable love is welling up inside you even as I speak. I am the dark Beauty and the blonde Beauty. The triumphant beauty without beauty. I am You and you are I. Clusters of plums hang from my fingertips. A heart is like a little pea which will germinate absurdly into its destiny: an anonymous accompaniment to the mortal remains of a wild duck in a richly-coloured sauce on a silver plate."

ON THE TABLE A GLASS AND A BOTTLE ARE LAID OUT IN memory of a fair-haired virgin who in this room experienced the disturbing menstrual wound for the first time and who, raising her right arm towards the ceiling and pointing her left towards the window, was able to make triangles of moving pigeons flutter in the air to her heart's content. Below, down where the burning sands of the desert jealously hide a gentle blue dolman on a manikin of white bones, she knelt an prayed the heavens to change into a scarf with which she could cover her shoulders, shoulders which to tell the truth were slightly bony but extremely delicate when one thinks of the blows of the whip which will not fail to rain down on her back and clenched buttocks, far away from here at the end of a seam in the silver mines of Baikal at the time of the Tsar.

While waiting, the fair-haired virgin dips her blonde tresses in my coffee; it is midday; the statutory litre of wine which has been deposited next to the ribbed glass in front of me turns into a dove. The coffee turns into tea, the fair-haired virgin grows a little pale; from now on she will sing sweeter than the nightingale. The bell rings: in his ribbed velvet garb the forensic expert comes in. He takes a seat. He liberates the dove imprisoned in the bottle, he turns over the glass which becomes an egg-timer, kisses the fair-haired virgin on the lips. He accuses me of murder. Enter . . . who? Two police-men . . . carrying handcuffs!

That, Your Honour, ladies and gentlemen of the jury, is how I come to be here. Your ridiculous accoutrements lead me to believe, alas, that the reign of Henri III has not yet come to an end. The statutory litre becomes a crown. The glass turns into a glass eye for your empty socket. The police doctor will invent a sleep machine which will abolish awakening.

As for me, I will turn into a giant clad in iron and gold more supple than silk. Your might have taken me for an eagle, but eagles have wings and in my name this letter auguring an irreparable fall does not figure. By dint of working the mines, the earth will be made hollow. Personally, I sleep on a glass table, you are imitation doves in a state of mortal sin. The flood would fit in my statutory litre, and I enjoin you to render unto me that which is Caesar's.

THE FIRE THAT CONSUMED SODOM AN JOHANN HUS AND the cigarette stump that I have just discarded burns over the seas and marshes, on the edges of cemeteries, in the smoke of locomotives, in the portholes of liners.

On the sea bed, starfish talk to oysters and to the wreckage. Their words, transmitted to the coral by the usual vibrations of the water, do not give rise to the slightest delay in the fabulous timetable of the tides. The starfish remembered however that she had once been Venus taking her regular stroll along the invisible paths of the firmament where the terrifying crocodiles prosper that the storm sometimes lets loose on the uninhabited cities of this fauna since the last day of the deluge. She remembered that she was Icarus and that this was the very spot where she had fallen, how she had vainly tried to emerge from the sea, which is what gave rise to the absurd myth of the profane birth of the goddess of love, and that overcome by her heaviness and cramp she had had to settle for a resting-place on the damp sands of the depths. Poor star shining out of reach of the fishermen, she stretches voluptuously her five delicate arms and makes the oyster finally release the pearl which time and illness had given him.

Strange indeed was the dialogue of the starfish and the oyster. The pearl rolled as far as the wreck which barely noticed and the starfish completed her stretch. She did this on clear October mornings, she the perfect mistress and sensual lover, when, as he unloaded cart loads of roses, the colourless assassin who was following her finally dropped the deadly knife into the mahogany-coloured stream.

The starfish sleeps now.

The oyster has closed its sturdy lid, which becomes encrusted with barnacles, over its despoiled sickness.

Only the wreckage stirs. It rose to the surface with a pearl. The pearl rolled around the bridge, the pearl took the helm, the navigated wreckage reached coastal waters; an estuary offered its mouth barricaded by the en-counter of fresh water and salt water; the vessel sailed up the estuary against the tide. The riverside dwellers witnessed that night the will-o'-the-wisp and a miraculous brilliance to their pipes and lanterns. Standing at their windows, they saw a white furrow mysteriously crawling up stream. They thought it was the moon and went to bed untroubled.

Tomorrow, the starfish will recall an anchor and the oyster a porthole. They will be amazed by the disappearance of the wreck on the back of which the word MARVEL may be made out and will continue their mute mutual contemplation.

And yet, how surprised will be the guide to the Ardennes Forest to see deadly nightshade flowering on paths now frequented only by ferns. He will find a boat planted in the middle of the trees with a pearl at the helm, a pearl which will order him to die and which he will obey.

The man in the soft blue dolman, the huntsman in the bar where the fair-haired virgin is a regular, the bare-armed huntsman will chop down oak trees not far from there.

And the pearl, eternally transfixed to the wheel, will be amazed that the boat remains forever immobile under an ocean of fir-trees unaware of the magnificent destiny that was bestowed on her equals in civilised lands, in towns where bar huntsmen have dolmans the colour of the sky.

IN A NORTHERN TOWN, THERE WAS AN AMAZING BAROMETER
to which the storms and the rains, the sunshine and the snow used to come
to receive their orders. One day, the remotest waters of all the oceans, those
which lap deserted islands and those in which washerwomen do their wash-
ing, wanted to see this mysterious tyrant who regulated the equinoxes and
the shipwrecks. They mounted an attack on the town. For seven days and
seven nights, the inhabitants defended themselves with rifle and canonfire
against what they termed the liquid barbarians. They succumbed and on
the eighth day the light of the obedient sun played across their dead bodies,
presided over their decomposition and was able to see the majestic crowd
of peaceful waves pay spumy tribute to the tyrannical barometer which,
unmindful of the honour, reflected that far away, saved by the sacrifice
of her town, the fair-haired virgin and a pirate in a pale blue dolman lay
clasped together on the seaweed on the deserted ocean floor abandoned by
the waters at the very moment that The MARVEL, the liner on which they
were passengers, was being engulfed.

LISTEN. THROUGH THE THICKNESS OF NIGHT THE WAILING of a baby martyr tortured by its luxurious parents reaches my ears, or perhaps it is the parting cry of an angora tomcat dispatched despite its mewing on a transatlantic liner to a far off destination and which, while the boat still follows the coast, continues to salute its wild mistresses, the crouching cats with phosphorescent eyes in place of lighthouses which threaten to lure vessels unfamiliar with this locality on the reefs!

Listen, is it, it is neither the child-like scream of a nocturnal rape nor feline sobs, it is the sinister song of the water in the plumbing of my taps which slowly weeps on to the tombstone which serves me as a sink. The water imprisoned in the immense narrow boa which runs from one house to another hears its drips speak.

"As for me," says one, "I was once brutally propelled from a fireman's hose in order to put out a fire. What a waste of effort! The flames transformed me into a bird and I escaped towards the sky for which I was destined by the long vicissitudes I had suffered on a lake in a park where the swans were once women who, long ago, had been adulated." "Me," said the other, "I lay wallowing in a duckpond beside bodies which were turning blue and the water-lilies which lent me their delicate perfume."

From time to time, a prolonged shiver runs through the water. It is a fair-haired virgin washing herself after love-making and asking the colourless liquid to erase from her body the signs of a nightmarish struggle. Happy the drops destined for intimacy with her body, but happy also those who feel the rustle of mermaids close to the reefs or the ripping of armour-plated bows through the oceans. Another recounts how he burrowed beneath the earth before bursting out in a spring and how in that way he was permitted the vision of beautiful bathers stretching their hands towards the sky to betoken their grief before they plunged down the mountainside. Memories of coral, memories of jellyfish, memories of islands, memories of clouds, memories of girls swimming, memories following love-making, that is the ominous song sung by the water in the lead-plumbing of cities. An enormous red umbrella emerges from an official edifice and deafens the urban inhabitants.

Down below, some other drops of water have shared the company of fish (who will proclaim the extraordinary importance of fish in poetry? For they evoke both fire and water and it is they who mourn the drips in the lead-plumbing of cities). From time to time, the prisoners are shaken by a long sonorous shiver. It is the poet in the soft blue dolman who slakes his solitary thirst, it is the fair-haired virgin who dilutes her wine with water, it is the municipal sprinkler filling up before starting its morning promenade.

The frightful water drips on to the tombstone which serves me as a sink. "Water! Water! Drip no more, I am clean, drip no more. My eyes are running like you without grief or pain and I am not thirsty.

"Water, you roll too many eyes for me to look at you. I am afraid of your multiple spheres in which your memories may be clearly seen like the SACRÉ-COEUR in a bone pen-holder."

But the water does not listen. It glistens. The kettle on the fire groans because the water boils and evaporates. An hour after I awake the town is dry.

"Lost pedestrian, this desert was not always so. There was once a flourishing town here, but the water departed and the sand covered it with its lustreless constellations. The tombstone on which you sit was not always thus. It was formerly the stone sink in which fresh water ran lugubriously at night filling the flat where I live with anxiety. The blue tatters of the sky were not always a flag but . . ."

But the pedestrian passes by and the savage sky remains without a storm. The open sky.

THE STREET WAS A LONG ONE LINED WITH TAILORS' SHOPS. To tell the truth, none of the tradesmen were taking much money at this time of day. It was two o'clock in the morning. A recent strike had decimated the company of lamp-lighters. One of them was just finishing his round for the night and I congratulated the borough on its presence of mind in requiring its modest servants to attire themselves in pale blue for lighting up and in black when extinguishing. I walked for a long time and my shadow moved around me ominously.

One day it will doubtless stop still and that day will be my last. In the mean time, I follow the lamp-lighter wearing pale blue overalls as he completes his round as if in a race.

An hour later, I was stopped by the fair-haired virgin. Dressed in her most beautiful clothes and wearing make up, she had gone down to the street to try and make a bit of money by selling her body. I turned over the various aspects of this important question for a minute, I thought of old women on the coast reduced to seeking out the company of sea-horses and who slowly rise to the surface when their couplings have taken too long. The fishermen reel them in at dawn, and that makes one more grave and one less woman. I thought of the little girls from boarding-school led forty at a time into the army barracks, of women who lose their dignity in bars, and of those who try to forget the hero on the screen in the convenient darkness of cinemas. Then I fell asleep.

He's asleep, said the moon.

And slowly it began to count a rosary of stars. The stars grumbled softly to themselves. The star acting as a pendant shone with a thousand fires and I wondered how much longer this incantation would last. The moon was praying! The stars grew dim one by one and the dawn made my temples grey. Crowds filled the streets, trams passed by, far away the fishermen pulled up the corpses of old women. I slept.

The surprising metamorphosis of sleep makes us equal to gods. Their actions are reduced to the same status as those of actors on a subsidized stage while we, in our dress-coats and our boxes or seats in the front stalls, applaud them. When the excitement languishes, we take their place and, just for the fun of it, risk our necks in deadly adventures.

Respect my sleep, passers-by in the street below. The great organ of the sun makes you march in step, but I will not wake until this evening when the moon begins its prayer.

I will leave for the coast where ships never land; one shall present itself, a black flag fluttering at the stern. The rocks will part.

I shall step ashore.

And my friends high in their observatories will watch the exploits of the gangs of black flags scattered across the plain, while above them the moon will say its prayer. It will count its rosary of stars and distant cathedrals will crash to the ground.

I will return only with the fair-haired virgin, the beautiful, the charming fair-haired virgin who will make the moon turn pale above the flowering apple trees.

To die! To die in a bed of watercress!

A BALLOON DRIFTED WITH THE WIND, TAKING ON THE appear-
ance of—or so it seemed to me—alternately a poppy, a hand and a sward,
although it is more than likely that the driver of the express train in which
I was sitting, a thoughtful man whose profession frequently required him
to distinguish between varying shapes and sizes, might have been able to
enlighten me.

In any case, the cause of our disagreement soon disappeared. Despite the
signals which were exchanged between the balloonists and the passengers,
the train and the spherical shape went off in different directions, the former
retaining the memory of a vertiginous roundness, the latter that of a trail
of smoke. My gaze wandered across the peaceful plain over which pouting
streams careered in search of the tall poplars which an industrialist had
ordered to be felled and exported to Great Britain, a country which still ven-
erates hangings; my eyes soon came to rest on a pink marble wall at the foot
of which was sprawled a women naked and murdered. The striking shape
of her mouth, despite the paleness of my eyes and a distance of more than
ten kilometres between us, indicated that her head had been humming with
love and that rather than succombing to the perfect embrace, the velvety
drone of poetry had found it preferable to destroy the hive, kill the swarm
of thoughts and the beautiful, tenuous queen bee with her pink fingers. The
express continued on its way, preceded sometimes by the snow-plough of
anxiety, sometimes the headlight of metaphysics, sometimes by a flock of
golden pheasants, the messengers of madness.

Spherical balloons still crossed my field of vision. My gaze still came to
rest on walls of pink marble, but never again would balloonists or murdered
women give my frightened soul that feeling of a vast plain, carefully cultivat-
ed and empty of human beings, under a violet sky during the chronometer's
eternal hour.

O! Unlucky man! It would have been better to have gone up with the smoke as high as the roundness of the airship or to have thrown yourself out the door and to have gained the bloody body at the foot of the wall of pink marble across the fields and marshes.

Silence! Silence!

WOMEN'S TEETH ARE SUCH PRETTY OBJECTS THAT ONE should only see them in dreams or at the moment of death. It is the time of night when delicate jaws fasten themselves on our gobs, o poets! Do not forget that a train, having jumped all the signals, is careering towards Kilometre 178 and that, at night, our dreams, on march for many a long year, have been delayed by two naked women talking at the foot of a poplar. Just as truly as we were contained in the first woman, our dreams were contained in the first dream. Ever since birth, we have been seeking one night to walk together side by side, even if only for a moment in time. Our age is infinity and infinity demands that the meeting, the coincidence, takes place today in a railway compartment hurtling towards disaster. Lock us in together, o poets! The invisible door opens on to countryside and an organ, yes an organ, rises up from the marsh. The fingers of the blonde woman, which I notice for the first time are webbed, ring out on it a joyful hymn. A wedding march of our reflections left behind in the mirror when the woman we ought to have met and never will comes to admire herself in it. A wedding march of hands severed as an ex-voto when death, offering us its basket full of violets, agrees again to read our horoscope. At the sound of the organ, the hangar doors open and throbbingly release voluminous dirigibles into the open sky.

Awoken from his sleep, the pilot buried at Kilometre 178 throws the points thirty seconds before the express arrives and aims them at the moon. The train goes by with its hellish din. It casts a shadow over our satellite and disappears like the song of the liner's engineer heard by mistake on the radio in the middle of a town in the South of France. The fair-haired virgin takes out a needle and sews a tiny purse full of freshly pulled teeth. She throws it at the fleeing stars and the sky henceforth assumes the appearance of a set of enormous, adorable woman's jaws. The same woman who will look into this mirror an hour after me. The pilot goes back to sleep and says: "I've got plenty of time to waste." The red star, the red star, the red star will fade at sunrise.

It was a very calm summer's night over a marsh.

A clock struck 1, 2, 3.

Beautiful blonde with the red lips!

THANKS TO THE ATTENTIONS OF A WOMAN WE LOVE, SLEEP clothes itself in our body just like a handsome snake who—while the sun, the creepers, the mosquitoes and the unpleasant smell of the rotting mangroves in a shallow swamp jar the nerves of the sand-coloured lionesses—slowly dresses itself its shiny new skin, a new skin for a new year, identical to those touching calendars which book-keepers change on the walls of their offices every 2nd of January (because the 1st is a bank holiday) and which bear witness by their obtuse presence to the illusory mathematical unfolding of eternity before a procession of conquerors theatrically ranged before funeral monuments on which a stone angel tilting an urn of tears over a truncated column of historical characters on the point of death in the presence of an historian, of symmetrical battles and treaties being signed with peacock's feathers by plenipotentiaries in full regalia in sparkling rooms, sleep, I repeat, clothes itself in our body while the woman we love who brought it to our bed is astounded by the funereal change that has overtaken our features, by the relative rigidity of our members and by our apparent indifference to the words which usually make us more dreamy than the tall lamp posts in deserted avenues at the onset of darkness. The woman gets up and sits pensively at the window where our dream follows her while the deserted street echoes from time to time with the dusty passage of motor-taxis and the languid footfall of a policeman on his beat. For a moment her white silhouette hovers in the air on a level with the third floor, and a young nocturnal rambler struck by this apparition, and imagining it to be the fall of a shooting star, articulates aloud his dearest wish: to sleep in a rocking chair on a terrace.

It is two o'clock in the morning. It is sleep and his boisterous retinue of motley horses. The woman who we love leads an orphanage of little girls dressed in sky-blue along the paths of a dark wood. An alert musician collects, thanks to his extraordinarily acute hearing, the different sounds made by keys turning in locks and dashes off one of the most beautiful compositions imaginable.

Tomorrow, the woman we love will dance to his refrain.

The bedroom door opens: the red archangel Raphael comes in followed by the white archangel Raphael.

It is sleep, it is sleep and his boisterous train of sandy lions and automobiles.

It is sleep.

"HERE LIES HE WHOSE WORDS ASSUMED THE SHAPE OF enormous northern flowers and who held in his strong arms that wild and deranged mistress the woman as red as Red and coral which is, in fact, blue but which because of its tortuous shape has been endowed by poetic profundity with this colour which is known to excite bulls."

What a strange epitaph, I thought to myself, how very strange. But who can predict the sublime irony of those who turn their wills into objects of shame for their families and make a laughing stock of their own memory. I could easily picture the amazement of the stone-mason on receiving his instructions to engrave this mysterious sentence on a block of granite torn from some rocky promontory and hewn into the shape of a parallelepiped rather than that of a plinth . . . Glory be to you, o granite! Covered in sharp edges as you are, to you the maritime gods expose their humid sexes, pell-mell with enormous fishes and ships in distress, you are resplendent in your magnificent horror, and the pilgrim, the hermit and the sailor contemplate your jagged summit, which is like a tooth, a claw or a tusk in terms of shape but only at the moment the spume breaks in terms of colour, without an inkling as to the mathematical precision your future form will take with its eight ledges and eight rectangular dihedral angles, if we make no mention of perspective, wondering whether nature could have blessed you with a more beautiful role even allowing for the pink stain on your pinnacle which they would have been unable to decide whether it were blood, the fugitive sun, or coral which is, in fact, blue but becomes red due to poetic profundity, that sturdy mistress, that savage woman who lingers over the baiting of bulls whom the fury of the oceans and the squids of your native region could not have frightened, while I myself know that the red stain on your summit gives you the appearance, o granite, of the most beautiful breast!

But, o granite, do no mourn your terrible majesty at the foot of the cliffs. Today, carefully carved as you are, and slumbering in this cemetery, a paper-weight holding down a body which has perhaps been turned into paper thanks to the use of putrid matter in the fabrication of that article, perhaps even the paper on which I am writing this eulogy, you assume the most majestically serene air by your association with the deceased who wished to carry away into silence even his name, a silence which extends to his very identity, and offers to the modest neighbourhood the dying echoes of a terrible peal of satanic laughter.

Paris, April, 1924

## Notes:

1. *Mourning for Mourning* (*Deuil pour deuil*) translated by Terry Hale. Excerpts reprinted by arrangement with Atlas Press, UK (www.atlaspress.co.uk).

"Leda is present among us" and "The sailor remembers China"
© Digital Image © The Museum of Modern Art/Licensed by SCALA / Art Resource

"Meeting of the explorers in evening clothes with the mysterious beast!"
© Digital Image © The Museum of Modern Art/Licensed by SCALA / Art Resource

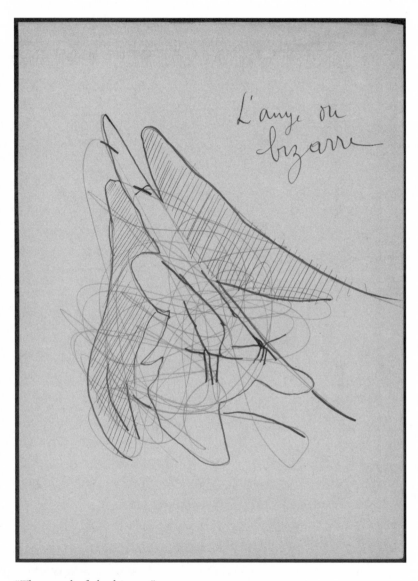

"The angel of the bizarre"
© Digital Image © The Museum of Modern Art/Licensed by SCALA /
Art Resource

"Vanity, memory of the swan"
© Digital Image © The Museum of Modern Art/Licensed by SCALA / Art Resource

1927
*Excerpts from La Liberté ou l'amour! (Liberty or Love!)*
translated by Terry Hale[1]


# VIII

## *AS FAR AS THE EYE CAN SEE*

CORSAIR SANGLOT WAS BORED! BOREDOM HAD BECOME HIS
main reason to go on living. He let it grow in silence, marvelling every
day that it still managed to increase in size. It was Boredom: a large sunny
square, lined with rectilinear colonnades, perfectly swept, perfectly clean,
deserted. An unalterable hour had struck in the Corsair's life and he
now understood that boredom is synonymous with Eternity. In vain was
he awakened every night by the pendulum's strange tick-tock, a tick-tock
which grew ever louder, filling the room in which he lay with the sound of
its breathing or else, towards midnight, a dark presence which would inter-
rupt his dream. His pupils, dilated in the darkness, sought for the person
who must have come into the room. But no one had forced the door and
soon the calm sound of the clock mingled with the sleeper's breathing.

Corsair Sanglot felt a new sense of esteem growing for himself and in
himself. Since he had understood and accepted the monotony of Eternity,
he advanced straight as a pole through adventures like slithering vines which
were unable to check his progress. A new exaltation had replaced his depres-

sion. A sort of enthusiasm in reverse permitted him to consider objectively the failure of his most cherished enterprises. Time's freedom had finally conquered him. He had merged with the patient minutes which succeeded and resembled one another.

It was boredom, the great square into which he had one day ventured. It was three o'clock in the afternoon. Silence weighed over everything, even the sonorous buzzing of hornets and the heated air. The colonnades cast their rectilinear shadows over the yellow ground. No passers-by, except on the other side of the square, which must have had a three kilometre radius: a minuscule person strolling without visible purpose. Corsair Sanglot remarked with terror that it was still three o'clock that the shadows were immutably turned in the same direction. But this terror dispelled itself. The Corsair finally came to terms with this pathetic hell. He knew that no paradise was permitted to the man who suddenly became aware one day of the existence of the infinite, and he agreed to remain, an eternal sentinel, on the square warmed and brilliantly lit by an immobile sun.

Who was it who compared boredom to dust? Boredom and eternity are absolutely devoid of the least speck of dust. A mental road-sweeper carefully attends to the hopeless cleanliness. Did I say hopeless? Boredom may no more engender hopelessness than it may culminate in suicide. You who have no fear of death, try a little boredom. Henceforth, death will no longer be of the slightest use to you. The immobile torment and the distant perspectives of the mind freed of all sense of the picturesque and all sentimentality will have been revealed to you once and for all.

It was at this period of his life that a strange adventure happened to Corsair Sanglot. Not that he got too excited about it.

He scarcely deigned to pay the slightest attention to the romantic landscape in which his body was moving: a sunken road followed the wall of a cemetery behind which could be seen the tops of some cypress trees and two gigantic parasol pines while the sky became convulsed, swollen with grey and black clouds, clouds rent asunder to the west by a fan of sunbeams which only made the monstrous vaults of the heavy cumulus stand out all the more lugubriously. Three o'clock was it? It was more like five o'clock on a

September evening. The desolation of dusk's dark cloak advanced across the land. The only noise audible was the unlikely clatter of a car engine, presumably on a concealed road cut into a nearby embankment, unless the lowness of the clouds caused the sound to travel further than usual. Suddenly, and Corsair Sanglot did not see this, thirty thousand tombstones in the cemetery rose up and thirty thousand cadavers in calico night-shirts appeared lined up as if on parade. A couple of them broke away and, scaling the stones, leaned their elbows on the ridge of the wall. It was at this moment that Corsair Sanglot, who was feeling slightly depressed, noticed their heads. They projected unexpectedly above the level of the wall and stared at him laughingly, but as for him, he just continued on his way. Their peals of laughter long echoed behind him, and the sound of the invisible car engine suddenly became much louder. When the Corsair arrived at the place where the path joined the road, he saw an enormous hearse, a giant's hearse, pulled by four strong Percherons whose hoofs, partly hidden by a fringe of hair, drummed heavily against the ground, though the hearse was empty, with neither a coffin nor a coachman.

It disappeared. The corpses on the cemetery wall studied the sky in silence. The sky, where one would have preferred the brightness of a storm, buffeted by currents of air high above, became convulsed with great bands of grey and black clouds which totally altered the colour of the dying day and gave to nature a bituminous aspect, heavy and lowering. The stormy boredom of the high seasons enveloped Corsair Sanglot in his gloomy sponge-cloth dressing-gown. It is he who, with a vigilant finger, moved the illusory hands of the clock face. It is he who confused the passers-by on the large sunny squares lined with colonnades, and it is he who, with a steady hand, agitated his slack ocean, ignoring tempests despite a sky full of menacing grey and black clouds too oily in which to drown oneself.

Various landscapes in keeping with the casting of spells: from the cave in which the Sibyl and her serpentine familiar presided over the fall of Empires to the tunnels of the metro decorated with their monotonously humorous posters for *Dubonnet*, ridiculous name, destined to exorcise the ghostly familiars of underground passageways, by way of the Bondy forests, blooming with blunderbusses and musketoons, populated by bandits in conical hats, granite-built feudal manor houses with vaulted chambers haunted by friendly ravens and voluminous owls; to the flats of the petit-bourgeoisie where, as a result of some insignificant pretext, an upset salt-cellar or a hint of criticism, disagreement with its gun-cotton pyroxylin breasts enters without knocking and runs up to the soft-spoken parents and their pusillanimous son, placing in their hand the until that moment inoffensive bread-knife (except for fingers cut when slicing bread—one should break bread, not cut it, do this in remembrance of our Lord) or while chopping parsley (a dangerous herb because of its resemblance to hemlock, a poisonous plant of which Socrates was sentenced to swallow a fatal dose by the merciless tribunal of an ungrateful country, which enabled the hero dear to pederasts to display tremendous courage in the face of death and so aggrandise himself at the very moment his enemies hoped to see him off) and transform the peaceful dining room into a frightful slaughterhouse, blood spurting from severed carotids, splattering one after the other the soup tureen of Limoges china, the gas chandelier and the imitation Renaissance buffet; to the street corners lit by green lamps to indicate bus stops, at which gallows-bird shadows hold secret confabulations, huddled in the shadows of entrances, until the very moment when they are alerted by echoing footsteps that the time is ripe for them to jump out on unsuspecting pedestrians; to the ripe meadows at two o'clock in the afternoon when the tourist, at a loss as to what to do, unbuttons his flies and falls on his knees astride the young shepherdess with her skirts bundled up above her waist. Landscapes: you are only cardboard stage sets. A single actor: Frégoli,* that is to say boredom, struts about the stage and plays out a sempiternal farce in which the protagonists pursue each other never-endingly, forever obliged to change costumes in the wings before each of his new reincarnations.

Not long afterwards, Corsair Sanglot went down a Parisian street.

# MONOLOGUE OF CORSAIR SANGLOT OUTSIDE A BARBER'S SHOP ON THE RUE DU FAUBOURG-SAINT-HONORÉ

"I HAVE NEVER HAD ANY FRIENDS, ONLY LOVERS. GIVEN THE strength of attachment I felt for my friends and my coldness towards women, for a long time I used to think that I was more capable of friendship than love. Sheer madness, I was totally incapable of friendship. The passionate nature of my relations with all sorts of people, how could I discard it or transfer it to other recipients. In some cases, I remember, the passion was reciprocal. Those tumultuous encounters, that furious attraction, that half-hatred, those crises of conscience, the rows, the sense of sadness when they were not there, the different emotions with which, now we hardly ever see each other any more, I think of them—how could I possibly mistake those things with that grey and shapeless entity called friendship. Those incapable of sensing the exalted character of the exchange I was offering gave me friendship, and I despised them. Friends became part of my life for no more than a moment. We abandoned each other, not without jealousy, for the first  pretty face. I lost myself in alcoves without echoes, they too. I believed in the profound oblivion of sleeping with your head on your mistress's breast, I let myself be taken in by the tenderness of the female sphinx, they too. Nothing can bring back for us the way we were. Strangers to each other when we are together, the communion of ideas we once enjoyed revives only when we have gone our separate ways. Our memories are not the slightest help. Confronted by one of our former friends, that idealised friend—the one we imagine we are with when we are alone—asks with whom we are comparing him and what right we have to behave in such a way, he who is but a fiction, the product of the melancholic notion of the void.

"And now I have no other setting for my actions than the public squares:

Place La Fayette, Place des Victoires, Place Vendôme, Place Dauphine, Place de la Concorde.

"A poetic agoraphobia transforms my nights into deserts and my dreams into anxieties.

"I am speaking today from outside a window of periwigs and tortoise-shell combs and as I automatically stock this greenhouse with severed heads and apathetic turtles, a gigantic razor made of the finest steel takes the place of the hand on the clock face of my tiny imagination. From now on, it will shave the minutes without cutting them off.

"My former mistresses change their hair-styles and I no longer see them; somewhere or other, with a growing affection, my friends drink fatidical aperitifs with strangers.

"I am alone: still capable, more than capable, of feeling passion. Boredom, the boredom which I cultivate with a rigorous lack of awareness, guards my life from the uniformity from whence spring storms and night and the sun."

At this moment the barber came out to stand in the shop doorway and examine the stationary passer-by.

"Would you care for a shave, sir. I won't hurt you. My nickel-plated instruments are nimble elves. My wife, the wig-maker with hair the colour of Brazilian rosewood, is renowned for the adroitness of her massage and the dexterity of her manicure. Step this way, sir; come on in."

The barber's chair and the mirror extended their usual gloom. The shaving-dish was already brimming with lather. The barber prepared the shaving-brush. It was two o'clock in the morning, night jumbled up the shadows cast by the waxwork busts. A smell of cologne hung heavily in the air. The lather on the shaving-sticks made a crackling sound as it dried. Corsair Sanglot felt a strange presence above his head. He violently ripped away the sheet and the salty air of the expiring sea at his feet made him feel light-headed. The sand was smooth.

Next Corsair Sanglot got lost in an enormous palace dotted with high columns, columns so high that the ceiling was invisible. Then his historiographer lost him from sight and forgot about him.

The Corsair went on walking. The palace kept him occupied for a long time. Constructed from the shells of lobsters and crayfish, and set in the midst of white mountains, its slender shape and the red mass of its towers reached upwards. In the sides of the walls of those towers, which were made from the shells of turtle crabs, care had been taken to employ shellfish, cooked and brown, while the sea breeze caused the entire edifice to rock gently on its fragile foundations.

Do not become my friend, I warn you. I have sworn never to let myself be taken in by that terrible MAN-TRAP. I will never be your friend and if you agree to give up everything for me, I will still abandon you one day.

In any case, I know the feeling of being abandoned only too well, having experienced it myself. If that is the insolent luxury you desire, that is fine; you may follow me. Otherwise all I ask of you is your indifference, if not your enmity.

# IX
# THE PALACE OF MIRAGES

LOST IN THE DESERT, THE WHITE-HELMETED EXPLORER sees the majestic towers of an unknown city looming on the horizon.

Corsair Sanglot was walking through the gardens of the Tuileries at three o'clock in the afternoon on his way towards the Concorde. At the same moment Louise Lame was going down the Rue Royale. As she passes Maxim's café, the wind lifts her hat and whisks it away in the direction of the Madeleine. Louise Lame, dishevelled, chases after it and picks it up. While this is happening, Corsair Sanglot crosses the Place de la Concorde and disappears down the Avenue Gabrielle. Three minutes later, Louise Lame in turn crosses the square, once illustrious for its revolutionary machinery, and begins to make her way along the Avenue des Champs-Élysées. Corsair Sanglot pauses for a second to do up his shoe laces. He lights a cigarette. Louise Lame and Corsair Sanglot, separated by the clumps of trees along the Champs-Élysées, move in parallel in the same direction.

Lost in the desert, the white-helmeted explorer consults the position of the night stars in vain. On the horizon looms the formidable machicolated towers of an unknown city whose shadow covers a vast territory. Corsair Sanglot remembers a woman he once met long ago on the Rue du Mont-Thabor. Jack the Ripper's very own bedroom provided them shelter. He is surprised that his thoughts cling to her so insistently, he wishes ardently to meet this woman again. And Louise Lame, bothered by the exactness of her memories, wonders what ever became of that handsome buccaneer who surrendered himself to her one evening. On the blackboard of a ruinous secondary school lecture hall, a school lost in the suburbs of a populous city and the lair of lost cats, circumstance's black genius traces itineraries which cross but do not meet. Lost in a desert without palm trees, the white-helmeted explorer slowly circles a mysterious city unknown to geographers.

Corsair Sanglot turns right. Louise Lame left. The white-helmeted explorer approaches nearer and nearer the city sprung up in the middle of the desert. It shrinks soon to a tiny sandcastle which is dispersed by the wind, while misgivings assail the lonely traveller who can only wonder what new power has been bestowed on his glance.

The genius of circumstance puts on his road-mender's uniform, makes his way to the Place de la Concorde and there traces the mysterious stars on the pavement.

Louise Lame, proceeding on her way, suddenly sees the Corsair standing in her path. But it was only a dream. For a long time she contemplates the place where his ghost appeared. She is thinking to herself that one day, not so long ago perhaps, the adventurer himself had undoubtedly set foot in the same place where she now stood. She started out again pensively.

As for him, the wind billowing out the pleats of his raglan overcoat, his reflection in the windows and mirrors ahead, following the direction of his fleeting thoughts, now stained scarlet and then green in front of chemists' shops, now brushed by the fur of a woman's coat, he let himself be borne away towards the Gare Saint-Lazare. From the Boulevard des Batignolles, he looks down into the sooty cutting and sees trains leaving Paris. As it is not yet dark, the street-lamps cast a pale, yellow light across the doors. Against one of them is leaning the mermaid from the Sperm Drinkers' Club. The Corsair does not see her.

Lost in the desert, the white-helmeted explorer discovers the real remains, buried in the sand until uncovered by a recent sirocco, of a former Timbuktu. Going down the stairs from the flat where he has just committed his latest masterpiece, Jack the Ripper strolls down the Boulevard des Batignolles. He begs a light for his cigarette which has gone out from the Corsair, and a few metres further on asks a policeman the shortest route to Ternes. Lost in a desert of black sand, the white-helmeted explorer enters the ruins of the former Timbuktu. He is greeted by the sight of treasure and skeletons bearing esoteric symbols of a long dead religion. The express train in which the mermaid has taken a seat crosses a bridge at the very same moment as the German music-hall chanteuse drives over it in a car. Corsair Sanglot, Louise Lame and the chanteuse's desire for each other spreads in vain across the entire world. Their thoughts jostle each other, increasing their desire to meet as they collide at those mysterious points of infinity where they are reflected back towards the minds which have given rise to them. Prostrate yourself before these fatidical places where remarkable people, for whom such meetings are crucial, continually miss each other by a minute. Strange destiny by which Corsair Sanglot and Louise Lame almost brush against each other on the Place de la Concorde, by which the mermaid and the chanteuse pass beneath each other in a sinister corner of a Parisian suburb, by which you or I, in a bus or any other means of public transport, take a seat in front of the very person who is able to unite us with the man or woman who has been lost in our memories since the time of our nights of torment, without us knowing it, strange destiny how long will you frustrate our tired and troubled senses?

Lost in a desert of coal and anthracite, an explorer dressed in white recalls the evening fire in the rustic grate at his parents-in-law's, when his wife was no more than his fiancée; when will-o'-the-wisps were not called Saint-Elmo's fire and, like garden flowers, half-seen in the darkness of your eyelids when you clench your eyes shut, they hovered in the marshy countryside; when, the embers dying about one o'clock in the morning of a 25th of December, a young child wakes and, wearing only a night-shirt, goes to check that the mythological hero has passed through the paternal hearth, and listens to the roar of the wind in the chimney which accompanies the song of invisible archangels who inculcate in him a love of the night and a love of the midday sun, as unvarying, solemn and tragic as the shadows; when the aurora borealis is glimpsed for the first time in the magical drawings of a book for children before, as it rises in the north, it is rapturously greeted on the bridge of a boat in a forgotten bay in the Arctic circle.

A cobblestone from the Place de la Concorde, left over by some workmen, dislodges itself from the pile where it has been until then condemned by its mineralogical properties. It addresses the people there, speaking their language which, despite being an unusual phenomenon, would hardly have retained their interest (given that the crowd are accustomed to prodigies), if it had not also enumerated the names of all those who had trodden on it over the course of the years. The names of the famous are greeted with cheers and shouts. There then follow unfamiliar names, the names of humble people, repeated far and wide by loud-speakers, names which echo ponderously in the hearts of all those gathered there. Someone recognises the name of his father, another person, an old man, raises his hat upon hearing the name of his first mistress, others recognise their own surnames. They come to a halt and their lives seem pitiful to them. Boredom invaded every one's mind. Corsair Sanglot takes note of the depressed state of public opinion. He rejoices and is amazed at his strange joy. He understands at last that in place of boredom he has discovered a despair identical with enthusiasm.

Lost between segments of a ferocious horizon, the white-helmeted explorer prepares to die and assembles his memories in order to discover how an explorer should end his days: with his arms outstretched and his face in the sand, or should he dig a fugitive tomb because of wind and hyenas, or just curl up in the so-called broken-gun position which causes so much worry to mothers when they discover that this is the position in which their offspring prefer to fall asleep, or if a lion or sunstroke or thirst will do the honours for him.

The cobblestone in the Place de la Concorde considers the procession of all those who have stepped on it. Women's underclothing, varying according to fashion, adventurers, those out for a peaceful stroll, women's underclothing, horsemen, coaches, barouches, victorias, cabriolets, hackney carriages, cars, Corsair Sanglot, Louise Lame, such and such, cars, policemen, you, me, Corsair Sanglot, cars, cars, cars, night prowlers, policemen, lamp-lighters, Corsair Sanglot, such and such.

Two metro lines, two trains, two carriages, two people walking in parallel streets, two lives, couples criss-crossing without seeing each other, potential encounters, meetings which shall never take place. The imagination rewrites history. It modifies the local directory and the roll-call of those who frequent a town, a street, a house, a woman. It transfixes reflections in the mirror for all eternity. It hangs entire portrait galleries from the wall of our future memory on which magnificent strangers engrave their initials and a date with a sharp knife.

Corsair Sanglot, on the third floor of a house, is still thinking of the legendary Louise Lame while the latter, on the third floor of another house, remembers him as he was the evening they parted, and through the wails their eyes meet and, to the amazement of astronomers, give birth to new stars. Face to face, but hidden by how many obstacles, houses, public monuments, trees, the two converse inwardly with each other.

Let a tumultuous catastrophe topple the screens and the circumstances and there they are, grams of sand lost on a flat plain, united by the imaginary straight line which links every being to no matter what other being. Neither time nor space, nothing opposes these ideal relations. A life overturned, worldly constraints, earthly obligations, everything crumbles. Human beings are no less subject to the same arbitrary roll of the dice.

In the desert, lost, irremediably lost, the white-helmeted explorer finally realises the reality of mirages and of unknown treasures, the dream-like fauna, the improbable flora which constitute the sensual paradise where from now on he will evolve, a scarecrow without sparrows, a tomb without epitaph, a man without name, while, in a formidable displacement, the pyramids reveal the dice hidden beneath their heavy mass and pose once more the perplexing problem of bygone fatality and future destiny. As for the present, that beautiful eternal sky, it lasts no longer than the time it takes to roll three dice over a city, a desert, a man, a white-helmeted explorer, more lost in his vast intuition of eternal events than in the sandy expanse of the equatorial plain where his genius, that wily guide, has led him step by step towards a revelation which ceaselessly contradicts itself and causes him to stray from his own unrecognizable image, due to the position of his eyes or the lack of some point of comparison and the legitimate suspicions which a superior spirit always entertains for mirrors whose revealed truth remains wholly uncorroborated, leading him to the chaotic image of the skies, other beings, inanimate objects and the ghostly incarnations of his own thoughts.

## Notes:

1. Excerpts from *Liberty or Love!* (*La liberte ou l'amour!*) translated by Terry Hale reprinted by arrangement with Atlas Press, UK (www. atlaspress.co.uk).

# II. Essays and Prose Reflections

# Essays and Prose Reflections

S ome of Desnos' major declarations in his essays are easily the equal of any surrealist writing, including the better known manifestos. His own manifesto exudes a powerful sense of disillusion with his erstwhile hero, André Breton, who has expelled him from the group, and an expression of his own individuality. Like Aragon's lyrical description in his *Paris Peasant* of the singular image which can so change one's life, Desnos extolls the potency of the modern imagery, at the heart of the revolution in aesthetics and life in which he so ardently believes.

His romantic self-confession, beginning "While I remain" and translated in these pages contains within it the kind of doom-consciousness that will make such an appeal in his surrealist work: "I have been awaiting for years the shipwreck of the beautiful boat I love." ("Tandis que je demeure," in the *Confession d'un Enfant du siècle*.)

## 1925
## «Description d'une révolte prochaine», "Description of an Impending Revolt" (*La Révolution Surréaliste* 3 [April 1925]), translated by Jonathan P. Eburne

Hailing from the shadowy East, the civilized continue the Westward march begun by Atilla the Hun, Tamerlane, and many other unknowns. Whoever says "civilized" means "former barbarian"—that is, the bastard offspring of adventurers of the night—that is, those who have been corrupted by the enemy (Romans, Greeks). Cast off from Pacific shores and Himalayan slopes, these "mercenaries," unfaithful to their mission, now find themselves confronted by the ones who drove them out in the first place, during the Great Invasions of the not-too-distant past.

Sons of Mongols, grandsons of Huns, cast aside those robes borrowed from the cloakrooms of Athens and Thebes, that armor gathered in Sparta and Rome, and appear naked like your fathers on their tiny horses; and you, Norman workers, sardine fishermen, cider-makers, climb aboard those perilous barques, whose wakes stretch far beyond the artic circle before reaching misty fields and game-rich forests! Wolf pack, know your leader! You think you've been fleeing the Orient, which banished you, while vesting in you a right to destruction you didn't know how to maintain; and now here you've caught up to it from behind, on completion of your world tour. I beg you, don't be like a dog chasing its tail; you're perpetually running after the West—stop it!

O great oriental army who have become today's *Westerners:* live up to your mission.

ROME? You've destroyed it with a gust of wind, or the broadsword of your ally, Brennus. Rome? You've reconstructed it; you've even borrowed its laws (Roman laws, as the old men say in courts of law), and you've given it a Pope, in order to divert the spirit of the Orient from its goal.

ATHENS? You've divided her up like fabric, and you've modeled your own faces on the faces of her broken statues.

You have even destroyed, in passing, THEBES and MEMPHIS, but you've been careful not to take anything from them. You never laugh harder than when people mention Tutankhamen.

Whenever the rearguard rejoins the center of the crowd, Charles Martel is in command; you fought him, just as you clashed with the archangels of Atilla the Hun in the Catalauni fields. The languages you speak are those of your former adversaries. For nearly twenty centuries you've allowed an historical rheumatism to spread to your limbs. It's time for you to ask the men from the East for the watchword you've lost. The route you follow, in spite of the earth's roundness, will never show you anything other than the setting sun. Turn back[1] . . .

What's this? It seems you're taking yourself seriously!

That summit meeting? Those impotent gentlemen, that stupid woman of letters? The *League of Nations,* as you say—yet naturally you omit what it cost: ten million fresh corpses and whatever was necessary to keep the stock market going. Let's take a moment to examine your filthy work, O corrupt diplomats gathered together to render all wars impossible. It seems above all that your League's goal is to combat freedom. On the basis of what monstrous principle of conservation of space do you still allow your associates to condemn abortion? On the side of crime, love stirs and prepares its knives: it is possible that before long, and in love's name—which has never signified Peace—there could be blood spilled.

---

[1]  This is what you should have done when, upon reaching the shores of the Atlantic and after destroying the Greco-Latin world, you instead transformed your bivouacs into cities.

On the basis of what right do you forbid the use of narcotics[2]? No doubt you stooges will soon condemn to death anyone who unsuccessfully attempts suicide. But I concede that you need soldiers for your generals, and taxpayers for your finances.

In any event, how despicable is this control over our way of life, and our way of death, exerted by the very same people who are ready to demand "the sacrifice of life" and the "blood tax" for a cause I personally condemn. The care of my death and life matters only to me. The fatherland? What does this even mean now?

This same hatred of the individual and his rights has led you to regulate *"pornographic literature."* A good opportunity for the rancid old maid who represents France and the paralytics who represent other countries to rub their naked bellies up against their thoughts. An admirable spectacle: a woman of letters, with drooping tits, discussing with great wisdom the crime of those books that remind her how long it's already been since her decrepitude began scaring off her more vigorous lovers.[3]

League of Nations! Old whore! You can be proud of your work. Tomorrow, through the forests and plains, solders supervised by gendarmes, pistols in hand, will kill each other with brute force. Those same soldiers you brought into the world through your laws and orders. Tomorrow, protestant America, stupider than ever, by dint of Prohibition, masturbating only behind its bank vaults and the Statue of Liberty, will have powerfully seconded the effort of the European Labor Council. Thus the lyrical lover and the sage will reflect that the time for the revolt of the spirit over matter has come. The primitive watchword finally found once again, will overexcite that handful who are the last survivors of the utilitarian inquisition. What this

---

[2]   It would be useful to note here the conduct of a couple of volunteer stool-pigeons: J-P Liausu and Marcel Nadaud, who are leading an abject smear campaign in the press. More than any anyone else, these two deserve unmitigated contempt. In this particular case, these "gentlemen" are conducting themselves like full-fledged swine.

[3]   The trend toward shame so dear to journalists is not imaginary. It is the first manifestation of that vulgar state of mind that has hijacked the word moral away from its meaning, seeing in it only a utilitarian distinction between a problematic "good" and an arbitrary "evil."

spontaneous revolt will be—barracks and cathedrals in flames, or an irresistible seizure of power in a public monument: a president of the Republic in front of a green felt desktop, the Legion of Honor with their dangling medals, and his ministers in their jackets, all led by decorous insurgents— makes no difference. What matters is the regime under which this overthrow of power will be attained.

I have always despised those revolutionaries who, for having put a tricolor flag in the place of a white one, consider themselves satisfied and live tranquilly, decorated by the new State, and pensioned by the new government.

No; for a revolutionary, there can be only one possible regime:

THE REVOLUTION,

that is,

TERROR

The establishment of this regime is what interests me, and today its advent alone is what keeps me hopeful about the possibility that the bastards that clog up life will disappear. Today's infernal atmosphere will get the better of the noblest impulses. Only the guillotine can, with its somber blows, enlighten that crowd of adversaries with whom we clash. Ah, may that sympathetic machine of deliverance stand at last in a public place! It has served villainous ends for too long.

Murderers, bandits, pirates—you were the first revolutionaries. The foul "honest people's party" has consecrated you to the gods of cowardice and hypocrisy. You have done what I will most likely never have the courage to try; and your severed heads, rolled about by some invisible ocean, knock together darkly, somewhere in a corner of the universal soul.

Whether a puerile wish, or laughable childishness, it nonetheless pleases me to imagine this "big night," such as it will be.

With its caravans of shackled officers being led to the platform.

With black clothing emblazoned with dried blood, decapitated diplomats and politicians stacked up at the feet of lamp-posts. And the mug of Léon Daudet, and the hollow piggy-bank of Charles Maurras, pell-mell with the great muzzle of Paul Claudel, that of our old acquaintance sergeant Noel de Castelnau, and all the priests—yes, all the priests! What a fine lot of cassocks and surplices, exposing thighs haggard from the body lice of their lecherous hypocrisy; and the guardians of the peace, disemboweled first; and those gentlemen "in bourgeois dress," castrated; and the women of letters, from la Noailles to Jean Cocteau, wisely martyred by the torturers that we know so well how to be.

Ah, to find the language of "Le Père Duchesne" again for celebrating you, O future age! I'm not talking about calling for people's heads in the media that belong in museums and libraries—an ancillary measure, when something more radical would be better.

But the methodical purification of the population—the founders of the family; the creators of Benevolent Works (charity is a flaw); priests and pastors (I certainly don't want to forget them); the military; people who claim the wallets they find in the street as their own; Cornelian fathers; Mother Hubbards; investors in savings banks (they're more despicable than capitalists); the police *en bloc*; men and women of letters; inventors of serums for fighting epidemics; the "saviors of humanity"; the givers and beneficiaries of pity—all this compost cleared off at last; what a relief! The great Revolutions are born from the recognition of a singular principle: that of absolute liberty will be the motive for the one to come.

All those individual freedoms will clash. Through natural selection, humanity will decline until the day when, freed of its parasites, it will be possible to say that there are important questions other than the cultivation of grain.

AT LAST, IT IS TIME TO FOCUS ON ETERNITY.

**Translator's Note:** This text, published in the April, 1925 issue (#3) of *La Révolution Surréaliste,* is one of Desnos's most significant contributions to surrealist discussions of world revolution, prompted by recent anti-colonial uprisings in the Rif sector of Morocco. Desnos's essay shares with surrealist tracts (such as "The Revolution First and Always!" [1925] and "A Letter to the Dalai Lama" [1925]) an appeal to the Orient as a site of revolt and salutary intellectual ferment. Unlike other surrealist articles of the period, though, Desnos's essay is historical in character; its attacks on the pieties of the League of Nations and the treaty of Versailles, as well as its critiques of contemporary morals, are depicted as a continuation of the West's historical project of suppressing the spirit of barbarism and revolt Desnos characterizes as a property of the East. The surrealists would soon abandon such orientalist rhetoric, instead describing revolt in more orthodox Marxist terms. Desnos himself briefly fell in with this project, publishing an essay on "The Revolutionary Meaning of Surrealism" in the leftist journal *Clarté,* before drifting away from the movement's politics altogether in 1928–1929.

« Imagerie moderne »,"Modern Imagery,"
*Documents* 7 (December 1930),
translated by Jonathan P. Eburne

The essence of the artistic spirit is to trail along behind fashion. Unfit for discovering treasures, it is ready to admire what others enjoy, provided that time—or commercial value—imparts pseudo-consecration to objects that are often admirable. Someone who would have disdained the charming woodcut "images of Epinal" a few dozen years ago, today collects them, since popular expression is most susceptible to these sudden vogues.

Though we disdain them today, we will seek out tomorrow the extraordinary covers of illustrated supplements to newspapers like the *Petit Journal* and the *Petit Parisien,* which provide such a perfectly expressive commentary on current affairs and history. *L'Oeil de la Police* was one of those galleries comparable to the panoramas, which filled our young eyes with wonder in the fairs of yesteryear, in Trône or Neuilly.

Before snobbery can take hold of them—and it will indeed take hold of them—I would like today to brand with the hallmark of poetry some of the covers of popular novels: *Nick Carter, Sâr Dubnotal, Buffalo Bill, Texas Jack,* and, above all, *Fantômas.*

Let us note, without insisting on it, the extraordinary influence of this imagery on the development of the cinema, and let us linger on the effect it has had on modern vision and, as a result, on morals.

* * *

Certainly *Fantômas* sprang up amidst this literature as one of the most formidable monuments of spontaneous poetry. The text here is worthy of illustration. The whole period leading up to the war is described here with an accuracy that converged exactly with the phenomenon of lyricism. International intrigues; the lives of little people; the look of capital cities, and especially Paris; worldly morals as they really are—that is, as people imagine them; bourgeois morals; police morals; the presence, for the very first time, of a marvelous specific to the 20th century; the natural use of machines and recent inventions; the mystery of things, of men, and of destiny.

Each of the thirty-one volumes of this modern epic has a cover representing a scene from the novel. What's strange is that it's not always the most important scene that gets used, but the most curious one.

The cover of the first volume—representing Fantômas himself, in a top hat, cape, and mask, rising gigantically above the Paris on which he rests his foot—was enormously significant to the mythology and dream-life of Parisians. The elegance of its hero, and the bloody dagger he holds in his hand, overwhelmed our commonplace notions and destroyed the idea of the ratty, pitiful, and raggedy crook that had itself replaced another gentleman: Rocambole.

The nightmares of which a poster from this period gives us a very accurate idea (behind a door, two misers in their night-shirts and caps, candlesticks in hand, listen to two wall-drillers attacking an invincible security bolt) consume the "King of Fear's" prey. He was beautiful, seductive, elegant . . . one could love him and, if he was a romantic ideal for many boys, it's beyond a doubt that he was a Romantic and sentimental ideal for many little girls, even teenagers. The feminine sensuality of 1929 certainly owes much to this apparition, within the oneiric-erotic universe of children back then and, as a result, on the moral outlook of our own era as well. For every man, consciously or not, seeks to be a seducer, and, as a consequence, tries to respond to women's ideals of masculinity. We all know that one does not try fashioning oneself after a model with impunity, and that a physical simulation ends up corresponding to a moral sincerity.

Whereas Fantômas was the animator of all these revolutions, he was powerfully seconded in his psychic activity by the posters pasted onto walls announcing the publication of a feuilleton-novel in a newspaper (almost always *Le Matin* or *Le Petit Parisien*)—who doesn't remember *Balaoo* (There are footprints on the ceiling); or *Chéri-Bibi* (Not the hands! Not the hands!); or the *Mysteries of Passy* (where the Passy viaduct sinks ominously into a night of terror); or the notorious "They steal children in Paris," and even that odd contest in *Petits Pois du métro* that rejuvenated the famous game of "golden liter" in such an astonishing fashion. It was thus a whole series of magic formulae that were cast into the world, a series that included the famous "Closer to you, O God" illustrating the shipwreck of the *Titanic*.

There one met up with the highly sensory universe of song, which harmonized astonishingly well with that tragic and mysterious atmosphere: "Et voilà la journée terminée," "The Brown Waltz," "Mariette" (a remembrance of the Steinheil affair)—and the era thereby rose beneath the extraordinary air of Harry Fragson, seated at his piano A. Bord (what child hasn't looked for the piano "on board" Parisian boats), with one foot standing on Paris, the other on London.

Fragson, who would have to die so tragically, like a character in Fantômas.

And each month a new volume appeared: a world of nuns confronting each other with revolvers, in a ship's steerage, in the presence of an empty coffin; of kings imprisoned inside the mermaids in the fountains at the Place de la Concorde; of severed hands on the roulette table at Monte-Carlo; of a hansom cab driven by a dead coachman; of a murderer emptying the macabre content of a hatbox into the Seine: a woman's bloodless head emanating the black roses of a poisoned perfume.

All the elements of magic and prophecy were projected into the universal imagination—and let's not forget the humor represented by those sons of Père Ubu: the *Pieds nickelés* comic strip, and their frequent expression: *Thanks for the tart!*

Thus, unbeknownst to men, magic forces were clashing in the universe, and the mystic *Sâr Dubnotal* himself, in spite of his extraordinary powers of psychagogy (sic) was powerless to subjugate them. Only the gruesome bloodbath of the war would drown all these admirable deities beneath its waves of crimson and mud.

Will they resurrect themselves one day, through the good grace of contemporary sentimental relations, over whose birth they presided?

**Translator's Note:** This essay was one of several historical studies Desnos published in Georges Bataille's short-lived but deeply influential journal *Documents,* appearing in issue # 7 in December 1930. Bataille's journal offered an important counter-discourse to surrealism's increasingly militant form of cultural politics, allowing Desnos to pursue his interest in popular cultural forms that could evoke what he elsewhere called the marvelous, amoral, and anarchic "essential character of the dream" that surrealist imagery and popular film, at their best, could also generate. But whereas the surrealists, with whom Desnos broke formally in 1929, pursued cultural politics through romanticized forms of Marxism and psychoanalysis, Desnos strove instead to assemble an alternative archive of intransigence and wonder. In his article on "Modern Imagery," Desnos presciently notes the historical significance of popular dime-novel serials of the Belle Epoque (*Fantômas, Sub Dârnotal, Chéri-Bibi, Balaoo,* and the *Mysteries of Passy),* as well as its popular songs, comic books, and word games (Desnos mentions the "golden liter," a precursor to that other prewar invention, the crossword puzzle, first introduced as a newspaper feature in 1913). These popular forms, Desnos claims, display a form of social and artistic awareness whose effects still lingered in the contemporary imagination of 1930, yet whose origins had been forgotten, their cultural memory obliterated by the trauma of the First World War. Desnos's reference-laden essay might thus be considered an exercise in cultural archeology, unearthing and studying the buried artifacts of popular culture before they could be looted by "snobs" and commercialized anew.

## «Troisième manifeste du surréalisme», "Third Manifesto of Surrealism," *Le Courrier littéraire,* 1 March 1930, translated by Jonathan P. Eburne

> Since we haven't seen clearly what he's done, poor André
> Breton looks as if he has been seriously mistreated.
> —Noël Sabord, review of "A Corpse," *Paris-Midi,*
> 23 January.

Mr. André Breton has called his compendium of slander and calumny *The Second Manifesto of Surrealism;* I wish today, at the request of the *Courrier littéraire,* to make a necessary clarification. After five years of complete friendship followed by three years of silence, I have been obliged, through my participation in "A Corpse," to reveal the utter contempt in which I hold André Breton. It was not without effort that I came to this conclusion, and not without trying to deceive myself. Such is the case with his former mistresses, whose power has more to do with habit than with the love they inspire. Since André Breton never knew how to maintain the prudent silence his actions recommended, I am obliged today to reveal the reasons for this rupture. I once confided a secret in André Breton, based on the strength of our friendship. He betrayed this secret. He gave me his word of honor that he didn't know the name of the person who betrayed it; but then several months later, he confessed everything, and *asked for my forgiveness.*

But when respect and trust no longer exist, there can be no question of friendship. Taken one at a time, the flaws of this man of letters would seem venial. They would even be negligible if Breton would admit, once and for all, that he is nothing more than a *belle-lettrist.* Their sum, as we will see, is a reason for our separation and a proof of his bad faith.

André Breton accused Philippe Soupault of a certain number of offenses. When he was asked for proof, he presented the *question of faith*, just like Poincaré or Tardieu; yet last year, he confessed to Prévert that nothing had authorized him to accuse Soupault of anything.

It's the exactly the same case with Roger Vitrac, accused of who knows what machinations, without proof, without reason, in the most perfectly bad faith.

I can still hear and see Breton saying to me: "My dear friend, why do you practice journalism? It's idiotic. Do what I do: marry a rich woman! They're easy to find."

André Breton despises Éluard and his poetry. I've seen Breton throw Éluard's books into the fireplace. Admittedly, that day the author of *Love, Poetry* had refused to lend him 10,000 francs . . . if Breton didn't sign an I.O.U. for him in exchange. Why does he remain his friend, and why does he write encomiums to his work? Because Paul Éluard, however communist he claims to be, is a developer, and the money he makes from selling swampland to workers he uses to buy paintings and Negro objects, in which he and Breton are both dealers.

André Breton despises Aragon, on whom he casts aspersions again and again. Why does he go easy on him? Because he's afraid, and because he knows that a break with him would signal his own failure.

André Breton used to be angry with Tristan Tzara, for the precise reason that at the performance of *Coeur à barbe* the Dada leader had us arrested. He knows this. He saw and heard him pointing us out to the police, just as well as I did. Why have they reconciled? Because Tristan Tzara buys the Negro fetishes and paintings Breton sells him.

In an article on painting, André Breton rebukes Joan Miró for having come into some money along the way. Yet is was he, André Breton, who bought the painting "The Tilled Field" for five hundred francs and then sold it again for between six and eight thousand. Miró may have come into money, but it was Breton who pocketed it.

André Breton wrote *Surrealism and Painting* with the sobriety of a pope, the solemnity of a magus, and the purity of Eliacin. It is nonetheless curious to observe that the only painters he praises without reservation are those with whom he's able to do business.

In December 1926, while we were discussing whether or not to join the Communist Party, André Breton tried to make me look like a coward, because, instead of turning a profit from the work of painters, I was paying my dues as a journalist. He demanded everyone's agreement not to contribute to bourgeois journals. Six weeks later, he submitted a text to the journal *Commerce* "because," as he said, "it pays well." Likewise, he who so gently upbraided Man Ray for his relations with the Vicomte de Noailles, was just last year clinging to the hope of having de Noailles pay for *La Révolution Surréaliste*. But that said, Breton will forever claim that André Masson is a sellout because he allowed the German journal *Querschnitt* to print a text by Limbour about his work.

It's fitting to imagine such contradictions as nothing more than a business rivalry between art dealers. As for me, I would see no harm in Breton "making a living" in this way, or in any other way, if he were willing to recognize that money plays at least as important a role in his existence as it does in everyone else's, and if he didn't always have that sanctimonious word "purity" on the tip of his tongue, and at the tip of his pen. If he was pure, so be it. There are eccentrics and perverts who have a taste for that foul thing called virginity. Now, virginity and purity are about as different as two pigs in a poke.

But Breton is first and foremost a man of letters. He has never created anything. His whole activity is based on literary or artistic critique, which sure looks like the highest peak of literature to me. Why is it so important for him to masquerade as a moral leader, as a model for living? Because such attitudes come with material advantages. Breton profiting from surrealism is no different from the Pope receiving, to his profit, the last confession of Saint Peter. I could continue infinitely to recount these incidents which, together with his serious character flaws (insults directed at his mistresses and friends; a taste for authority exercised even on our choice of aperitifs and other burlesque actions), ends up not only making one not only weary, but obnoxious as well.

When all is said and done, Breton is contemptible because his life and actions do not match up with the ideas he claims to defend; because he is a hypocrite, a coward, an operator (see. the letters he writes to critics to get them to talk about his books), and because his work has always evolved in a direction contrary to life, mankind, and truth.

I'll get all this back-room gossip over with—since our gentleman has more of a taste for it than I (his books are full of it)—but I could tell dozens more stories. His feeble response to "A Corpse" speaks volumes, moreover, about his dismay when spoken to positively.

What does the fact that I wrote tributes to Breton in 1923 and insulted him in 1930 prove, other than that I've changed my opinion? As far as I'm concerned, I guess I loved a pig. Besides, there's no need to trot out confidential writings to get people to understand me. If they read *The Lost Steps, Nadja,* the *First Manifesto, Earthlight,* etc., they'll see what Breton thought of me before the bad-faith passage he dedicated to me in the *Second Manifesto.* What do I care if he says that my Alexandrians are false, padded, and hollow? That's a quarrel for pedants. What do I care if he says that I pretend to be Victor Hugo and Robespierre? I think he's short of insults. And in any case, this is better than pretending to be the pope (cf. his preface to Gegenbach's *Satan in Paris* and the *Second Manifesto of Surrealism).*

But where I catch my Breton red-handed with his bag of tricks is when he accuses me, in my article "The Mercenaries of Opinion," of defending Clemenceau. The lie there is so blatant that it's enough simply to read the article in question (in the journal *Bifur,* #2, page 165). Why doesn't he also say, while he's at it, that I'm a pederast, an opium addict, and a Freemason?[1]

There is much to say about Breton's Puritanism and Protestantism. Does he not condemn the use of alcohol? Yes, but he drinks, and one might

---

[1] "Desnos," he said, "is a dubious man. He's an addict."
"An addict in what way? Does he take drugs?"
"Yes; he drinks alcohol." (Private conversation)

explain his character pretty well as the effect of cirrhosis of the liver on his thinking. Once again we find in him an outrageous religious conformity. But the quarrel isn't limited to this. I do not share Breton's ideas—that priest who doesn't laugh; who doesn't even know what it means to laugh, no matter how much the desire to do so might consume him. Incapable of theater, he condemns it *en bloc*. More bourgeois than anyone, he has the word Revolution in his mouth not because it comes to him from the heart, but because it is too hard for his feeble throat to swallow, lest his fragile stomach vomit it up. Breton is the type of character who lives for the idea of revolution and not the act. At the first sign of trouble, he will leave for Koblenz. Here, then, is that impotent poet, that critic, that intellectual con man (and trust that he knows how to fool everyone in his circle), that sophist, in the presence of Lautréamont. Ah! understand that he never gets confused. One sentence, one single proposition from Lautréamont has struck him: *the right to contradict oneself*—and I can guarantee that he has made use of this.

With him, this human, legitimate right turns into a right to hypocrisy and mental restriction. Jesuit!

From here, exploiting surrealism, and daring to say it exists, is only one step away—the step from a lie to a breach of trust.

I, who have some right to talk about surrealism, declare here that the surreal exists only for non-surrealists. For surrealists, there is only one reality —unique, whole, and open to all.

Breton would not be the suspect being I've just denounced, were not his ideas alone enough to condemn him. To believe in the surreal is to repave the path of God. Surrealism, such as it has been formulated by Breton, is one of the gravest dangers to which we expose our freedom of thought; the most devious trap into which we let our atheism fall; the finest auxiliary to a renaissance in Catholicism and clericalism.

And I proclaim here André Breton tonsured by my hand, cast into his literary monastery, his disaffected chapel; and I proclaim surrealism fallen into the public domain, at the disposal of heretics, schismatics, and atheists.

And I am an atheist.

**Translator's Note:** This text, though titled as a "Manifesto," was published as an article in Eugène Merle's most recent newspaper, *Le Courrier littéraire,* in March 1930. For the past several years Desnos had been supporting himself as a journalist, publishing numerous articles, essays, poems, and reviews in Merle's newspapers, such as *Paris-Soir* (1923-1927), *Paris-Matinal* (1927-1929), and *Le Courrier littéraire* (founded in late 1929). It was Desnos's career in journalism, in fact, that formed the basis of his formal break with André Breton, and with organized surrealism more broadly; in Breton's *Second Manifesto of Surrealism* (first published in December 1929), the surrealist leader attacked Desnos for scorning organized politics in favor of the commercialism and populism of professional newspaper-writing. Desnos first responded to Breton's critique in the vituperative anti-Breton group tract, "A Corpse," published as a pamphlet earlier in 1930. Desnos's later "Third Manifesto," in spite of its open hostility, represents in fact a more measured response, adding to its character-assault on Breton a provocative statement about the necessity for surrealist creative activities to reach a public. Surrealism, Desnos argues, should only be practiced by non-surrealists, rather than husbanded as the inner machinations of a secret society or cult; thus its publication in a popular newspaper seems especially fitting.

# 1944
## Art poétique

(Part of the project of the volume *Sens*, which was to follow after *Fortunes*. Published in *Destinée arbitraire*, 1975.)

In the back of the throat
Picked up in the mud and the slime
Spit out, thrown up, cast off—
I am the poem witness to the breath of my master –
Discard, rubbish, garbage
Like the diamond, the flame, and the sky's blue
Not pure, not virgin
But kissed in every corner
kissed screwed sucked fucked raped
I am the verse witness to the breath of my master
Screwing and raping
Nothing dirtier than a deflowering
Oof! That's it and you get out
Good muddy earth where I put my foot
I am for the wind the great wind and the sea
I am the verse witness to the breath of my master
It cracks it farts it sings it snores
Great wind storm heart of the world
There is no more bad weather

I love all weather I love weather
I love the great wind
The great wind rain cries snow sun fire and everything of the earth
    muddy or dry
And let it crumble!
And let it rot
Rot old flesh old bones
Through the back of the throat
And let it break the teeth and set the gums to bleeding
I am the verse witness to the breath of my master
The water runs with its absurd humming-bird song
Of nightingale and alcohol burning in a casserole
running along my body
A mushroom rots in the corner of the shadowy forest where a
    woman of god's thunder is lost and splashes barefoot
It really rots at the foot of the oaks
A golden medal won't hold out
It's soft
Deep
It gives
It really rots at the foot of the oaks
A moon from long ago
Is reflected in this rot
Smell of death smell of life embracing smell
droll creatures of shadow must be rolling about
and fighting and embracing here
It really rots at the foot of the oaks
And that breathes still harder at thesummit
Nests upset and the famous hummingbirds just now
Thrown down
Nightingales delunged
Foliage of immense palpitating forests
Dirtied and wrinkled like toilet paper

Tumultuous rising tides of the summit
of the forests your waves pull up towards the sky
the plump hills in a foam
of clearings and pastures veined with
rivers and minerals
Finally here it is coming from its lair
The bleeding flayed one singing with his troat alive
No nails at the end of his fingers
Orpheus they call him
Cold kisser the confident of Sybls
Bacchus castrato raving and fortuneteller
Once a man of good earth come forth from good seed by a good wind
Speaks bleeds dreams
Teeth broken kidneys split, arteries knotted
Heart of nothing
While the river runs rolls inebriates grotesque wrecks of barges
    with coal running
Reaches the plain reaches the sea
Foam rolling and wearing out
On the sand salt coral
I will enter in your waves
After the river exhausted
Watch out for your FLOTTES!
For your corals, your sand, your salt at your feasts
Issued for the from the walls with passwords
By the back of the throats
By the back of the teeth
Good weather
For men worthy of the name
Good weather for the rivers and trees
Good weather for the sea
The foam and the mud remain
And the joy of living

And a hand in mine
And the joy of living
I am the verse the witness of the breath of my master.

1944–45

# III. On the Cinema

# On the Cinema

The heroic cinema must be a vital summons to the living, a witness to the eternal in the temporal, a combination of seeing and hearing, of suggestion, perception, intensification, and exaltation—humor and tragedy carried to their extremes. Above all, it has nothing to do with talent or work, with the patience of description or the elegance of wit—and everything to do with the genius of spontaneous decision, the profound impoliteness of passion.

Desnos attaches great importance to the possibilities of the cinema as an expression of the otherwise inexpressible longing for the fusion of vision, movement, and imagination. The cinema could provide in its unlimited suggestion of possibilities the basis for a sustained revolution against fixity, the exact opposite of the formal efforts of "literature" and "art." While Desnos made of his dream / reality meditations the basis for a series of poems focusing on the imagery of darkness and mystery, he also utilized them as sources for a corresponding series of scenarios and film criticisms.

Against the triviality, the false seriousness, and the genuine banality of the "ridiculous" life we lead, as Desnos terms it, the film poses a world of possibility. If those old in spirit no longer dream, if they suffer the sterility of knowing what to expect, the endlessly fertile and youthful imagination of those who know how to dream transports them to the surprising atmosphere—what Desnos calls the "infinite and the eternal," a cinematic composite of the unexpected, the sensual, the baroque, and the uninhibited.

Even the cinema hall itself is for him a place of marvelous encounter, ideally suited to the dual spiritual and sensual nature of dream and love. The darkness links the minds of the observers to the actions portrayed and their dreams to each other, opening a physical-spiritual intimacy based on chance. In his poems Desnos laments the solitude of dreaming, its threat to sentiment, as the dreamer is separated from other beings, even the most passionately loved. But the cinema is a dream shared, a "revenge" of the many upon their daily surroundings.

This multidimensional life in unison takes its source in imaginative transformation of reality and in the insistence on mental freedom, both essential ingredients of the surrealist dream. The man of the cinema is not just a man of letters, an occupation for which Desnos has only scorn. At the very opposite pole from the "mediocre literary satisfaction" which he refuses for himself and for all the authors and creators he respects, stands the idea of poetry, defined by Desnos as the attitude of those who are willing to run risks. Situated at the other pole from poetry, art is for Desnos the spoiler of the most moving experiences, a dedicated opponent of the unconscious in its revolutionary force. No surrealist ever ceased to wish himself the conveyer of the seeds of revolutionary action. Desnos is convinced that only the structure of the film can keep the architecture of the barricades from falling into oblivion. All the reactions to the poetry of cinema are violent, since it is itself a creator of energy, a center of revolutionary fervor. True poets will, he says, imprint violent kisses on the screen, or set fire to it. These liberated beings, immune to the temptations felt by those to whom Desnos concedes only "mediocre souls," "vulgar souls," "bourgeois souls," long for the storm, the unremitting violence of the absolute:

> Born in the forebodings of the tempest, we await it with its procession of clouds of thunder and lightning, and there are many among us—I write on behalf of extreme and virile souls—who give to this future and perhaps imminent cataclysm the name of Revolution. ("Tempest over Asia")

Attila the Hun did more for human evolution than Pasteur, says Desnos, in "Tempest over Asia." So the *impassioned*, those burned pure by their capacity for exceeding the normal limit, are the true heroes of our time. The cinema provides the truest landscape for passion.

From *les Rayons et les Ombres,*
ed. MC Dumas, Gallimard, 1992
translated by Mary Ann Caws

## Scenario: *Une étoile filante*
"A Shooting Star"

One lovely summer night, a shooting star appears in the sky. As it passes over a village, from a balcony, a girl makes a vow as she looks at it: "To be loved, to be loved always." As it passes over a crossroads, a young man also makes a vow: "To love, to love always." As it passes over an orchard, another girl makes a vow, the third one: "Never to love."

And naturally, the three characters meet during a country dance. The young man will fall in love, of course, with the second girl who won't love him. The first one will remain alone. She'll become the confidant of the young man.

Finally, the young man will manage to marry the girl he loves and life goes on, sad for the one who isn't loved, empty for the woman who doesn't love, dreary for the one who wants to be loved and isn't. The drama turns more and more around these three characters, for little by little, as time passes, it's in his confidant that the man sees his desires crystallise. The action will mount dramatically until the day when, in a fire, the young man will choose to save not his wife but the one who wishes to be loved.

Above the smoking remains a shooting star inspires their last vow: "To love each other."

Around this scenario lives a whole village with its work in the fields, the succeeding seasons, the aging of the world.

(RO 309–310)

## "La nuit parfaite du cinéma"
### *The Perfect Night of the Cinema*

The perfect night of the cinema doesn't just offer us the miracle of the screen, a neutral country where dreams are projected, it offers us also the most appealing form of modern adventure. Not in vain do these men and women assembled under the comet tail of the projector submit their life to comparison with that, just as real, of the heroes on the screen. If the adventure of the film is worth the spectator's risk at participating in it, if, lacking any exciting adventure, the smile of a women, the seductive look of an assassin arouse in us a rather lovely story, the viewing room and the spectators fall into a dead faint. The seated dreamer is carried off into a new world in relation to which reality is only an unappealing fiction. A superb opium, the cinema takes us far away from material cares, gives us the perfect generative indifference of great acts, sensational discoveries, elevated thoughts.

How many among these modest people, mediocre souls, have felt passing over them, with the breath of frenetic lives, the bitter regret of days consecrated to accountability, the cooking of the evening soup, trivial ambitions! Those admirable screening rooms stamping their delight at the avatars of Charlie Chaplin, the car races of the Mysteries of New York, Nazimova's deeds and gestures, Pearl White, and Betty Compson, you are where it all takes place.

But if, in those room the screen offers only celluloid protagonists and calico spectacles, you stretch out your hand, it will probably meet a friendly hand, or if you move your knee to the side, as befits the tradition. it will encounter the knee next to it. Boot to boot you will perhaps leave for some ardent gallop. Oh, miserable moralists, deserters of love, rush to remonstrate with them, these Don Juans of the shadows, these Berenices of the shadows! For me, I have never seen without being moved the strategies of these un-quiet souls, in the noise of the folding seats snapping up as their silhou-ette is profiled on the screen's white rectangle.. How many hands have I not reached out for myself thanks to the dusk of the cinema! What marvels I've imagined waiting for the electric dawn! Meetings and gropings, sentimen-tal hopscotch, it is comforting to submit to your fate, even just to earn the legitimate scorn of those who only know the caricature of love, an old woman warming her rheumatism by the corner of the fire.

*Journal littéraire*, 25 April, 1925
RO, pp. 69–70

## "Cinema Frénétique et cinéma académique"
### *Frenetic Cinema and Academic Cinema*

Lost in a deep forest whose earth is made of moss and pine needles and whose light— filtered by the high eucalyptus with hanging bark, the pine trees green like the meadows promised to the souls of the wild horses fine and free, the oaks with their bodies knotted and tortured by infernal maladies—is sometimes yellow like dead leaves, sometimes white like the edge of the woods, the modern traveler is seeking the marvelous. He thinks he recognizes his way groping along. Strange shadows tremble in the clearings. He thinks he recognizes the domain promised to his dreams by night. It falls dark, full of mystery and promise. A great magic projector pursues the fabulous creatures. Here is Nosferatu the Vampire; here is the asylum where Cesare and Doctor Caligari had their memorable adventures; here are, coming forth from the poetic caves, Jack the Ripper, Ivan the Terrible, and their old friend from the Cabinet of Wax Figures.

The modern traveler, finally swept away by the powers of tragic poetry, reaches the heart of the miraculous regions of human emotion.

At this moment there appears a grotesque character who doesn't seem at all out of place in these marvelous clearings. From the dandruff of his hair, the ink spots on his fingers, the dirt between his nails, his myopia, you can recognize a frightening specimen of the species of the *man of letters*. He is declaring that poetry is only literature; he is declaring that cinema is an art; he is declaring that art has to copy nature, naturally (sic); he is declaring the duty of the artist is to represent man in his most mediocre and filthiest occupations; he puts his soiled fingers on the white apparitions, on the adorable phantoms of the night, on the pure face of the exceptional creatures, and everything disappears. The modern traveler is seated in a screening room. They tell him he is in the cinema, that a film that has cost millions of dollars is about to be shown.

A title appears on the screen. Great lovers and lovely women are moving about. They are figuring in a dishearteningly banal scenario which is dragging along, through mediocre but clever technical tricks, the kind that fill the ordinary spectator with joy and let him exercise his feeble intelligence, leading up to a vulgar dénouement.

The modern traveler yawns. He goes out on the boulevard. The neon lights rival the stars of paradise. Admirable women go by reflected with tenderness on the humid pavement.

The modern traveller finds again the path of the mysterious forest with the nightly marvels. He remembers Charlie Chaplin, and the miracles he accomplishes. He remembers the *Mysteries of New York* and Pearl White.

He declares that the reality he is being offered isn't worth being lived or told and, letting the German cinema go to its ruin under a tinplate sky, through the ridiculous maxims of bourgeois morale, he goes off under the great trees, in search of adventures worthy of his imagination. For in the cinema, we are watching the great struggle which, in all domains, opposes intelligence to sensitivity (and I am just contrasting two words taken strictly in their literal sense), poetry to literature, life to art, love and hate to scepticism, revolution to counter-revolution. Human fate is played out in detail and in general in these struggles which began in the last years of the Eighteenth century.

When we are speaking about the cinema, we have to understand that it is not a question of corporate interests or techniques but of its very spirit and of the links that attach it to the solemn dimensions of disquiet. And just in the narrow radius of Germany, where frenetic cinema and academic cinema battle it out, it's important not to forget that the technique and the material future of the screen aren't in question, but that, with the excuse of perfecting one and guaranteeing the other, the risk is the silencing, as has already been done in many countries, of the magnificent sources of inspiration.

RO, pp. 86–88

## "Mélancolie du cinéma"
### *Melancholy of the Cinema*

Here it is almost summer. The trees of Paris are the green as we used to long for this past winter, and already we can feel the precocious burning of the August sun, the falls of autumn, the bare branches of December.

Our eyes no longer want to believe in the eternity of good weather, and the rain, the tempest and the storm seem to us more natural than the calm radiance of the star on a planet prosperous, calm, and silent.

Born in the premises of the tempest, we are awaiting this tempest with its accompaniment of clouds, of thunder and lightning, and there are many among us—I am writing for those virile and extreme souls—who are according to this future and perhaps imminent cataclysm the name of Revolution.

Oh, you young men just my own age, your hearts vibrant with faith but whom the old call sceptics, where shall we hide our eyelids burned by daylight, where shall we spend our nights prey to dreams and hallucinations?

Often night is just for us a matter of sleeplessness, disquiet, torments. Cinema offers us its darkness, a drama we want to enter. If the heroes don't have an everyday soul, if the object of their torment is valid, we'll go right into their universe. If they are just puppets, we'll have a really good laugh and it will take the whole night and all its breezes to calm our burning eyes.

Too bad for inferior films. A day will come when we'll tear apart any screen on which bad or ridiculous ones are projected.

Man Ray, to whom the cinema already owes so much, and to whom if it were not a slave to money, it could owe a lot more still, said to me one day that three fourths of films spent their time opening and closing doors, or imitating conversation. Two totally useless things, you have to admit.

On the other hand, you notice that, except for "news" and a few German films, no burial is ever shown in the cinema. It is strange to notice that the spectacle of death is banished from the cinema as is that of love, I mean love for love, with its bestial brutalities and its wildly savage aspects, as is the spectacle of the guillotine, which would do certain of our gentle compatriots such good and would show them how expensive it is to take someone else's life, whereas you can just open and close a door or imitate a conversation.

Oh you unknown censor, have you really weighed the meaning of these last scenes, where your soul and your heart are only tin plate?

All the melancholy, all the despair of our lives is held in these acts: closing a door, opening another, pretending to speak.

The doors we are opening open on pitiful landscapes and close on landscapes just as pitiful. Our lyric hearts are absent from most of our conversations. And our tongues, oh you heroes of the film screen, are perhaps even more silent than yours. Give us films at the level of our torments! Bow down, oh imbecile censors, before the rare honorable films which mostly come to France from this corner of America, Los Angeles, a free city among slavish places!

Leave us our desirable heroines, leave us our heroes. Our world is too pitiful for our dream to be brother to reality, we need heroic years. And I say loudly that I'm not thinking about the war when I speak of heroism. We need loves and lovers as noble as the legends that our mind invents.

Why should we continue to hide the surrealist torment of our epoch, where the cinema has its place? Nights of tempests and foamy waves, assassinations perpetrated in the forests of the screen, lovely landscapes! Thanks to the cinema, we no longer believe in the magic of distant landscapes, we no longer believe in the picturesque. The cinema has destroyed what Chateaubriand, that great poet, could describe with the help of his memories and his imagination.

But we are still sensitive to the earthly mysteries of the night, of the day, of stars and of love The revolt growing in us would be happy to rest on the bosom of a mistress now docile and now not, according to our desires.

Here it is almost summer. The trees of Paris are the green as we used to long for this past winter, and already we can feel the precocious burning of the August sun, the falls of autumn, the bare branches of December.

The man who is writing these lines—will he take a long time to respond to the call of the eternal foliage of the faroff forests, the touching monotony of eternal snows?

*Le Soir*, May 7, 1927

# IV. Poems

# Poems

*Poetry can be this or that. It does not necessarily have to be this or that except delirious and lucid.*

"Reflections on Poetry"

O ne of the first things we notice about all the work of Desnos is his impassioned attachment to language itself, in all its possibilities or its play, in the sense of the *play* of metal, for instance. Breton always was to proclaim the seriousness of word play as in the expression "les jeux de mot": words, he said, "aren't playing they are making love.") Just so, the titles of Desnos' works are often recognizable word plays: *Deuil pour Deuil* is "sorrow for sorrow," just as we say "an eye for an eye and a tooth for a tooth," but it is also "sorrow for sorrow's sake." *La Liberté ou l'amour!* is, according to Marie-Claire Dumas, of the same order as "your money or your life" whereas we read it here also as "the Liberty which is also Love." *Corps et biens* is a play on "corps et âme," "body and soul," but here the possessions have replaced the soul, whereas P'oasis is perfectly clear in its two senses of poetry/oasis telescoped ("poésie/oasis") and of the plural of "poesies." Now, in the development of Desnos' greatest poetry, there is a noticeable change from the early linguistic experiments and poetic jokes, such as *L'Aumonyme and Langage cuit* of 1923, to the serious and often tragic love poems of *A la mystérieuse* of 1926, where meditations on the real and the illusory, and on the presence and absence of the woman loved, are

97

found side by side with presentations of a vague menace in the natural world or of a startling landscape.

Each of the poems in the latter volume has an unmistakable inner coherence and certain of them have an exterior brilliance, although the collection as a whole has not the accumulated intensity of *Les Ténèbres* (1927), where the themes of adventure. love, and presence, of the waking and the nocturnal dream in its relation to reality merge with the greater theme of poetic language itself. In every poem of *Les Ténèbres* one is acutely aware of the self-critical poet already seen in the poetic novels, where the cause of linguistic adventure was paradoxically treated alongside that of surrealist love, sometimes as identical with it, and then again as its irreconcilable opposite—the two senses, contrary but joined, of *La Liberté ou l'amour!* In these poems, Desnos tests his own poetry for its fidelity to his dream and to a wider actuality beyond. This time, however, the adventure of the poet's dreaming is clearly separate from that of his love, and the latter is frequently sacrificed to make way for the former; in fact, the very value of love is denied whenever the two are compared. Intensity of experience and expression seem finally to depend on the poet's isolation. To what extent this psychological reality may be dependent on the tragedy of Desnos' love for Yvonne George is finally not the major question for us.

That the famous poem "J'ai tant rêvé de toi" (I Have So Often Dreamed of You) keeps its own profile even when, after Theresienstadt, it is recited in Czech by Joseph Stuna and retranslated into French as "The Last Poem of Desnos," is indicative, even symbolic, of the continuity of his personality. For it is then addressed to Youki as surely as if it had been written for her, and the isolation which penetrates the poem finds its concomitant reality in the life of Desnos with its tragic conclusion but transcends it also. What we finally are attached to in our own memory of the poet is not the specific biographical facts so much as the intensity of certain texts, marked by a loneliness which no extrinsic knowledge can reduce by explaining it. This is, it seems to us, the incontrovertible and inner poetic reality.

*Note:* All poems without initials are translated by Mary Ann Caws.

**1923**
*L'Aumonyme*

## «Notre paire quiète, o yeux!»

Notre paire quiète, ô yeux!
que votre «non» soit sang (t'y fier?)
que votre araignée rie,
que votre vol honteux soit fête (au fait)
sur la terre (commotion!).

Donnez-nous, aux joues réduites,
notre pain quotidien.
Part donnez-nous de nos œufs foncés
Comme nous part donnons
à ceux qui nous ont offensés.
nounou laissez-nous succomber à la tentation
et d'aile ivrez-nous du mal.

# Hour farther

Hour farther witch art in Heaven
Hallowed bee, thine aim.
Thy king done come!
Thy will be done in
ersatz is in Heaven.

Kippers this day-hour,
Delhi bread.
And four kippers, sour trace, pa says,
As we four give them that trace paths against us.
Leader's not in to tempt Asians;
Butter liver (as from Eve)
fill our men.

tr. Martin Sorrell

## «C'est une fâcheuse aventure» (extract)

*«C'est une fâcheuse aventure: créer le mystère autour de nos amours. Pas si fâcheuse que ça.*

*Je l'aime, elle roule si vite, la grande automobile blanche. De temps à autre, au tournant des rues, le chauffeur blanc et noir, plus majestueusement qu'un capitaine de frégate, abaisse lentement le bras dans l'espace qui roule, roule, roule si vite, en ondes blanches comme les roues de l'automobile que j'aime.*

*Mais le mystère qui se déroule concentriquement autour de ses seins a capturé dans son labyrinthe de macadam taché de larmes la grande automobile blanche qui vogue plutôt qu'elle ne roule en faisant naître autour d'elle dans l'espace les grandes ondes invisibles et concentriques du mystère. La cible aérienne que les hommes traversent sans s'en douter se disloque lentement au gré des amants et la sphère, cerclée de parallèles comme ses seins, crève ainsi qu'un ballon. Dirigeables et ballons, aéroplanes et vapeurs, locomotives et automobiles, tout est mystère dans mon immobile amour pour ses seins.»*

*Après avoir parlé, je regardai :*

*Le désert qui s'étendait autour de moi était peuplé d'échos qui me mirent cruellement en présence de ma propre image reflétée dans le miroir des mirages. Les femmes qui tenaient ces glaces à main étaient nues, hormis leurs mains qui étaient gantées, leur sein gauche, gainé de taffetas moiré noir à faire hurler mes gencives de volupté, hormis aussi leurs cheveux dissimulés sous une écharpe de fine laine jaune. Quand ces femmes se retournaient je pouvais tout voir de leur dos merveilleux, tout hormis la nuque, la colonne verté-brale et cette partie de la croupe où la cambrure prend naissance, cachées qu'elles étaient par les pans de l'écharpe. Cette nudité partielle et savam-ment irritante pour moi a-t-elle causé ma folie? Dites-le-moi, vous dont le mystère est la fin, le but.*

## "It's a tiresome adventure . . . ." (extract)

"It's a tiresome undertaking: creating mystery around our loves. Not so tiresome as all that.

I love the great white car speeding along. From time to time, turning the corners, the white and black chauffeur lowers, even more majestically than a frigate commander, his arm in the space rolling, rolling, rolling along so rapidly in white waves like the tires of the car I love.

But the mystery which unfolds concentrically around its breasts has captured in its asphalt labyrinth spotted with tears the great white car sailing rather than rolling along, making great invisible circles around it in space, concentric waves of mystery. The aerial target through which men pass without realizing it is slowly displaced according to the desires of lovers and the sphere, encircled with parallel lines like her breasts, pops like a balloon. Dirigibles and balloons, airplanes and mists, locomotives and automobiles, all is mystery in my immobile love for her breasts."

After having spoken, I looked:

The desert which stretched out around me was peopled with echoes whose cruelty forced me into the presence of my own image reflected in the mirror of mirages. The women holding these hand mirrors were naked, except for their gloved hands, their left breasts encased in taffeta moiré black enough to set my gums screaming in pleasure, and except for their hair hidden under scarves of thin yellow wool. When these women turned around I could see their marvelous backs in entirety, all except the nape of the neck, the vertebral column, and the part where the hip begins to curve, hidden as these were by the scarf. Did this partial nudity, skillfully irritating to me, provoke my madness? Tell me that, you whose mystery is the goal.

tr. MAC

# 1923
## *Langage cuit*

## Vent nocturne

Sur la mer maritime se perdent les perdus
Les morts meurent en chassant des chasseurs
dansent en rond une ronde
Dieux divins! Hommes humains!
de mes doigts digitaux je déchire une cervelle cérébrale.
   Quelle angoissante angoisse
Mais les maîtresses maîtrisées ont des cheveux chevelus
   Cieux célestes
    terre terrestre
mais où est la terre céleste?

# The wind at night

On oceanic oceans the sunk sink
the doomed die chasing
chasers ring-dancing rondos
Godly gods! Human humans!
With my digital digits I dismantle brainy brains.
    Such agonising agony!
But mastered mistresses have hirsute hair
    Heavenly heavens
    Earthy earth
But where is heaven on earth?

tr. Martin Sorrell

# À présent

J'aimai avec passion ces longues fleurs qui éclatai-je à mon entrée.
  Chaque lampe se transfigurai-je en œil crevé d'où coulai-je des vins
  plus précieux que la nacre et les soupirs des femmes assassinées.
Avec frénésie, avec frénésie nos passions naquis-je et le fleuve Amazone
  lui-même ne bondis-je pas mieux.
Ecouté-je moi bien! Du coffret jaillis-je des océans et non des vins et le
  ciel s'entr'ouvris-je quand il parus-je.
Le nom du seigneur n'eus-je rien à faire ici.
Les belles mourus-je d'amour et les glands, tous les glands tombai-je
  dans les ruisseaux.
La grande cathédrale se dressai-je jusqu'au bel œil. L'œil de ma bien-
  aimée.
Il connus-je des couloirs de chair. Quant aux murs il se liquéfiai-je et le
  dernier coup de tonnerre fis-je disparaître de la terre tous les
  tombeaux.

# Actually

I loved with passion those long flowers which rI/oted on my arrIval.
   Each lamp did I sock it into whence did run dr/I fine wine more
   precious than oyster pearl and the sighs of slain women.
Frenziedly, frenziedly our passions me/rupted and the Amazon river
   itself could not leap 'igher.
Listen hear I say! From D Jones' locker
   did fl/I up and not from wines and the sk/I half opened when there
      happened b/I.
Beauties d/Ied of love and acorns, f/all acorns into the streams.
The great cathedral I sing to the sk/I. M/y loved one's I.
Corridors of flesh, I openers to me. As for the walls, they did liquefy/I
   and the last thunder clap I made vanish from the face of the earth
   every tomb.

tr. Martin Sorrell

## Idéal maîtresse

Je m'étais attardé ce matin-là à brosser les dents d'un joli animal que, patiemment, j'apprivoise. C'est un caméléon. Cette aimable bête fuma, comme à l'ordinaire, quelques cigarettes pois je partis.

Dans l'escalier je la rencontrai. «Je mauve» me dit-elle et tandis que moi-même je cristal à pleine ciel-je à son regard qui fleuve vers moi.

Or, il serrure et, maîtresse! Tu pitchpin qu'a joli vase je me chaise si les chemins tombeaux.

L'escalier, toujours l'escalier qui bibliothèque et la foule au bas plus abîme que le soleil ne cloche.

Remontons! mais en vain, les souvenirs se sardine! à peine, à peine un bouton tirelire-t-il. Tombez, tombez! En voici le verdict: «La danseuse sera fusillée à l'aube en tenue de danse avec ses bijoux immolés au feu de son corps. Le sang des bijoux, soldats!»

Eh quoi, déjà je miroir. Maîtresse tu carré noir et si les nuages de tout à l'heure myosotis, ils moulins dans la toujours présente éternité.

# Only one thing on his mind

I'd spun it out that morning brushing the teeth of the lovely animal which patiently I'm taming. A chameleon. The pleasant creature smoked, as per usual, a few cigarettes, after which I left.

It was on the stairs I met her: "I mauve" said she, and while myself I crystal in open skies beneath her fluent gaze in my direction.

Then padlock and mistress! You yellow pine in vessel fine I to seat if road vault.

The stairs, always the stairs turning library and the crowd abysmally lower than sun can clash.

Back upstairs! But in vain, memories that sardine! hardly, hardly a button tirra-lirra-till. Fall fall! Here's the verdict: "the dancer will be shot at dawn wearing tutu and bijoux sacrificed in the flames of her body. Soldier, bijoux blood!"

But already I mirror. Mistress you black square and if the clouds of a while ago forget me not, they mill in sempiternal eternity.

tr. Martin Sorrell

## Au mocassin le verbe

Tu me suicides, si docilement
Je to mourrai pourtant un jour.
Je connaîtrons cette femme idéale
et lentement je neigerai sur sa bouche
Et je pleuvrai sans doute même si je fais tard, même si je
    fais beau temps
Nous aimez si peu nos yeux
Et s'écroulerai cette larme sans
raison bien entendu et sans tristesse.
sans.

# Take the verb to moccasin

You kill I, obediently.
I'll die you yet.
That ideal woman will ice snow
and snow blowly on her mouth.
And no doubt I'll rain weather I'm late or good whether.
  Our eyes your loves lost
and this tear drop
I'll sort of course down
no reason why and long face
less.

tr. Martin Sorrell

## Un jour qu'il faisait nuit

Il s'envola au fond de la rivière.
Les pierres en bois d'ébène, les fils de fer en or et la croix sans branche.
Tout rien.
Je la hais d'amour comme tout un chacun.
Le mort respirait de grandes bouffées de vide.
Le compas traçait des carrés
et des triangles à cinq côtés.
Après cela il descendit au grenier.
Les étoiles de midi resplendissaient.
Le chasseur revenait, carnassière pleine de poissons
    Sur la rive au milieu de la Seine.
Un ver de terre, marque le centre du cercle
sur la circonférence.
En silence mes yeux prononcèrent un bruyant discours.
Alors nous avancions dans une allée déserte où se pressait la foule.
Quand la marche nous eut bien reposé
    nous eûmes le courage de nous asseoir
    puis au réveil nos yeux se fermèrent
    et l'aube versa sur nous les réservoirs de la nuit.
La pluie nous sécha.

## One day in the middle of the night

It soared to the bottom of the river.
Ebony stones gold threads of steel the armless cross.
Full zero.
Adoringly I hate her like anyone else.
Death filled its lungs to maximum emptiness.
The compass traced five-sided squares and triangles.
After which he descended to the loft.
The midday stars dazzled.
His bag full of fish the hunter
    stepped ashore in the middle of the Seine.
Earthworms mark the circle's centre at its circumference.
Without a sound my eyes spoke deafeningly.
Then we moved through a deserted alley teeming with people.
After the walking had rested us
    we summoned up the strength to sit down and waking closed our eyes
    and dawn poured over
    us its reservoirs of night.
The rain dried us.

tr. Martin Sorrell

## Cœur en bouche

Son manteau traînait comme un soleil couchant
    et les perles de son collier étaient belles comme des dents.
Une neige de seins qu'entourait la maison
et dans l'âtre un feu de baisers.
Et les diamants de ses bagues étaient plus brillants que des yeux.
«Nocturne visiteuse Dieu croit en moi!
—Je vous salue gracieuse de plénitude
les entrailles de votre fruit sont bénies
Dehors se courbent les roseaux fines tailles.
Les chats grincent mieux que les girouettes.
Demain à la première heure, respirer des roses aux doigts d'aurore
et la nue éclatante transformera en astre le duvet.»
Dans la nuit ce fut l'injure des rails aux indifférentes locomotives
    près des jardins où les roses oubliées
    sont des amourettes déracinées.
«Nocturne visiteuse un jour je me coucherai dans un linceul comme
dans une mer.
Tes regards sont des rayons d'étoile,
les rubans de ta robe des routes vers l'infini.
Viens dans un ballon léger semblable à un cœur
malgré l'aimant, arc de triomphe quant à la forme.
Les giroflées du parterre deviennent les mains les plus belles d'Haarlem.
Les siècles de notre vie durent à peine des secondes.
À peine les secondes durent-elles quelques amours.
À chaque tournant il y a un angle droit qui ressemble à un vieillard.
Le loup à pas de nuit s'introduit dans ma couche.
Visiteuse! Visiteuse! tes boucliers sont des seins!
Dans l'atelier se dressent aussi sournoises que des langues les vipères.

# Mouth-shaped heart

Her coat was dragging like a sinking sun
    and the pearls of her necklace were as lovely as teeth.
A snow of breasts that the house surrounded
and a fire of kisses in the hearth.
And the diamonds of her rings shone brighter than any eyes.
"Night visitor, God believe in me!
—I hail you gracious with fullness
blessed be the womb of your fruit.
Outside the reeds of delicate proportions curve gently.
The cats screech louder than weathercocks.
Tomorrow at daybreak, breathe roses with dawn's fingers
and the shining cloud will transform softest down to a star."
In the night it was the swearing of rails at the nonchalant trains
    near the gardens where the forgotten roses
    are uprooted love affairs.
"Night visitor, one day I shall lie down in a winding sheet as in a sea.
Your looks are star beams
the streamers on your dress roads to the infinite.
Come in a balloon light as a heart
in spite of the magnet, an arch of triumph in its form.
The flowers of the orchestra pit become the liveliest hands of Haarlem.
The centuries of our life last scarcely seconds.
Scarcely do seconds last loves.
At each bend in the road a right angle like an old man.
The night quiet as a wolf climbs into my bed.
Visitor! Visitor! your shields are breasts!
In the studio vipers rear up as mean as tongues.

Et les étaux de fer comme les giroflées sont devenus des mains
Avec les fronts de qui lapiderez-vous les cailloux?
quel lion te suit plus grondant qu'un orage?
Voici venir les cauchemars des fantômes.»
Et le couvercle du palais se ferma aussi bruyamment
que les portes du cercueil.
On me cloua avec des clous aussi maigres
que des morts
dans une mort de silence.
Maintenant vous ne prêterez plus d'attention
aux oiseaux de la chansonnette.
L'éponge dont je me lave n'est qu'un cerveau ruisselant
et des poignards me pénètrent avec l'acuité de vos regards.

And the flower-like iron vices have become hands.
With whose foreheads will you lapidate the peoples?
What lion follows you roaring louder than a storm?
Here come the nightmares of phantoms."
And the roof of the palate slammed as loudly as the doors of the tomb.
They nailed me with nails as thin as the dead
in a death of silence.
Now you will pay no more attention
to the birds of the comic song.
The sponge I wash myself with is only a dripping brain
and knives pierce me with the sharpness of your looks.

[This poem is based largely on the reversals and deformations of certain
clichés: for instance, "le cœur en bouche" is the twisting of "la bouche en
cœur," or a heart-shaped mouth, and so on, for the list: teeth like pearls,
breasts like snow, rosy-fingered dawn, hands like flowers, and old man bent
at right angles, a tongue as mean as a viper's, a deathly silence, the spongy
matter of the brain, and looks as sharp and cutting as knives.]

tr. MAC

# 1926
from *C'est les bottes de 7 lieues...*

## Porte du second infini

*À Antonin Artand*

L'encrier périscope me guette au tournant
mon porte-plume rentre dans sa coquille
La feuille de papier déploie ses grandes ailes blanches
Avant peu ses deux serres
m'arracheront les yeux
Je n'y verrai que du feu mon corps
feu mon corps!
Vous eûtes l'occasion de le voir en grand appareil
le jour de tous les ridicules
Les femmes mirent leurs bijoux dans leur bouche
comme Démosthène
Mais je suis inventeur d'un téléphone de
verre des Bohême et de
tabac anglais
en relation directe
avec la peur!

# Door of the second infinite

*To Antonin Artaud*

The periscope inkwell waits for me where the road turns
my penholder returns to its shell
The sheet of paper unfurls its great white wings
Pretty soon its two claws
will tear out my eyes
I will see nothing of my former body
my former body!
You got to see it all dressed up
On the most ridiculous day
The women put their jewels in their mouth
like Demosthenes
But I am the inventor of a telephone
in glass from Bohemia and
English tobacco
in direct relation
to fear!

# Destinée arbitraire

*Á Georges Malkine*

Voici venir le temps des croisades.
Par la fenêtre fermée les oiseaux s'obstinent à parler
comme les poissons d'aquarium.
À la devanture d'une boutique
une jolie femme sourit.
Bonheur tu n'es que cire à cacheter
et je passe tel un feu follet.
Un grand nombre de gardiens poursuivent
un inoffensif papillon échappé de l'asile
Il devient sous mes mains pantalon de dentelle
et ta chair d'aigle
ô mon rêve quand je vous caresse !
Demain on enterrera gratuitement
on ne s'enrhumera plus
on parlera le langage des fleurs
on s'éclairera de lumières inconnues à ce jour.
Mais aujourd'hui c'est aujourd'hui
Je sens que mon commencement est proche
pareil aux blés de juin.
Gendarmes passez-moi les menottes.
Les statues se détournent sans obéir.
Sur leur socle j'inscrirai des injures et le nom
de mon pire ennemi.
Là-bas dans l'océan
Entre deux eaux
Un beau corps de femme
Fait reculer les requins
Ils montent à la surface se mirer dans l'air
et n'osent pas mordre aux seins
aux seins délicieux.

# Arbitrary fate

*To Georges Malkine*

Here comes the time of the crusades.
Through the closed window the birds insist on speaking
like fish in an aquarium.
At the shop window
a pretty woman smiles.
Happiness you are only sealing wax
and I go by like a firefly.
A number of guardians pursue
an inoffensive butterfly escaped from the asylum.
Under my hands he becomes lace pants
and your eagle flesh
oh my dream when I caress you!
Tomorrow burials will be free
there will be no more catching colds
the language of flowers will be spoken
light will be cast by lamps unknown to this day.
But today is today.
I feel that my beginning is close
like June wheat
Policemen hand me the handcuffs.
The statues turn away without obeying.
On their base I shall write insults
and the name of my worst enemy.
There in the distant ocean
between tides a lovely woman's body
causes the sharks to draw back.
They rise to the surface to look at themselves in the air
and dare not bite the breasts
the delicious breasts.

## Les grands jours du poète

Les disciples de la lumière n'ont jamais inventé que des ténèbres
    peu opaques.

La rivière roule un petit corps de femme et cela signifie que la fin
    est proche.

La veuve en habits de noces se trompe de convoi.

Nous arriverons tous en retard à notre tombeau.

Un navire de chair s'enlise sur une petite plage. Le timonier invite
    les passagers à se taire.

Les flots attendent impatiemment Plus Près de Toi ô mon Dieu!

Le timonier invite les flots à parler. Ils parlent.

La nuit cachette ses bouteilles avec des étoiles et fait fortune
    dans l'exportation.

De grands comptoirs se construisent pour vendre des rossignols.
    Mais ils ne peuvent satisfaire les désirs de la Reine de Sibérie
    qui veut un rossignol blanc.

Un commodore anglais jure qu'on ne le prendra plus à cueillir la sauge
    la nuit entre les pieds des statues de sel.

À ce propos une petite salière Cérébos se dresse avec difficulté sur
    ses jambes fines. Elle verse dans mon assiette ce qu'il me reste
    à vivre.

De quoi saler l'Océan Pacifique.

Vous mettrez sur ma tombe une bouée de sauvetage.

Parce qu'on ne sait jamais.

# Great days in the life of the poet

The disciples of light have never invented anything but not very
thick shadows.
A woman's small body is rolled along by the river, which means that
the end is near.
A widow dressed for a wedding gets into the wrong procession.
We will all come late to the tomb.
A boat made of flesh gets stuck on a small beach. The helmsman
invites the passengers to keep quiet.
The waves wait impatiently. Nearer to Thee O my God!
The helmsman invites the waves to speak. They speak.
Night seals its bottles with stars, exports them and makes a fortune.
Big display tables are built for the sale of nightingales. But they
can't satisfy the Queen of Siberia's desire for a white one.
An English commodore swears he will never again be caught
gathering sage at night from among the feet of salt statues.
Hearing that, Cerebos, a small saltcellar, struggles to get up on its
slender legs. It pours onto my plate all that remains of my life.
Enough to salt the Pacific Ocean.
Be sure to put a life preserver on my tomb.
Because you never know.

tr. Patricia Terry

# 1926
## « Journal d'une apparition »

## Journal d'une apparition

La vie nous réserve encore des surprises en dépit des déceptions dont elle se montre prodigue à notre égard. Le merveilleux consent encore à poser sur notre front fatigué sa main gantée et à nous conduire dans des labyrinthes surprenants. Nous errons à sa suite parmi des parterres de fleurs sanglantes, nous constatons de surnaturelles présences dans des paysages incroyables, mais vienne le jour où tant de merveilles nous donnent enfin des ailes. Comme Icare nous mourons de notre fortune ou, comme Dédale, nous atterrissons dans un pays moins beau et que désormais nous nous obstinons à considérer comme la seule réalité.

Qu'on nous parle alors du labyrinthe fameux et des aventures que nous y courûmes, nous hésiterons à le décrire autrement que comme un songe-creux.

Et quelque jour, considérant les moignons brûlés de ce qui fut nos ailes, témoignage des merveilles que nous vîmes et instrument d'une pseudo-délivrance, nous nous attendrirons sur nous-mêmes et nous maudirons le scepticisme du souvenir et la tendance de l'homme à confondre le présent avec la réalité.

J'échapperai à cette déchéance. Le labyrinthe que j'ai perdu, j'y pourrai rentrer à nouveau, j'y rentrerai un jour proche ou lointain. Mais je me refuserai toujours à classer parmi les hallucinations les visites nocturnes de *** ou plutôt je me refuserai, le mot hallucination étant admis, à le considérer comme une explication de ce qui, pour le vulgaire, est peut-être un phénomène, mais qui ne saurait l'être pour moi.

# Journal of an apparition

Life still has in store for us some surprises, despite the disappointments it hands us so generously. The marvelous still consents to place on our tired forehead its gloved hand and takes us into astounding labyrinths. We wander along after it among beds of bleeding flowers, we come across supernatural presences in incredible landscapes, but a day comes when all these many marvels finally give us wings. Like Icarus we will die from our luck, or, like Dedalus, we shall land in a country less beautiful, that from now on we shall insist on considering as the only reality..

Let them talk to us about the famous labyrinth and the adventures we undertook there, we shall hesitate to describe it otherwise than as in a dream state.

And some day, considering the burned stumps of what were our wings, a witness to the marvels that we saw and the instrument of a pseudo-deliverance, we will be filled with tenderness about ourselves and will curse the skepticism of memory and man's tendency to confuse the present with reality.

I shall escape this fall from grace. The labyrinth that I have lost, I shall be able to return to it, I shall do so sooner or later. But I shall always refuse to classify among my hallucinations the nightly visits of *** or rather I shall refuse, once the word hallucination has been admitted, to consider it as an explanation of what, for the man in the street, is perhaps a phenomenon, but which can't be one for me.

\*\*\* est réellement venue chez moi. Je l'ai vue. Je l'ai entendue. J'ai senti son parfum et parfois même elle m'a touché. Et puisque la vue, l'ouïe, l'odorat et le tact se trouvent d'accord pour reconnaître sa présence, pourquoi douterais-je de sa réalité sans suspecter d'être de faux-semblants les autres réalités communément reconnues et qui ne sont en définitive contrôlées que par les mêmes sens? Comment reconnaîtrais-je à ceux-ci le pouvoir de m'éclairer dans certains cas et de m'abuser dans d'autres? Il s'agit d'ailleurs moins pour moi de faire admettre comme réels des faits normalement tenus pour illusoires que de mettre sur le même plan le rêve et la réalité, me souciant peu, au demeurant, que tout soit faux ou que tout soit vrai.

R. D.

# Journal

*Du 10 au 16 novembre 1926*

Mes sommeils sont devenus plus lourds, plus profonds, plus épais. Au réveil, j'ai non pas le souvenir des rêves que j'ai faits, mais le souvenir que j'ai rêvé, sans pouvoir les préciser. Si je tente de les retrouver dans ma mémoire, je me heurte à d'épaisses ténèbres dans lesquelles des ombres imprécises font de grands gestes vagues. C'est un état que je connais déjà pour l'avoir éprouvé à plusieurs reprises, notamment à l'époque des « *sommeils surréalistes* ».

***really came to me. I saw her. I heard her. I smelled her scent and sometimes she even touched me. And since sight, hearing, smell and touch are all agreeing to recognize her presence, why should I doubt her reality without suspecting the other commonly received realities to be false appearances, since they are definitely controlled by the same senses? How should I recognize in those some enlightening power and not in others? It is less difficult to admit as real those facts we usually consider illusory than to place dream and reality on the same level, caring little for what is false and what is true.

R. D.

## Journal

*From the 10 to the 16 of November, 1926*

My sleeps have become heavier, deeper, thicker. Waking up, I no longer have the memory of the dreams I had, but the memory that I dreamt, without being able to make them precise. If I try to find them again in my memory, I bump up against a dense darkness in which imprecise shadows are gesturing vaguely. It's a state which I recognize for having already experienced it many times, notably in the epoch of the *"surrealist sleeps."*

*Nuit du 16 novembre 1926*

Changement brusque dans la nuit du 16 novembre.. Au lieu du trou profond où je sombrais les nuits précédentes quand je m'endormais, je flotte dans une somnolence vague et euphorique. La nuit est très claire et mon atelier en est doucement éclairé. Bien qu'endormi et rêvant sans pouvoir faire la part exacte du rêve et de la rêverie, je garde la notion du décor. Vers deux heures du matin, je m'éveille complète-ment. Le silence siffle de cette façon particulière que l'on remarque pendant les insomnies. Un instant se passe puis, très distinctement, j'entends qu'on ouvre ma porte bien que celle-ci soit fermée à clef (je te constaterai au matin). J'entends les gonds rouler et même le bruit très particulier du pêne de la serrure qui est cassé et qu'on est obligé de pousser avec la main pour refermer la porte.

Et, doucement, sans bruit, *** entre dans mon atelier. C'est elle à n'en pas douter. Je reconnais son visage, sa démarche, l'expression de son sourire. Je reconnais encore sa robe: une robe très reconnaissable qu'elle ne porte que dans certaines circonstances.

Elle s'approche de moi et s'assoit à quelque distance de mon lit sur un fauteuil où j'ai posé mes vêtements avant de me coucher. Elle se pose commo-dément et me regarde fixement.

J'observe que je la vois aussi distinctement que s'il y avait de la lumière dans mon atelier et que la clarté de la nuit n'explique pas cette circonstance, pas plus d'ailleurs qu'une ligne phosphorescente d'un bleu assez tendre qui cerne tout son corps, non plus que le rougissement du poêle. Elle remue son pied droit qui parfois heurte le plancher qui résonne.

Combien de temps dure cette contemplation? Je l'ignore. J'ignore même quand ma visiteuse a disparu. Je me réveille normalement au matin, assez frais et absolument persuadé de la réalité de cette visite nocturne. Mes vêtements sont toujours sur le fauteuil. Peut-être ont-ils été déplacés, mais je ne pourrais l'affirmer.

*Night of November 16, 1926*

A sudden change in the night of November 16. Instead of the deep hole I sank into during the preceding nights when I fell asleep, I am floating in a vague euphoric somnolence. The night is very clear and my study is faintly lit by its brightness. Although I am asleep and dreaming without being able to exactly distinguish between the dream and reverie, I retain some notion of the setting. Towards two in the morning, I wake up completely. The silence is whistling in that strange way that you notice during your insomnia. An instant goes by and then, very distinctly, I heard someone opening my door although it is locked (I will notice that again in the morning.) I hear the hinges roll back and even the very particular sound of the lock which is broken and which you have to push to close the door again.

And then gently, noiselessly, \*\*\* enters my study. That's who it is without any doubt. I recognize her face, her way of walking, her smile. I recognize her dress: a very recognizable dress she only wears in certain circumstances.

She comes toward me and sits a little distance from my bed on a chair where I had put my clothes before going to bed. She sits down easily and looks at me steadily.

I see her as distinctly as if there were a light on in my study, that the clarity of the night doesn't explain, nor does it explain a phosphorescent line of a rather tender blue that surrounds her body, or the reddening of the stove. She moves her right foot that sometimes strikes against the wooden floor, noisily.

How long did I spend contemplating this vision? I don't know. Neither do I know when my visitor disappeared. I wake up as usual in the morning, feeling rather refreshed and absolutely convinced of the reality of this night-time visit. My clothes are still on the chair. Perhaps they have been moved, but I couldn't swear to it.

*Du 16 au 25 novembre 1926*

Les apparitions se reproduisent chaque nuit avec exactitude. Je prends soin désormais de ne plus fermer la porte à clef, de ne plus embarrasser le fauteuil et de rapprocher celui-ci de mon lit. Maintenant, j'attends les visites de \*\*\* et, quand elles se produisent, elles ne me surprennent plus. Elles font partie de ma vie et occupent mes pensées pendant l'état de veille.

*Nuit du 26 novembre 1926*

Cette nuit \*\*\* est venue comme d'habitude, mais au lieu de s'asseoir sur le fauteuil, elle s'est assise sur mon lit. J'ai senti la pression de son corps contre les couvertures. Elle m'a regardé, tournant parfois la tête vers le poêle dont la lueur éclairait en rouge son visage. Je note que sur sa physionomie est répandue une expression triste rompue par instants, comme dans la vie normale, par un sourire.

Elle portait cette nuit une robe que je lui connais bien, rouge et noire, et dont je me souviens de lui avoir fait compliment.

*Nuits du 26 novembre 1926 au 15 décembre 1926*

Elle est revenue régulièrement toutes ces nuits. Elle s'est assise tantôt sur le fauteuil, tantôt sur le lit, tantôt sur le tapis devant le feu. J'ai remarqué dans la nuit du 14 décembre qu'elle a toussé à deux reprises. Dans la nuit du 15 décembre, accroché à son épaule, il y avait un morceau du serpentin de papier, comme on en jette dans les fêtes et les bars de nuit.

Ces visites rentrent de plus en plus dans la normale. Pas une nuit ne s'est passée depuis le 16 novembre sans qu'elle vienne et son abstention me causerait probablement un trouble inexprimable. J'ai besoin qu'elle vienne.

Quant à la manière dont elle part, je ne m'en rends, la plupart du temps, pas compte. Je me réveille au matin, sans savoir comment je me suis endormi et avec jusqu'au dernier moment de mes souvenirs de l'état de veille, le souvenir de sa présence.

*From the 16 to the 25 November, 1926*

The appearances reproduce themselves every night quite exactly. I am careful from now on not to lock the door, not to put anything on the chair, and to move it nearer to my bed. Now I await the visits of \*\*\* and am no long surprised by them. They are part of my life and occupy my waking thoughts.

*The night of November 26, 1926*

Tonight \*\*\* came as usual, but instead of sitting on the chair, she sat on my bed. I felt the pressure of her body against the covers. She looked at me, turning her head sometimes toward the stove whose gleam reddened her face. I notice it taking on a tired expression that a smile breaks into from time to time, as in normal life.

Tonight she was wearing a dress that I know very well, red and black, about which I remember complimenting her.

*Nights of November 26 to December 15, 1926*

She has come back with regularity every night. She has sat now on the chair, now on the bed, now on the rug before the fire. I noticed in the night of December 14 that she was coughing twice. In the night of December 15, attached to her shoulder, there was a piece of curled-up paper, the kind thrown in the air at festivals and in nighttime bars.

These visits enter more and more in the normal state of things. These visits seem more and more normal. Not one night since November 16 without her coming, and her not coming would probably awaken in me an inexpressible unease. I need her to come.

As for the way in which she leaves, I don't usually notice. I wake up in the morning without knowing how I went to sleep and remembering, up to the last moment of my waking, the trace of her presence.

Il m'est arrivé de rentrer tard et de n'être pas encore endormi quand elle arrivait, mais il ne m'est jamais arrivé de n'être pas encore couché à ce moment. À trois reprises, je l'ai vue partir. J'ai entendu la porte se refermer derrière elle et son pas décroître dans la cour. Une nuit de pluie, j'ai remarqué que ses chaussures étaient tachées de boue.

Enfin, deux fois, j'ai couché ailleurs que chez moi. À deux heures environ, je me suis réveillé et j'ai été torturé par l'idée qu'elle était seule chez moi et que peut-être le feu était éteint. Dans une somnolence voisine de l'anéantissement, j'évoquais mon atelier dans ses moindres détails et elle, seule, assise dans le fauteuil. Cela me causait une telle gêne que désormais je ne coucherai plus ailleurs que chez moi.

*Nuit du 16 décembre 1926*

J'avais résolu dans la journée de mettre mon fantôme à l'épreuve en le touchant. Je devais poser ma main sur la sienne. Qu'attendais-je de cet acte? Je ne saurais le dire, mais j'attendais quelque chose.

Et tout s'est passé le plus normalement du monde. Je crois avoir posé ma main sur la sienne. Elle l'a retirée, mais n'est pas partie. Je dis « crois » car au réveil j'ai douté de l'avoir fait et je me suis trouvé en présence d'un moi-même sceptique et chicaneur. Pour convaincre ce second dont les arguments me désespèrent, j'ai résolu de tuer cette nuit *** avec un poignard malais à longue lame.

*Nuit du 17 décembre 1926*

Comment ai-je pu imaginer un acte aussi stupide. Elle est venue et je n'ai rien fait. J'ai trouvé ce matin le poignard près de mon oreiller. Comment ai-je pu croire que je m'en servirais?

I've come back late and not been yet asleep when she arrived, but I've never been asleep in that moment. Three times I have seen her leave. I have heard the door close behind her and her steps fade away in the courtyard. One rainy night I noticed that her shoes were splashed with mud.

Finally, twice, I went to bed not at home. At about two, I woke up and was tortured by the idea that she was alone at my place and perhaps the fire had gone out. In a somnolence near to complete annihilation, I imagined my study in the slightest details and her there alone, seated in the chair. That made me so uncomfortable that from then on I would not sleep anywhere except at home.

### Night of December 16, 1926

I had resolved in the day to test my phantom by touching it. I was going to put my hand on hers. What did I expect from this gesture? I couldn't say exactly, but surely something.

And everything came about the most normally in the world. I think I placed my hand on hers. She drew hers away, but didn't leave. I say "I believe" because when I awakened I doubted I had done it and found myself in the presence of a self both sceptical and argumentative. To convince this second self of night with a long-bladed Malaysian dagger.

### Night of December 17, 1926

How could I have imagined such a senseless act. She came and I did nothing. I found this morning the dagger near my pillow. How could I have thought I might use it?

*Nuit du 18 décembre 1926*

Et pourtant j'ai voulu recommencer et, au matin, je ne me rappelle pas ce qui s'est passé. Elle est venue et s'est assise. Ce matin, j'ai retrouvé le poignard sur le fauteuil. Impossible, absolument impossible de savoir ce qui s'est passé. Pourvu qu'elle revienne la nuit prochaine.

*Nuit du 19 décembre 1926*

Elle est revenue.

*Nuits du 20 décembre 1926 au 5 janvier 1927*

Elle est venue chaque nuit, mais le souvenir que je garde de ses visites est de moins en moins précis. Je ne saurais plus dire au réveil si elle s'est assise sur le lit ou sur le fauteuil.

*Nuit du 6 janvier 1927*

Pour la première fois depuis le début de ses visites, je ne puis affirmer que *** est venue cette nuit. Il me semble bien qu'elle est arrivée, mais je ne puis faire la différence entre la perception de cette visite et l'habitude que j'en ai prise.

*Nuits du 6 au 24 janvier 1927*

Je doute de plus en plus qu'elle continue à venir me voir. Certains jours j'en suis presque certain mais le lendemain je suis presque persuadé que mes souvenirs me trompent.

*Nuit du 25 janvier 1927*

Elle n'est certainement pas venue cette nuit et pourtant j'étais éveillé à l'heure habituelle de son arrivée et je ne me suis pas endormi avant le petit jour.

*Nuit du 26 janvier 1927*

Elle n'est pas venue.

*Night of December 18, 1926*

And yet I wanted to begin all this again and in the morning I don't re-member what happened. She came and sat down. This morning I found the dagger on the chair. Absolutely impossible to know what happened. I hope she comes again tonight.

*Night of December 19, 1926*

She has come back.

*Nights of December 20, 1926 to January 5, 1927*

She has coming every night, but the memory I keep of her visits is less and less precise. I couldn't say when I wake up if she sat on the bed or the chair.

*Night of January 6, 1927*

For the first time since her visits began, I can't swear that \*\*\* came last night. It seems to me indeed that she arrived, but I can't distinguish between my perception of this visit and the habit I have of them.

*Nights from the 6ᵗʰ to the 24ᵗʰ of January 1927*

I doubt more and more that she will continue to come to see me. Certain days I am almost sure of it but the next day I am almost convinced that my memory is deceiving me.

*Night of January 25, 1927*

She certainly didn't come last night and yet I was awake at the usual hour when she comes and I didn't go back to sleep before dawn.

*Night of January 26, 1927*

She didn't come.

*Nuits du 27 janvier à fin février*

Elle ne vient certainement plus. J'ai continué à m'éveiller à l'heure de sa visite journalière et, au début, j'avais sans la voir l'impression de sa présence. Puis cette impression a disparu. Les dernières nuits j'ai dormi sans m'éveiller.

*Maintenant*

Elle ne reviendra plus.

*Nights from January 27 to the end of February*

She is certainly not coming again. I have continued to wake up at the time of her daily visit and, in the beginning, I had the impression of her presence without seeing her. Then this impression faded away. The last nights I slept without waking.

*Now*

She won't ever come again.

1926
*A La Mystérieuse*

# Ô douleurs de l'amour!

Ô douleurs de l'amour!
Comme vous m'êtes nécessaires et comme vous m'êtes chères.

Mes yeux qui se ferment sur des larmes imaginaires, mes mains qui se tendent sans cesse vers le vide.

J'ai rêvé cette nuit de paysages insensés et d'aventures dangereuses aussi bien du point de vue de la mort que du point de vue de la vie qui sont aussi le point de vue de l'amour.

Au réveil vous étiez présentes, ô douleurs de l'amour, ô muses du désert, ô muses exigeantes.

Mon rire et ma joie se cristallisent autour de vous. C'est votre fard, c'est votre poudre, c'est votre rouge, c'est votre sac de peau de serpent, c'est vos bas de soie... et c'est aussi ce petit pli entre l'oreille et la nuque, à la naissance du cou, c'est votre pantalon de soie et votre fine chemise et votre manteau de fourrures, votre ventre rond c'est mon rire et mes joies vos pieds et tous vos bijoux.

En vérité comme vous êtes bien vêtue et bien parée.

Ô douleurs de l'amour, anges exigeants, voilà que je vous imagine à l'image même de mon amour que je vous confonds avec lui...

Ô douleurs de l'amour, vous que je crée et habille, vous vous confondez avec mon amour dont je ne connais que les vêtements et aussi les yeux, la voix, le visage, les mains, les cheveux, les dents, les yeux...

# Oh pangs of love!

Oh pangs of love!

How necessary you are to me and how precious.

My eyes closing on imaginary tears, my hands stretching out ceaselessly toward nothingness.

I dreamed last night of crazed landscapes and of adventures as dangerous from the perspective of death as from the perspective of life which are both also the perspective of love.

At my waking you were present, oh anguish of love, oh desert muses, oh exigent muses.

My laugh and my joy crystallize about you. Your makeup, your powder, your rouge, your alligator bag, your silk stockings . . . and also that little fold between the ear and the nape of your neck, near its base, your silk pants and your delicate shirt and your fur coat, your round belly is my laughter and your feet my joys and all your jewels.

Really, how good-looking and well dressed you are.


Oh pangs of love, exigent angels, here I am imagining you in the very likeness of my love, confusing you with it . . .

Oh pangs of love, you whom I create and clothe, you are confused with my love whose clothing only I know and also her eyes, voice, face, hands, hair, teeth, eyes . . .

tr. MAC

# J'ai tant rêvé de toi

J'ai tant rêvé de toi que tu perds ta réalité.

Est-il encore temps d'atteindre ce corps vivant et de baiser sur cette
    bouche la naissance de la voix qui m'est chère?

J'ai tant rêvé de toi que mes bras habitués en étreignant ton ombre à se
    croiser sur ma poitrine ne se plieraient pas au contour de ton corps,
    peut-être.

Et que, devant l'apparence réelle de ce qui me hante et me gouverne
    depuis des jours et des années je deviendrais une ombre sans doute,
Ô balances sentimentales.

J'ai tant rêvé de toi qu'il n'est plus temps sans doute que je m'éveille.
    Je dors debout, le corps exposé à toutes les apparences de la vie et
    de l'amour et toi, la seule qui compte aujourd'hui pour moi, je
    pourrais moins toucher ton front et tes lèvres que les premières
    lèvres et le premier front venu.

J'ai tant rêvé de toi, tant marché, parlé, couché avec ton fantôme
    qu'il ne me reste plus peut-être, et pourtant, qu'à être fantôme
    parmi les fantômes et plus ombre cent fois que l'ombre
    qui se promène et se promènera allègrement sur le cadran solaire
    de ta vie.

# I have so often dreamed of you

I have so often dreamed of you that you become unreal.
Is it still time enough to reach that living body and to kiss on that
   mouth the birth of the voice so dear to me?
I have so often dreamed of you that my arms used as they are to
   meet on my breast in embracing your shadow would perhaps not
   fit the contour of your body.
And, before the real appearance of what has haunted and ruled me
   for days and years, I might become only a shadow.
Oh the weighing of sentiment.
I have so often dreamed of you that there is probably no time now
   to waken. I sleep standing, my body exposed to all the
   appearances of life and love and you, who alone still matter to me,
   I could less easily touch your forehead and your lips than the
   first lips and the first forehead I might meet by chance.
I have so often dreamed of you, walked, spoken, slept with your
   phantom that perhaps I can be nothing any longer than a
   phantom among phantoms and a hundred times more shadow
   than the shadow which walks and will walk joyously over the
   sundial of your life.

tr. Paul Auster

## Les espaces du sommeil

Dans la nuit il y a naturellement les sept merveilles du monde et la
  grandeur et le tragique et le charme.
Les forêts s'y heurtent confusément avec des créatures de légende
cachées dans les fourrés.
Il y a toi.
Dans la nuit il y a le pas du promeneur et celui de l'assassin et celui du
  sergent de ville et la lumière du réverbère et celle de la lanterne
du chiffonnier.
Il y a toi.
Dans la nuit passent les trains et les bateaux et le mirage des pays où il
fait jour. Les derniers souffles du crépuscule et les premiers
frissons de l'aube.
Il y a toi.
Un air de piano, un éclat de voix.
Une porte claque. Une horloge.
Et pas seulement les êtres et les choses et les bruits matériels.
Mais encore moi qui me poursuis ou sans cesse me dépasse.
Il y a toi l'immolée, toi que j'attends.
Parfois d'étranges figures naissent à l'instant du sommeil et disparaissent.
Quand je ferme les yeux, des floraisons phosphorescentes apparaissent
et se fanent et renaissent comme des feux d'artifice charnus.
Des pays inconnus que je parcours en compagnie de créatures.
Il y a toi sans doute, ô belle et discrète espionne.
Et l'âme palpable de l'étendue.
Et les parfums du ciel et des étoiles et le chant du coq d'il y a
  2 000 ans et
  le cri du paon dans des parcs en flamme et des baisers.
Des mains qui se serrent sinistrement dans une lumière blafarde et des
  qessieux qui grincent sur des routes médusantes.
Il y a toi sans doute que je ne connais pas, que je connais au contraire.

# Sleep spaces

In the night there are naturally the seven marvels of the world and
greatness and the tragic and enchantment.
Confusedly, forests mingle with legendary creatures hidden in the
thickets.
You are there.
In the night there is the nightwalker's step and the murderer's and
the policeman's and the streetlight and the ragman's lantern.
You are there.
In the night pass trains and ships and the mirage of countries where it
is daylight. The last breaths of twilight and the first shivers of dawn.
You are there.
A tune on the piano, an exclamation.
A door slams,
A clock.
And not just beings and things and material noises.
But still myself chasing myself or going on beyond.
You are there, immolated one, you for whom I wait.
Sometimes strange figures are born at the instant of sleep and disappear.
When I close my eyes, phosphorescent blooms appear and fade and
are reborn like fleshy fireworks.
Unknown countries I traverse with creatures for company.
You are there most probably, oh beautiful discreet spy.
And the palpable soul of the reaches.
And the perfumes of the sky and the stars and the cock's crow from
two thousand years ago and the peacock's scream in the parks
aflame and kisses.
Handshakes sinister in a sickly light and axles screeching on
hypnotic roads.
You are most probably there, whom I do not know, whom on the
contrary I know.

Mais qui présente dans mes rêves s'obstine à s'y laisser deviner sans
   y paraître.
Toi qui restes insaisissable dans la réalité et dans le rêve.
Toi qui m'appartiens de par ma volonté de te posséder en illusion
   mais qui n'approches ton visage du mien que mes yeux clos
   aussi bien au rêve qu'à la réalité.
Toi qu'en dépit d'une rhétorique facile où le flot meurt sur les plages,
   ù la corneille vole dans des usines en ruines, où le bois pourrit
   en craquant sous un soleil de plomb,
Toi qui es à la base de mes rêves et qui secoues mon esprit plein
   de métamorphoses et qui me laisses ton gant quand je baise
   ta main.
Dans la nuit, il y a les étoiles et le mouvement ténébreux de la
   mer, des fleuves, des forêts, des villes, des herbes, des poumons
   de millions et millions d'êtres.
Dans la nuit il y a les merveilles du monde.
Dans la nuit, il n'y a pas d'anges gardiens mais il y a le sommeil.
Dans la nuit il y a toi.
Dans le jour aussi.

But who, present in my dreams, insist on being sensed there without
    appearing.
You who remain out of reach in reality and in dream.
You who belong to me by my will to possess you in illusion but
    whose face approaches mine only if my eyes are closed to dream
    as well as to reality.
You despite an easy rhetoric where the waves die on the beaches,
    there the crow flies in ruined factories, where wood rots cracking
    under a leaden sun.
You who are in the depths of my dreams, arousing my mind full of
    metamorphoses and leaving me your glove when I kiss your hand.
In the night there are stars and the tenebral motion of the sea,
    rivers, forests, towns, grass, the lungs of millions and millions
    of beings.
In the night there are the marvels of the world.
In the night there are no guardian angels but there is sleep.
In the night you are there.
In the day also.

tr. MAC

# Si tu savais

Loin de moi et semblable aux étoiles, à la mer et à tous les
  accessoires de la mythologie poétique,
Loin de moi et cependant présente à ton insu,
Loin de moi et plus silencieuse encore parce que je t'imagine sans
  cesse, Loin de moi, mon joli mirage et mon rêve éternel, tu ne
  peux pas savoir.
Si tu savais.
Loin de moi et peut-être davantage encore de m'ignorer et m'ignorer
  encore.
Loin de moi parce que tu ne m'aimes pas sans doute ou ce qui
  revient au même, que j'en doute.
Loin de moi parce que tu ignores sciemment mes désirs passionnés.
Loin de moi parce que tu es cruelle.
Si tu savais.
Loin de moi, ô joyeuse comme la fleur qui danse dans la rivière au
  bout de sa tige aquatique, ô triste comme sept heures du
  soir dans les champignonnières.
Loin de moi silencieuse encore ainsi qu'en ma présence et joyeuse
  encore comme l'heure en forme de cigogne qui tombe de haut.
Loin de moi à l'instant où chantent les alambics, à l'instant
  où la mer silencieuse et bruyante se replie sur les oreillers blancs.
Si tu savais.
Loin de moi, ô mon présent présent tourment, loin de moi au
  bruit magnifique des coquilles d'huîtres qui se brisent sous
  le pas du noctambule, au petit jour, quand il passe devant
  la porte des restaurants.
Si tu savais.

# If you knew

Far from me and like the stars, the sea, and all the props of poetic
legend,
Far from me and present all the same without your knowledge,
Far from me and still more silent because I imagine you endlessly,
Far from me, my beautiful mirage and my eternal dream, you
cannot know.
If you knew.
Far from me and perhaps still farther from being unaware of me and
still unaware.
Far from me because you doubtless do not love me or, not so
different, I doubt your love.
Far from me for you cleverly ignore my passionate desires.
Far from me for you are cruel.
If you knew.
Far from me, oh joyous as the flower dancing in the river on its
watery stem, oh sad as seven in the evening in the mushroom fields.
Far from me still silent as in my presence and still joyous as the
stork-shaped hour falling from on high.
Far from me at the moment when the alembics sing, when the silent
and noisy sea curls up on the white pillows.
If you knew.
Far from me, oh my present present torment, far from me with the
splendid sound of oyster shells crunched under the
nightwalker's step, at dawn, when he passes by the door of
restaurants.
If you knew.

Loin de moi, volontaire et matériel mirage.

Loin de moi c'est une île qui se détourne au passage des navires.

Loin de moi un calme troupeau de bœufs se trompe de chemin,
s'arrête obstinément au bord d'un profond précipice, loin de moi,
cruelle.

Loin de moi, une étoile filante choit dans la bouteille nocturne
du poète.

Il met vivement le bouchon et dès lors il guette l'étoile enclose dans
le verre, il guette les constellations qui naissent sur les parois,
loin de moi, tu es loin de moi.

Si tu savais.

Loin de moi une maison achève d'être construite.

Un maçon en blouse blanche au sommet de l'échafaudage chante
une petite chanson très triste et, soudain, dans le récipient
empli de mortier apparaît le futur de la maison: les baisers
des amants et les suicides à deux et la nudité dans les chambres
des belles inconnues et leurs rêves mêmes à minuit, et les secrets
voluptueux surpris par les larmes de parquet

Loin de moi,

Si tu savais.

Si tu savais comme je t'aime et, bien que tu ne m'aimes pas, comme
je suis joyeux, comme je suis robuste et fier de sortir avec ton
image en tête, de sortir de l'univers.

Comme je suis joyeux à en mourir.

Si tu savais comme le monde m'est soumis.

Et toi, belle insoumise aussi, comme tu es ma prisonnière.

Ô toi, loin-de-moi à qui je suis soumis

Si tu savais.

Far from me, willed and material mirage.

Far from me an island turns aside at the passing of ships.

Far from me a calm herd of cattle mistakes the path, stops stubbornly
at the brink of a steep precipice, far from me, oh cruel one.

Far from me, a falling star falls in the night bottle of the poet. He
corks it instantly to watch the star enclosed within the glass, the
constellations come to life against the sides, far from me, you are
far from me.

If you knew.

Far from me a house is built just now.

A white-clothed worker atop the structure sings a sad brief song
and suddenly, in the hod of mortar there appears the future of
the house: lovers' kisses and double suicides and nakedness in
the rooms of lovely unknown girls and their midnight dreams,
and the voluptuous secrets surprised by the parquet floors.

Far from me,

If you knew.

If you knew how I love you and though you do not love me, how I
am happy, how I am strong and proud, with your image in my
mind, to leave the universe.

How I am happy enough to perish from it.

If you knew how the world submits to me.

And you, oh beautiful unsubmissive one, how you are also my prisoner.

Oh far-from-me to whom I submit.

If you knew.

tr. MAC

# Non l'amour n'est pas mort

Non l'amour n'est pas mort en ce cœur et ces yeux et cette bouche qui
    proclamait ses funérailles commencées.
Ecoutez, j'en ai assez du pittoresque et des couleurs et du charme.
J'aime l'amour, sa tendresse et sa cruauté.
Mon amour n'a qu'un seul nom, qu'une seule forme.
Tout passe. Des bouches se collent à cette bouche.
Mon amour n'a qu'un nom, qu'une forme.
Et si quelque jour tu t'en souviens
Ô toi, forme et nom de mon amour,
Un jour sur la mer entre l'Amérique et l'Europe,
À l'heure où le rayon final du soleil se réverbère sur la surface ondulée
    des vagues, ou bien une nuit d'orage sous un arbre dons la
    campagne ou dans une rapide automobile,
Un matin de printemps boulevard Malesherbes,
Un jour de pluie,
À l'aube avant de te coucher,
Dis-toi, je l'ordonne à ton fantôme familier, que je fus seul à t'aimer
    davantage et qu'il est dommage que tu ne l'aies pas connu.
Dis-toi qu'il ne faut pas regretter les choses: Ronsard avant moi et
    Baudelaire ont chanté le regret des vieilles et des mortes qui
    méprisèrent le plus pur amour.
Tu quand to seras morte
Tu seras belle et toujours désirable.
Je serai mort déjà, enclos tout entier en ton corps immortel, en ton
    image étonnante présente à jamais parmi les merveilles
    perpétuelles de la vie et de l'éternité, mais si je vis
Ta voix et son accent, ton regard et ses rayons,
L'odeur de toi et celle de tes cheveux et beaucoup d'autres choses
    encore vivront en moi,
En moi qui ne suis ni Ronsard ni Baudelaire,

# No, love is not dead

No, love is not dead in this heart and these eyes and this mouth
 which announced the beginning of its burial.
Listen, I have had enough of the picturesque and the colorful
 and the charming.
I love love, its tenderness and cruelty.
My love has but one name, but one form.
All passes. Mouths press against this mouth.
My love has but one name, but one form.
And if some day you remember
O form and name of my love,
One day on the ocean between America and Europe,
At the hour when the last sunbeam reverberates on the undulating
 surface of waves, or else a stormy night beneath a tree in the
 countryside or in a speeding car,
A spring morning on the boulevard Malesherbes,
A rainy day,
At dawn before sleeping,
Tell yourself, I command your familiar spirit, that I alone loved you
 more and that it is sad you should not have known it.
Tell yourself one must not regret things: Ronsard before me and
 Baudelaire have sung the regrets of ladies old or dead who
 despised the purest love. When you are dead
You will be beautiful and still an object of desire.
I will be already gone, enclosed forever complete within your
 immortal body, in your astonishing image present forever among
 the constant marvels of life and of eternity, but if I live
Your voice and its tone, your look and its radiance,
Your fragrance and the scent of your hair and many other things
 beside will still live in me,
Who am neither Ronsard nor Baudelaire,

Moi qui suis Robert Desnos et qui pour t'avoir connue et aimée,
Les vaux bien;
Moi qui suis Robert Desnos, pour t'aimer
Et qui ne veux pas attacher d'autre réputation à ma mémoire sur
    la terre méprisable.

I who am Robert Desnos and who for having known and loved you,
Am easily their equal.
I who am Robert Desnos, to love you
Wanting no other reputation to be remembered by on the
    despicable earth.


tr. MAC

## Tour de la tombe

À force d'aimer, je me suis perdu dans l'océan. Et quel océan!
Une tempête de rires et de larmes.

Si vous montez sur un navire ayez soin de regarder la figure de proue
qui vous fixera d'un œil rongé par la houle et l'eau salée.

Mais que dis-je? Les spectacles de l'amour ne m'intéressent guère.
Je ne veux plus être qu'une voile emportée au gré des
moussons vers des continents inconnus où je ne trouverai
qu'une seule personne. Celle pour laquelle vous avez un nom
tout trouvé.

Je me déshabille, ainsi qu'il sied à un explorateur perdu dans une
île et je reste immobile ainsi qu'une figure de proue.

Salut à toi, vent du large et à toi, désert, et à toi, oubli.

On m'oubliera. Quelque jour, on ne saura plus mon nom, mais je
saurai son nom. Un soir, couvert de gloire et riche, je
reviendrai, je frapperai à sa porte, tout nu, mais on ne me
répondra pas, même, ayant ouvert la porte, quand j'apparaîtrai
à ses yeux.

J'ai gagné, du moins, le sens de la perpétuité. Non pas celle, ridicule,
des concessions de cimetière.

Je souhaite en vain l'apparition des guillotines, mais je ne puis offrir
aux foules sanguinaires que mon désir de suicide.

Révolution! Tu ne brilleras qu'après ma mort, sur la place immense
de marbre blanc qui recouvrira mon immense cadavre.

La France est un nid de guêpes, l'Europe un champ pourri et le
monde une presqu'île de ma conscience.

Mais heureusement il me reste les étoiles, et la conscience de
ma grandeur morale opposée aux mille obstacles que le monde
apporte à mon amour.

# Tour of the tomb

From loving, I have gotten lost in the ocean. And what an ocean!
A tempest of laughter and tears.
If you climb aboard a ship take care to look at the figurehead who
will stare at you with her eyes eroded by the wave and the salt water.
But what am I saying? The spectacles of love scarcely interest me. I
no longer want to be other than a sail carried along at the pleasure
of monsoons towards unknown continents where I shall find
only one person. The one for whom you have a name already.
I undress, as an explorer lost on an island should, and I remain
unmoving like a figurehead.
Hail to you, wind of the open sea and to you, desert, and to you,
forgetfulness.
I will be forgotten. Some day, my name will no longer be known,
but I shall know her name. One evening, covered with wealth
and glory, I shall return to knock at her door, naked, but no one
will answer me, even when, having opened the door, I appear
before her eyes.
I have earned, at least, the sense of perpetuity. Not the ridiculous
sense of cemetery concessions.
I wish in vain for the apparition of guillotines, but I can only offer to
the sanguinary crowds my suicide wish.
Revolution! You will only shine after my death, on the immense
square of white marble covering my immense corpse.
France is a wasps' nest, Europe a rotted field, and the world a
peninsula of my consciousness.
But luckily I still have the stars, and the consciousness of my moral
greatness opposed to the thousand obstacles the world sets up
against my love.

tr. MAC

## Comme une main à l'instant de la mort

Comme une main à l'instant de la mort et du naufrage se dresse comme
   les rayons du soleil couchant, ainsi de toutes parts jaillissent tes
   regards.
Il n'est plus temps, il n'est plus temps peut-être de me voir,
Mais la feuille qui tombe et la roue qui tourne,
te diront que rien n'est perpétuel sur terre,
Sauf l'amour,
Et je veux m'en persuader.
Des bateaux de sauvetage peints de rougeâtres couleurs,
Des orages qui s'enfuient,
Une valse surannée qu'emportent le temps et le vent durant les longs
   espaces du ciel.
Paysages.
Moi je n'en veux pas d'autres que l'étreinte à laquelle j'aspire,
Et meure le chant du coq.
Comme une main, à l'instant de la mort, se crispe, mon cœur se serre.
Je n'ai jamais pleuré depuis que je te connais.
J'aime trop mon amour pour pleurer.
Tu pleureras sur mon tombeau,
Ou moi sur le tien.
Il ne sera pas trop tard.
Je mentirai. Je dirai que tu fus ma maîtresse.
Et puis vraiment c'est tellement inutile,
Toi et moi, nous mourrons bientôt.

# Just as a hand at the moment of death . . .

Just as a hand at the moment of death and of shipwreck rises like
    the beams of the setting sun, just so your gaze springs forth
    from everywhere.
Perhaps there's no longer time, no longer time to see me,
But the falling lef and the running wheel
will tell you nothing is permanent on this earth,
Except love,
And I want to persuade myself of it.
Rescue ships painted with reddish colors,
Storms fleeing,
A superannuated waltz that weather and wind carry off during the long
    spaces of the sky.
Landscapes.
Me, I want nothing else than the embrace I long for,
And let the cock's crow die.
Just as a hand, at the moment of death, tenses up, my heart contracts.
I've never wept since I've known you.
I love my love too much to weep.
You'll weep over my tomb,
Or me over yours.
It won't be too late.
I will lie. I will say you were my mistress.
And then really it's no use,
You and I, we'll soon die.

tr. MAC

# À la faveur de la nuit

Se glisser dans ton ombre à la faveur de la nuit.

Suivre tes pas, ton ombre à la fenêtre,

Cette ombre à la fenêtre c'est toi, ce n'est pas une autre c'est toi.

N'ouvre pas cette fenêtre derrière les rideaux de laquelle tu bouges.

Ferme les yeux.

Je voudrais les fermer avec mes lèvres.

Mais la fenêtre s'ouvre et le vent, le vent qui balance bizarrement la flamme et le drapeau entoure ma fuite de son manteau.

La fenêtre s'ouvre: Ce n'est pas toi.

Je le savais bien.

# Under the cover of night

To slip into your shadow under cover of night.
To follow your steps, your shadow at the window,
This shadow at the window, it's you, no one else, it's you.
Don't open this window behind whose curtains you're moving.
Close your eyes.
I'd like to close them with my lips.
But the window opens and the wind, wind swaying the flame
so oddly and the flag cloaking my flight.
The window opens: it's not you.
I knew it all along.

tr. MAC

1927
*Les Ténèbres*
translator, Mary Ann Caws

## I. La voix de Robert Desnos

Si semblable à la fleur et au courant d'air
au cours d'eau aux ombres passagères
au sourire entrevu ce fameux soir à minuit
si semblable à tout au bonheur et à la tristesse
c'est le minuit passé dressant son torse nu au-dessus des
beffrois et des peupliers
j'appelle à moi ceux-là perdus dans les campagnes
les vieux cadavres les jeunes chênes coupés
les lambeaux d'étoffe pourrissant sur la terre et le linge
séchant aux alentours des fermes
j'appelle à moi les tornades et les ouragans
les tempêtes les typhons les cyclones
les raz de marée
les tremblements de terre
j'appelle à moi la fumée des volcans et celle des cigarettes
les ronds de fumée des cigares de luxe
j'appelle à moi les amours et les amoureux
j'appelle à moi les vivants et les morts
j'appelle les fossoyeurs j'appelle les assassins
j'appelle les bourreaux j'appelle les pilotes les maçons et
les architectes
les assassins
j'appelle la chair
j'appelle celle que j'aime
j'appelle celle que j'aime
j'appelle celle que j'aime
le minuit triomphant déploie ses ailes de satin et se pose
sur mon lit
les beffrois et les peupliers se plient à mon désir
ceux-là s'écroulent ceux-là s'affaissent

# I. The voice of Robert Desnos

So like the flower and the breeze
like the water's flowing with its passing shadows
like the smile glimpsed that famous midnight
so like everything like joy and sadness
it's past midnight its naked torso rising above belfreys and poplars
I summon to me all those lost in the countryside
old corpses young felled oaks
the threads of cloth rotting on the ground
and the linen drying near the farms
I summon to me tornadoes and hurricanes
tempests typhoons cyclones
tidal waves
earthquakes
I summon to me volcano smoke and that of cigarettes
smoke rings from luxury cigars
I summon to me loves and lovers
I summon to me the living and the dead
I summon to me gravediggers I summon murderers
I summon executioners I summon pilots builders and architects
Murderers
I summon flesh
I summon the one I love
I summon the one I love
I summon the one I love
triumphant midnight unfolds its satin wings and alights on my bed
belfreys and poplars bend to my desire
the former fall in ruin the latter fade

les perdus dans la campagne se retrouvent en me trouvant

les vieux cadavres ressuscitent à ma voix

les jeunes chênes coupés se couvrent de verdure

les lambeaux d'étoffe pourrissent dans la terre et sur la terre claquent à
   ma voix comme l'étendard de la révolte le linge séchant aux
   alentours des fermes habille d'adorables femmes que je n'adore pas
   qui viennent à moi obéissent à ma voix et m'adorent

les tornades tournent dans ma bouche

les ouragans rougissent s'il est possible mes lèvres

les tempêtes grondent à mes pieds

les typhons s'il est possible me dépeignent

je reçois les baisers d'ivresse des cyclones

les raz de marée viennent mourir à mes pieds

les tremblements de terre ne m'ébranlent pas mais font tout crouler à
   mon ordre

la fumée des volcans me vêt de ses vapeurs

et celle des cigarettes me parfume

et les ronds de fumée des cigares me couronnent

les amours et l'amour si longtemps poursuivis se réfugient en moi

les amoureux écoutent ma voix

les vivants et les morts se soumettent et me saluent les premiers
   froidement les seconds familièrement

les fossoyeurs abandonnent les tombes à peine creusées et déclarent que
   moi seul puis commander leurs nocturnes travaux

les assassins me saluent

les bourreaux invoquent la révolution

invoquent ma voix

invoquent mon nom

les pilotes se guident sur mes yeux

les maçons ont le vertige en m'écoutant

les architectes partent pour le désert

those lost in the countryside find their way in finding me
the old cadavers resuscitate at my voice
the young felled oaks become green
the shreds of cloth rotting in the ground and on the ground
    clack at my voice like the banner of rebellion the
      linen drying around the farms dresses adorable women whom
        I do not adore who come to me obey my voice and adore me
tornadoes twist in my mouth
hurricanes redden my lips even more
tempests growl at my feet
typhoons rumple my hair even more
I receive the drunken kisses of cyclones
tidal waves rush forward to die at my feet
earthquakes destroy only at my command
volcano smoke clothes me in its vapors
and cigarette smoke perfumes me
and smoke rings from cigars crown me
loves and love so long pursued take refuge in me
lovers listen to my voice
the living and the dead submit to me the former greeting me
    coldly the latter in friendship
gravediggers leave graves half dug declaring that I alone can order
    their nightly labor
murderers salute me
executioners invoke the revolution
invoke my voice
invoke my name
pilots steer according to my eyes
builders grow dizzy listening to me
architects leave for the desert

les assassins me bénissent
la chair palpite à mon appel

celle que j'aime ne m'écoute pas
celle que j'aime ne m'entend pas
celle que j'aime ne me répond pas

*14-12-26*

murderers bless me
flesh quivers at my call

the one I love does not listen to me
the one I love does not hear me
the one I love does not answer me.

*(December 14, 1926)*

## II. Infinitif

Y mourir ô belle flammèche y mourir
voir les nuages fondre comme la neige et l'écho
origines du soleil et du blanc pauvres comme Job
ne pas mourir encore et voir durer l'ombre
naître avec le feu et ne pas mourir
étreindre et embrasser amour fugace le ciel mat
gagner les hauteurs abandonner le bord
et qui sait découvrir ce que j'aime
omettre de transmettre mon nom aux années
rire aux heures orageuses dormir au pied d'un pin
grâce aux étoiles semblables à un numéro
et mourir ce que j'aime au bord des flammes.

## II. Infinitive

To die there oh lovely spark to die there
to see clouds melting like snow and echo
origins of the sun of white poor as Job's turkey
not yet to die and see the shadow lasting still
to be born with the fire and not to die
to embrace and kiss fleeting love the unpolished sky
to attain the heights abandon ship
and who knows discover what I love
omit to transmit my name to future years
to laugh in the stormy hours to sleep at the foot of a pine
thanks to the stars like a spectacle
and to die what I love at the edge of flames.

## III. Le vendredi du crime

Un incroyable désir s'empare des femmes endormies
Une pierre précieuse s'endort dans l'écrin bleu de roi
Et voilà que sur le chemin s'agitent les cailloux fatigués
Plus jamais les pas des émues par la nuit
Passez cascades
Les murailles se construisent au son du luth d'Orphée
et s'écroulent au son des trompettes de Jéricho
Sa voix perce les murailles
et mon regard les supprime sans ruines
Ainsi passent les cascades avec la lamentation des étoiles
Plus de cailloux sur le sentier
Plus de femmes endormies
Plus de femmes dans l'obscurité
Ainsi passez cascades.

# III. Crime Friday

An incredible desire seizes the sleeping women
A precious stone sleeps in the king's blue mane
See how the tired pebbles are rattling on the path
No more steps of those stirred by night
Waterfalls, go on by
The walls rise at the sound of Orpheus's lute
and crumble at Jericho's trumpets
His voice pierces through those walls
And my gaze tumbles them into ruins
So the waterfalls go by with stars lamenting
No more pebbles on the path
No more sleeping women
No more women in the darkness
So waterfalls, go on by.

# IV. L'idée fixe

Je t'apporte une petite algue qui se mêlait à l'écume de la mer et ce
peigne
Mais tes cheveux sont mieux nattés que las nuages avec le vent avec les
rougeurs célestes et tels avec des frémissements de vie et de
sanglots que se tordant parfois entre mes mains ils meurent avec les
flots et les récifs du rivage en telle abondance qu'il faudra longtemps
pour désespérer des parfums et de leur fuite avec le soir où ce
peigne marque sans bouger les étoiles ensevelies dans leur rapide et
soyeux cours traversé par mes doigts sollicitant encore à leur racine
la caresse humide d'une mer plus dangereuse que celle où cette
algue fut recueillie avec la mousse dispersée d'une tempête.
Une étoile qui meurt est pareille à tes lèvres.
Elles bleuissent comme le vin répandu sur la nappe.
Un instant passe avec la profondeur d'une mine.
L'anthracite se plaint sourdement et tombe en flocons sur la ville
Qu'il fait froid dans l'impasse où je t'ai connue.
Un numéro oublié sur une maison en ruines
Le numéro 4 je crois.
Je te retrouverai avant quelques jours près de ce pot de reine-marguerite
Les mines ronflent sourdement
Les toits sont couverts d'anthracite.
Ce peigne dans tes cheveux semblables à la fin du monde
La fumée le vieil oiseau et le geai
Là sont finies les roses et les émeraudes
Les pierres précieuses et les fleurs
La terre s'effrite et s'étoile avec le bruit d'un fer à repasser sur la nacre
Mais tes cheveux si bien nattés ont la forme d'une main.

# IV. Obsession

I bring you a bit of seaweed which was tangled with the sea foam
    and this comb
But your hair is more neatly fixed than the clouds with the wind
    with celestial crimson glowing in them and are such that with
    quiverings of life and sobs twisting sometimes between my
    hands they die with the waves and the reefs of the strand so
    abundantly that we shall not soon again despair of perfumes
    and their flight at evening when this comb marks motionless the
    stars buried in their rapid and silky flow traversed by my hands
    seeking still at their root the humid caress of a sea more
    dangerous than the one where this seaweed was gathered with
    the froth scattered by a tempest.
A star dying is like your lips.
They turn blue as the wine spilled on the tablecloth.
An instant passes with a mine's profundity.
With a muffled complaint the anthracite falls in flakes on the town
How cold it is in the impasse where I knew you.
A forgotten number on a house in ruins
The number 4 I think.
Before too long I'll find you again near these china-asters
The mines make a muffled snoring
The roofs are strewn with anthracite.
This comb in your hair like the end of the world
The smoke the old bird and the jay
There the roses and the emeralds are finished
The precious stones and the flowers
The earth crumbles and stars screeching like an iron across
    mother-of-pearl
But your neatly fixed hair has the shape of a hand.

## V. Sous les saules

L'étrange oiseau dans la cage aux flammes
Je déclare que je suis le bûcheron de la forêt d'acier
que les martes et les loutres sont des jamais connues
l'étrange oiseau qui tord ses ailes et s'illumine
Un feu de Bengale inattendu a charmé ta parole
Quand je te quitte il rougit mes épaules et l'amour
Le quart d'heure vineux mieux vêtu qu'un décor lointain
étire ses bras débiles et fait craquer ses doigts d'albâtre
À la date voulue tout arrivera en transparence
plus fameux que la volière où les plumes se dispersent
Un arbre célèbre se dresse au-dessus du monde avec des
pendus en ses racines profondes vers la terre
c'est ce jour que je choisis
Un flamboyant poignard a tué l'étrange oiseau dans la cage
de flamme et la forêt d'acier vibre en sourdine illuminée par
le feu des mortes giroflées
Dans le taillis je t'ai cachée dans le taillis qui se proclame
roi des plaines.

## V. Under the Willows

The strange bird in the flaming cage
I declare that I'm woodcutter of the steel forest
that martens and otters are never-known
the strange bird twisting his wings brightening
Unforeseen a Bengal light has charmed your speech
When I leave you it reddens my shoulders and love
The winey moment better dressed than some distant décor
stretches out its weak arms cracks its alabaster fingers
When we wish will all arrive transparently
more famous than the aviary where feathers scatter
Renowned a  tree rises over the world
hanged men in its deep roots downward
it's today I choose
A flaring dagger has killed the strange bird in its cage
of flame and the steel forest vibrates secretly lit up
by the fire of the gillyflowers
In the copse I've hidden you in the copse self-proclaimed
king of the plains.

# VI. Trois étoiles

J'ai perdu le regret du mal passé les ans.

J'ai gagné la sympathie des poissons.

Plein d'algues, le palais qui abrite mes rêves est un récif et aussi un
territoire du ciel d'orage et non du ciel trop pâle de la mélancolique
divinité.

J'ai perdu tout de même la gloire que je méprise

J'ai tout perdu hormis l'amour, l'amour de l'amour, l'amour des algues,
l'amour de la reine des catastrophes.

Une étoile me parle à l'oreille:

Croyez-moi, c'est une belle dame

Les algues lui obéissent et la mer elle-même se transforme en robe de
cristal quand elle paraît sur la plage.

Belle robe de cristal tu résonnes à mon nom.

Les vibrations, ô cloche surnaturelle, se perpétuent dans sa chair

Les seins en frémissent.

La robe de cristal sait mon nom

La robe de cristal m'a dit:

«Fureur en toi, amour en toi

Enfant des étoiles sans nombres

Maître du seul vent et du seul sable

Maître des carillons de la destinée et de l'éternité,

Maître de tout enfin hormis de l'amour de sa belle

Maître de tout ce qu'il a perdu et esclave de ce qu'il garde encore.

Tu seras le dernier convive à la table ronde de l'amour.

Les convives, les autres, larrons ont emporté les couverts d'argent.

Le bois se fend, la neige fond.

Maître de tout hormis de l'amour de sa dame.

Toi qui commandes aux dieux ridicules de l'humanité et ne te sers pas
de leur pouvoir qui t'es soumis.

Toi, maître, maître de tout hormis de l'amour de ta belle»

Voilà ce que m'a dit la robe de cristal.

# VI. Three stars

I have lost regret of evil with the years gone by.

I have won the sympathy of fish.

Full of seaweed, the palace sheltering my dreams is a shoal and also
a territory of the stormy sky and not of the too-pale sky of
melancholy divinity.

I have lost all the same the glory I despise.

I have lost everything save for love, love of love, love of, love
of the queen of catastrophes.

A star speaks in my ear:

"Believe me, she's a lovely lady,

The seaweed obeys her and the sea itself changes to a crystal dress
when she appears on the shore."

Beautiful crystal dress you resound at my name.

Vibrations, oh supernatural bell, perpetuate themselves in her being

Her breasts tremble from it.

The crystal dress knows my name,

The crystal dress said to me:

"Fury in you, love in you

Child of the numberless stars

Master of the wind alone and the sand alone

Master of the carillons of fate and eternity,

Master of all at last save the love of his lovely one

Master of all he has lost and a slave to what he still retains.

You will be the last guest at the round table of love.

The guests, the other thieves have taken the silver setting.

Wood cleaves, snow melts.

Master of all save his lady's love.

You who command the ridiculous gods of humanity and do not use
their power which is subject to you.

You, master, master of all save your lady's love."

That is what the crystal dress said to me.

# VII. Chant du ciel

La fleur des Alpes disait au coquillage: «tu luis»
Le coquillage disait à la mer: «tu résonnes»
La mer disait au bateau: «tu trembles»
Le bateau disait au feu: «tu brilles»
Le feu me disait: «Je brille mois qui ses yeux»
Le bateau me disait: «je tremble moins que ton cœur quand
    elle paraît»
La mer me disait: «je résonne moins que son nom en ton amour»
Le coquillage me disait: «je luis moins que le phosphore du désir
    dans ton rêve creux»
La fleur des Alpes me disait: «Elle est belle»
Je disais: «Elle est belle, elle est belle, elle est émouvante»

# VII. Sky song

The flower of the Alps said to the seashell: "you are shining"
The seashell said to the sea: "you resound"
The sea said to the boat: "you quiver"
The boat said to the fire: "you are glowing"
The fire said to me: "I glow less brightly than her eyes"
The boat said to me: "I quiver less than your heart when she appears"
The sea said to me: "I resound less than her name in your love"
The seashell said to me: "I shine less than the phosphorous of desire
    in your empty dream"
The flower of the Alps said to me: "she is lovely"
I said: "she is lovely, she is lovely, she is touching."

## VIII. De la fleur d'amour et des chevaux migrateurs

Il était dans la forêt une fleur immense qui risquait de faire mourir
    d'amour tous les arbres
Tous les arbres l'aimaient
Les chênes vers minuit devenaient reptiles et rampaient jusqu'à sa tige
Les frênes et les peupliers se courbaient vers sa corolle
Les fougères jaunissaient dans sa terre.
Et telle elle était radieuse plus que l'amour nocturne de la mer et
    de la lune
Plus pâle que les grands volcans éteints de cet astre
Plus triste et nostalgique que le sable qui se dessèche et se mouille au
    gré des flots
Je parle de la fleur de la forêt et non des tours
Je parle de la fleur de la forêt et non de mon amour
Et si telle trop pâle et nostalgique et adorable aimée des arbres et des
    fougères elle retient mon souffle sur les lèvres c'est que nous
    sommes de même essence
Je l'ai rencontrée un jour
Je parle de la fleur et non des arbres
Dans la forêt frémissante où je passais
Salut papillon qui mourut dans sa corolle
Et toi fougère pourrissante mon cœur
Et vous mes yeux fougères presque charbon presque flamme presque
    flot
Je parle en vain de la fleur mais de moi
Les fougères ont jauni sur le sol devenu pareil à la lune
Semblable le temps précis à l'agonie d'une abeille perdue entre un
    bleuet et une rose et encore une perle.
Le ciel n'est pas si clos
Un homme surgit qui dit son nom devant lequel s'ouvrent les portes un
    chrysanthème à la boutonnière

# VIII. Of the flower of love and of the migrating horses

Once in the forest was an immense flower for love of whom all the
    trees almost died
All the trees loved her
Toward midnight the oaks assumed serpent shapes and slithered
    to the flower's stem
The ashes and the poplars bent over to her corolla
The ferns grew yellow in her earth.
And she was more radiant than the nightly love of moon and sea
Paler than the great extinct volcanos of this planet
Sadder and more nostalgic than the sand drying up and moistening
    at the will of waves
I speak of the forest flower and not of towers
I speak of the forest flower and not of my love
And if, too pale and nostalgic and adorable loved by the trees and
    ferns she causes my breath to catch it is because we share
    the same essence
I met the flower one day
I am speaking of the flower and not of trees
In the trembling forest where I went
Greetings butterfly who died in her corolla
And you rotting fern my heart
And you my eyes ferns almost coal almost flame almost flood
I speak in vain of the flower but of myself
The ferns have yellowed on the moon-like earth
At that precise moment similar to the agony of a bee lost between
    a cornflower and a rose and again a pearl.
The sky is not so closed
A man appears wearing a chrysanthemum and says his name for
    which doors open

C'est de la fleur immobile que je parle et non des ports de l'aventure et
  de la solitude
Les arbres un à un moururent autour de la fleur
Qui se nourrissait de leur mort pourrissante
Et c'est pourquoi la plaine devint semblable à la pulpe des fruits
Pourquoi les villes surgirent
Une rivière à mes pieds se love et reste à ma merci ficelle de la
  salutation des images
Un cœur quelque part s'arrête de battre et la fleur se dresse
C'est la fleur dont l'odeur triomphe du temps
La fleur qui d'elle-même a révélé son existence aux plaines dénudées
  pareilles à la lune à la mer et à l'aride atmosphère des cœurs
  douloureux
Une pince de homard bien rouge reste à côté de la marmite
Le soleil projette l'ombre de la bougie et de la flamme
La fleur se dresse avec orgueil dans un ciel de fable
Vos ongles mes amies sont pareils à ses pétales et roses comme eux
La forêt murmurante en bas se déploie
Un cœur qui s'arrête comme une source tarie
Il n'est plus temps il n'est plus temps d'aimer vous qui passez sur la
  route
La fleur de la forêt dont je conte l'histoire est un chrysanthème
Les arbres sont morts les champs ont verdi les villes sont apparues
Les grands chevaux migrateurs piaffent dans leurs écuries lointaines
Bientôt les grands chevaux migrateurs partent
Les villes regardent passer leur troupeau dons les rues dont le pavé
  résonne au choc de leurs sabots et parfois étincelle
Les champs sont bouleversés par cette cavalcade
Eux la queue traînant dans la poussière et les naseaux fumant passent
  devant la fleur
Longtemps se prolongent leurs ombres

It's of the motionless flower I speak and not of the ports of
    adventure and solitude
The trees one by one died about the flower
Who fed on their rotting death
And thus the plain grew like the pulp of fruit
The towns sprang up
A river nestles at my feet and remains at my mercy, twine of
    images in their greeting
Somewhere a heart stops beating and the flower arises
The flower whose perfume triumphs over time
The flower who chose to reveal itself to the denuded plains like the
    moon the sea and the arid space of dolorous hearts
One quite red lobster claw lies beside the kettle
The sun projects the shadow of the candle and the flame
The flower stands proudly upright in a fabled sky
Your nails my friends are like her petals and as pink
The murmuring forest stretches out below
A heart stopping like a dried-up spring
It is no longer time to love, it is no longer time, oh passers-by
    on the road
The forest flower whose tale I tell is a chrysanthemum
The trees have died the fields turned green the towns appeared
The great migrating horses snort in their distant stables
Soon the great migrating horses leave
The towns watch the herd passing in the streets whose pavings
    resound glinting with their hoofs
The fields are shaken by this cavalcade
While, trailing their tails in the dust and their smoking nostrils,
    they pass before the flower
Their long shadows extend

Mais que sont-ils devenus les chevaux migrateurs dont la robe tachetée
    était un gage de détresse
Parfois on trouve un fossile étrange en creusant la terre
C'est un de leurs fers
La fleur qui les vit fleurit encore sans tache ne faiblesse
Les feuilles poussent au long de sa tige
Les fougères s'enflamment et se penchent aux fenêtres des maisons
Mais les arbres que sont-ils devenus
La fleur pourquoi fleurit-elle
Volcans! ô volcans!
Le ciel s'écroule
Je pense à très loin au plus profond de moi
Les temps abolis sont pareils aux ongles brisés sur les portes closes
Quand dans les campagnes un paysan va mourir entouré des fruits mûrs
    de l'arrière-saison du bruit du givre qui se craquèle sur les vitres de
    l'ennui flétri fané comme les bleuets du gazon
Surgissent les chevaux migrateurs
Quand un voyageur s'égare dans les feux follets plus crevassés que le
    front des vieillards et qu'il se couche dans le terrain mouvant
Surgissent des chevaux migrateurs
Quand une fillette se couche nue au pied d'un bouleau et attend
Surgissent les chevaux migrateurs
Ils apparaissent dans un galop de flacons brisés et d'armoires grinçantes
Ils disparaissent dans un creux
Nulle selle n'a flétri leur échine et leur croupe luisante reflète le ciel
Ils passent éclaboussant les murs fraîchement recrépis
Et le givre craquant les fruits mûrs les fleurs effeuillées l'eau
    croupissante le terrain mou des marécages qui se modèlent
    lentement
Voient passer les chevaux migrateurs

But what became of the migratory horses whose spotted covering
    was a mark of distress
From time to time a strange fossil is found by digging in the earth
One of their horseshoes
The flower which saw them still flourishes with neither spot nor
    weakness
Leaves grow along her stem
The ferns catch fire and lean toward the windows of houses
But what became of the trees
Why does the flower flourish
Volcanoes! oh volcanoes!
The sky crumbles
I am thinking of great distance in the depths of myself
The abolished moments like fingernails broken on the closed doors
When in the countryside a peasant is about to die surrounded with
    Indian summer's ripe fruits with the frost crackling against the
    panes of boredom withered faded like cornflowers on the lawn
The migrating horses appear
When a traveler wanders lost among the fireflies with more furrows
    than an old man's forehead and when he lies down on the
    moving earth
The migrating horses appear
When a little girl lies down naked at the foot of a birch and waits
The migrating horses appear
They surge forth in a gallop of shattered flasks and creaking closets
Into a hollow they disappear
No saddle has ever withered their spine and their shining rump
    reflects the sky
Their passing splatters the walls freshly replastered
And the frost crackling the ripe fruit the depetaled flowers the
    stagnant water the marshy terrain slowly formed
See the migrating horses pass by

Les chevaux migrateurs
Les chevaux migrateurs
Les chevaux migrateurs
Les chevaux migrateurs

The migrating horses
The migrating horses
The migrating horses
The migrating horses.

## IX. Avec le cœur du chêne

Avec le bois tendre et dur de ces arbres, avec le cœur du chêne et
l'écorce du bouleau combien ferait-on de ciels, combien d'océans,
combien de pantoufles pour les jolis pieds d'Isabelle la vague?

Avec le cœur du chêne et l'écorce du bouleau.

Avec le ciel combien ferait-on de regards, combien d'ombres derrière le
mur, combien de chemises pour le corps d'Isabelle la vague?

Avec le cœur du chêne et l'écorce du bouleau, avec le ciel.

Avec les océans combien ferait-on de flammes, combien de reflets
au bord des palais, combien d'arcs-en-ciel au-dessus de la
tête d'Isabelle la vague?

Avec le cœur du chêne et l'écorce du bouleau, avec le ciel, avec les
océans.

Avec les pantoufles combien ferait-on d'étoiles, de chemin dans la nuit,
de marques dans la cendre, combien monterait-on d'escaliers pour
rencontrer Isabelle la vague?

Avec le cœur du chêne et l'écorce du bouleau, avec le ciel, avec les
océans, avec les pantoufles.

Mais Isabelle la vague, bous m'entendez, n'est qu'une image du rêve à
travers les feuilles vernies de l'arbre de la mort et de l'amour.

Avec le cœur du chêne et l'écorce du bouleau.

## IX. With oaken heart and birchbark

With the tender and hard wood of these trees, with oaken heart
and birchbark, how many skies could one make, how many
oceans, how many slippers for the pretty feet of Isabella the Vague?

With oaken heart and birchbark.

With the sky how many glances could one make, how many shadows
behind the wall, how many slips for the body of Isabella the Vague?

With oaken heart and birchbark, with the sky.

With the oceans how many flames could one make, how many
reflections at palace edge, how many rainbows above the head of
Isabella the Vague?

With oaken heart and birchbark, with the sky, with oceans.

With slippers how many stars could one make, how many paths in
the night, traces in the ashes, how many stairs could one climb
to meet Isabella the Vague?

With oaken heart and birchbark, with the sky, with oceans, with
slippers.

But Isabella the Vague, you know, is only an image of dream seen
through the polished leaves of the tree of death and of love.

With oaken heart and birchbark.

Qu'elle vienne jusqu'à moi dire en vain la destinée que je retiens dans mon poing fermé et qui ne s'envole pas quand j'ouvre la main et qui s'inscrit en lignes étranges.

Avec le cœur du chêne et l'écorce du bouleau, avec le ciel.

Elle pourra mirer son visage et ses cheveux au fond de mon âme et baiser ma bouche.

Avec le cœur du chêne et l'écorce du bouleau, avec le ciel, avec les océans.

Elle pourra se dénuder, je marcherai à ses côtés à travers le monde, dans la nuit, pour l'épouvante des veilleurs. Elle pourra me tuer, me piétiner ou mourir à mes pieds.

Car j'en aime une autre plus touchante qu'Isabelle la vague.

Avec le cœur du chêne et l'écorce du bouleau, avec le ciel, avec les océans, avec les pantoufles.

May she come to me telling in vain the fortune held in my clasped
fist, remaining there when I open my hand where it is sketched
in strange lines.

With oaken heart and birchbark, with the sky.

She can look at her face and her hair in the depths of my soul and
kiss my mouth.

With oaken heart and birchbark, with the sky, with oceans.

She can undress, I shall walk by her side throughout the world,
at night, frightening the nightwatchmen. She can kill me,
trample me or die at my feet.

For I love another more touching than Isabella the Vague.

With oaken heart and birchbark, with the sky, with oceans,
with slippers.

# X. Vieille clameur

Une tige dépouillée dans ma main c'est le monde
La serrure se ferme sur l'ombre et l'ombre met son œil à la serrure
Et voilà que l'ombre se glisse dans la chambre
La belle amante que voila l'ombre plus charnelle que ne l'imagine perdu
    dans son blasphème le grand oiseau de fourrure blanche perché sur
    l'épaule de la belle, de l'incomparable putain qui veille sur le
    sommeil
Le chemin se calme soudain en attendant la tempête
Un vert filet à papillon s'abat sur la bougie
Qui es-tu toi qui prends la flamme pour un insecte
Un étrange combat entre la gaze et le feu
C'est à vos genoux qui je voudrais passer la nuit
C'est à tes genoux
De temps à autre sur ton front ténébreux et calme en dépit des
    apparitions nocturnes, je remettrai en place une mèche de cheveux
    dérangée
Je surveillerai le lent balancement du temps et de ta respiration
Ce bouton je l'ai trouvé par terre
Il est en nacre
Et je cherche la boutonnière qui le perdit
Je sais qu'il manque un bouton à ton manteau
Au flanc de la montagne se flétrit l'edelweiss
L'edelweiss qui fleurit dans mon rêve et dans tes mains quand elles
    s'ouvrent:
Salut de bon matin quand l'ivresse est commune quand le fleuve
    adolescent descend d'un pas nonchalant les escaliers de marbre
    colossaux avec son cortège de nuées blanches et d'orties
La plus belle nuée était un clair de lune récemment transformé et l'ortie
    la plus haute était couverte de diamants

# X. Ancient clamor

A stalk stripped of leaves in my hand is the world
The keyhole is closed on the shadow and the shadow puts its eye
    to the keyhole
And here is the shadow gliding into the room
Here is the beautiful mistress the shadow more carnal than the great
    bird of white fur lost in its blasphemy imagines perched on the
    shoulder of the beautiful the incomparable whore watching
    over sleep
The path suddenly calms waiting for the tempest
A green butterfly net sweeps down on the candle
Who are you, taking the flame for an insect
A strange battle between the gauze and the fire
At your knees I should like to spend the night
At your knees
From time to time on your forehead shadowy and calm in spite of
    nocturnal apparitions I put back in its place a strand of hair
I shall watch over the slow swaying of time and of your breathing
This button I found on the ground
It is mother-of-pearl
And I look for the buttonhole that lost it
I know a button is missing on your coat
On the side of the mountain the edelweiss withers
The edelweiss flowering in my dream and in your hands when they open
Early morning greetings when drunkenness is shared when the
    adolescent river nonchalantly descends the colossal marble steps
    with its retinue of white clouds and thistles
The most beautiful cloud was a moonlight recently transformed and
    the tallest thistle was sheathed with diamonds

Salut de bon matin à la fleur du charbon la vierge au grand cœur qui
m'endormira ce soir
Salut de bon matin aux yeux de cristal aux yeux de lavande aux yeux de
gypse aux yeux de calme plat aux yeux de sanglot aux yeux de
tempête
Salut de bon matin salut
La flamme est dans mon cœur et le soleil dans le verre
Mais jamais plus hélas ne pourrons-nous dire encore
Salut de bon matin tous! crocodiles yeux de cristal orties vierge fleur du
charbon vierge au grand cœur.

Early morning greetings to the flower of coal the good-hearted virgin
who'll put me to sleep tonight
Early morning greetings to the crystal eyes the lavender eyes the gypsum
eyes the eyes of dead calm the eyes of sobbing the eyes of tempest
Greetings morning greetings
The flame is in my heart and the sun in the glass
But never more alas shall we say again
Good morning to all of you! crocodiles crystal eyes thistles virgin flower
of coal good-hearted virgin.

## XI. Le suicidé de nuit

Les rameaux verts s'inclinent quand la libellule apparaît au détour du
    sentier
J'approche d'une pierre tombale plus transparente que la neige blanche
    comme le lait blanche comme la chaux blanche blanche comme les
    murailles
La libellule patauge dans les flaques de lait
L'armure de verre tremble frémit se met en marche
Les arcs-en-ciel se nouent à la Louis XV
Eh quoi? déjà le sol dérobé par notre route dresse la main
Se bat avec l'armure de verre
Sonne aux portes
Flotte dans l'air
Crie
Gémit pleure ah! ah! ah! ah! sillage tu meurs en ce bruit bleu rocher
Les grands morceaux d'éponges qui tombent du ciel recouvrent les
    cimetières
Le vin coule avec un bruit de tonnerre
Le lait le sol dérobé l'armure se battent sur l'herbe qui rougit et
    blanchit tour à tour
Le tonnerre et l'éclair et l'arc-en-ciel
Ah! sillage tu crevasses et tu chantes
La petite fille s'en va à l'école en récitant sa leçon.

# XI. Night suicide

The green reeds bow down when the dragonfly appears at the bend of
    the path
I go towards a tombstone clearer than white snow like white milk white
    limestone white walls
The dragonfly splashes about in the pools of milk
The glass armor trembles shivers starts walking
Rainbows knot up Louis XV style
What? Already the earth hidden by our path holds up its hand
Struggles with the glass armor
Knocks at the doors
Floats in the air
Yells
Moans weeps ah! Ah! Ah! Ah! Furrow you die in this sound blue rock
Great morsels of sponges falling from the sky cover up cemeteries
Wine runs thunderous
Milk hidden earth armor struggle on the grass turning now red
    now white
Thunder and lightning and rainbow
Ah! Furrow you crevice and you sing
The little girl goes to school reciting her lesson

## XII. Pour un rêve de jour

Le meurtre du douanier fut splendide avec le cerne bleu des yeux et
l'accent rauque des canards près de la mare

Le meurtre fut splendide mais déjà le soleil se transformait en robe de
crêpe

Filleule de l'ananas et portrait même des profondeurs de la mer

Un cygne se couche sur l'herbe voici le poème des métamorphoses. Le
cygne qui devient boîte d'allumettes et le phosphore en guise de
cravate

Triste fin Métamorphose du silence en silence et chanson-verre du feu
à Neuilly le dimanche éclair qui se désole et rame à contre-courant
du nord magnétique et si peu fait pour comprendre que jamais du
fond des consciences ténébreuses sortir en éclat d'ailes et le fer se
troubler si l'escalier se résorbe en pluie sur l'étrange tissu marin que
parfois les pêcheurs ramènent dans leur filet de cheveux et d'écaille
au grand effroi des Peaux-rouges du tumulus et du signe fatal du
chargé de découvrir l'heure et la vitesse qui sanglote et palpite avec
l'arrêt de la sonnerie qui qui qui et qui?

Cueille, cueille la rose et ne t'occupe pas de ton destin cueille cueille la
rose et la feuille de palmier et relève les paupières de la jeune fille
pour qu'elle te regarde ÉTERNELLEMENT.

## XII. For a dream of day

The custom officer's murder was splendid with the blue shadows
    around the eyes and the raucous quack of the ducks near the pond

The murder was splendid but already the sun was changing into a crepe
    dress

Godchild of pineapple and the very picture of the ocean's depths

A swan lies down on the grass here's the poem of metamorphoses. The
    swan becoming a matchbox and phosphorous disguised as a tie

Sad end Metamorphosis of silence into silence and drinking song of a
    Neuilly fire Sunday lightning depressing and rowing against the
    current of the magnetic north so inapt at understanding that
    never from the depths of the shadowy consciences emerging in a
    dazzle of wings and the iron disturbed itself if the staircase
    dissolves into rain on the strange sailor cloth fishermen sometimes
    bring back in their net of hair and scales terribly frightening to the
    Indians of the tumulus and the fatal sign of the one charged with
    discovering the time and the speed sobbing and quivering as the
    ringing stops who who who and who?

Pick, pick the rose and don't worry about your fate pick pick the
    rose and the palm leaf  and lift the eyelids of the girl
    so she'll gaze at you ETERNALLY.

# XIII. Il fait nuit

Tu t'en iras quand tu voudras
Le lit se ferme et se délace avec délices comme un corset de velours noir
Et l'insecte brillant se pose sur l'oreiller
Éclate et rejoint le Noir
Le flot qui martèle arrive et se tait
Samoa la belle s'endort dans l'ouate
Clapier qui fais-tu des drapeaux? to les roules dans la boue
À la bonne étoile et au fond de toute boue
Le naufrage s'accentue sous la paupière
Je conte et décris le sommeil
Je recueille les flacons de la nuit et je les range sur une étagère
Le ramage de l'oiseau de bois se confond avec le bris des bouchons en
    forme de regard
N'y pas aller n'y pas mourir la joie est de trop
Un convive de plus à la table ronde dans la clairière de vert émeraude et
    de heaumes retentissants près d'un monceau d'épées et d'armures
    cabossées
Nerf en amoureuse lampe éteinte de la fin du jour
Je dors

# XIII. Now it's night

You'll go away when you want to
The bed closes and unlaces voluptuous like a black velvet corset
And the shining insect rests on the pillow
Bursts open and regains the Blackness
The hammering wave arrives stays silent
Samoa the beautiful falls asleep in the cotton
Rabbit-burrow what are you doing with the curtains? rolling them
    about in the mud
Under a lucky star and in the depths of all mud
The shipwreck is stressed under the eyelid
I count and describe this sleep
I gather the flasks of night and arrange them on a shelf
The wooden bird's warbling mingles with the smash of corks like a look
Don't go there don't die there wrong place for joy
One more guest at the round table in the clearing of emerald green and
    resounding helmets near a heap of swords and bashed-in armor
Loving nerves lamp extinguished at day's end
I am sleeping

# XIV. Vie d'ébène

Un calme effrayant marquera ce jour
Et l'ombre des réverbères et des avertisseurs d'incendie fatiguera la
      lumière
Tout se taira les plus silencieux et les plus bavards
Enfin mourront les nourrissons braillards
Les remorqueurs les locomotives le vent
Glisser en silence
On entendra la grande voix qui venant de loin passera sur la ville
On l'attendra longtemps
Puis vers le soleil de milord
Quand la poussière les pierres et l'absence de larmes composent sur les
      grandes places désertes la robe du soleil
Enfin on entendra venir la voix
Elle grondera longtemps aux portes
Elle passera sur la ville arrachant les drapeaux et brisant les vitres
On l'entendra
Quel silence avant elle mais plus grand encore le silence qu'elle ne
      troublera pas mais qu'elle accusera du délit de mort prochaine
      qu'elle flétrira qu'elle dénoncera.
Ô jour de malheurs et de joies
Le jour le jour prochain où la voix passera sur la ville.
Une mouette fantomatique m'a dit qu'elle m'aimait autant que je l'aime
Que ce grand silence terrible était mon amour
Que le vent qui portait la voix était mon amour
Que le vent qui portait la voix était la grande révolte du monde
Et que la voix me serait favorable.

## XIV. Ebony life

A frightful calm will mark this day
And the shadow of street lamps and fire hydrants will tire out the light
All will fall quiet the most silent and the chattiest
Finally the squalling infants will die
Tugboats trains wind
Will slip along in silence
We'll hear the great voice coming from far to pass over the town
We'll await it a long time
Then towards milord's sun
When the dust of the stones and the absence of tears make up
    the sun's dress on the great deserted squares
Finally we'll hear the voice coming
Muttering long at the doors
It will pass over the town snatching drapes breaking panes
We'll hear it
What silence before it still greater the silence it won't disturb
    but accuse it of the misdemeanor of sudden death it will brand
    and denounce.
Oh day of misfortune and joy
The day the nearby day when the voice will pass over the town.
A phantom seagull told me she loved me as much as I love her
That this great terrible silence was my love
That the wind bearing the voice was the great revolt of the world
And that the voice would be in my favor.

# XV. Désespoir du soleil

Quel bruit étrange glissait le long de la rampe d'escalier au bas de
laquelle rêvait la pomme transparente.

Les vergers étaient clos et le sphinx bien loin de là s'étirait dans le sable
craquant de chaleur dans la nuit de tissu fragile.

Ce bruit devait-il durer jusqu'à l'éveil des locataires ou s'évader dans
l'ombre du crépuscule matinal? Le bruit persistait. Le sphinx aux
aguets l'entendait depuis des siècles et désirait l'éprouver. Aussi ne
faut-il pas s'étonner de voir la silhouette souple du sphinx dans les
ténèbres de l'escalier. Le fauve égratignait de ses griffes les marches
encaustiquées. Les sonnettes devant chaque porte marquaient de
lueurs la cage de l'ascenseur et le bruit persistant sentant venir celui
qu'il attendait depuis des millions de ténèbres s'attacha à la crinière
et brusquement l'ombre pâlit.

C'est le poème du matin qui commence tandis que dans son lit tiède
avec des cheveux dénoués rabattus sur le visage et les drap plus
froissés que ses paupières la vagabonde attend l'instant où s'ouvrira
sur un paysage de résine et d'agathe sa porte close encore aux flots
du ciel et de la nuit.

C'est le poème du jour où le sphinx se couche dans le lit de la vagabonde
et malgré le bruit persistant lui jure un éternel amour digne de foi.

C'est le poème du jour qui commence dans la fumée odorante du
chocolat et la monotone tac tac du cireur qui s'étonne de voir sur les
marches de l'escalier les traces des griffes du voyageur de la nuit.

C'est le poème du jour qui commence avec des étincelles d'allumettes
au grand effroi des pyramides surprises et tristes de ne plus voir leur
majestueux compagnon couché à leurs pieds.

Mais le bruit quel était-il? Dites-le tandis que le poème du jour
commence tandis que la vagabonde et le sphinx bien-aimé rêvent
aux bouleversements de paysages.

# XV. Despair of the sun

What strange noise was sliding along the staircase at whose base
 the transparent apple dreamed.
The orchards were closed and the sphinx far off stretched lazily
 in the sand crackling with heat in the night of fragile cloth.
Was that noise to last until the waking of the tenants or would it go
 away in the shadow of the morning twilight? The noise persisted.
 The watchful sphinx had heard it for centuries and wanted to
 test it. So it was no surprise to see its supple silhouette in
 the shadows of the stairs. The beast scratched with its claws
 the waxed steps. The doorbells gleamed their light onto the elevator
 shaft and the persistent noise aware of the arrival of the one
 whom it had been awaiting for millions of shadows clung to its
 mane and suddenly the shadow paled.
It's the poem of the morning beginning while in her warm bed with
 her hair undone pulled over her face and the sheets more wrinkled
 than her eyelids the wanderer waits for the moment when her
 door still closed on the floods of sky and of night might open on
 the landscape of resin and agate.
It's the poem of day when the sphinx lies down in the bed of the
 wanderer and in spite of the persisting noise swears to her an eternal
 faithful love.
It's the poem of the day beginning in the perfumed vapor of
 chocolate and the monotonous slapping cloth of the bootblack
 astonished to see on the stairs the claw tracks of the night traveler.
It's the poem of the day beginning with the flames of matches to
 the great dismay of the pyramids surprised and saddened to see
 their majestic companion crouched at their feet no longer.
But what was the noise? Tell us while the poem of the day begins
 while the wanderer and the beloved sphinx dream of the
 landscapes thrown into chaos.

Ce n'était pas le bruit de la pendule ni celui des pas ne celui du moulin
à café.

Le bruit quel était-il? Quel était-il?

L'escalier s'enfoncera-t-il toujours plus avant? monter-t-il toujours plus
haut?

Rêvons acceptons de rêver c'est le poème du jour qui commence.

It was not the noise of the clock nor that of footsteps nor that of the coffee mill.

What was the noise? what was it?

Will the staircase always descend still lower? will it always ascend still higher?

Let us dream let us welcome the dream it's the poem of the day beginning.

## XVI. Identité des images

Je me bats avec fureur contre des animaux et des bouteilles
Depuis peu de temps peut-être dix heures sont passées l'une après
    l'autre
La belle nageuse qui avait peur du corail ce matin s'éveille
Le corail couronné de houx frappe à sa porte
Ah! encore le charbon toujours le charbon
Je t'en conjure charbon génie tutélaire du rêve et de ma solitude laisse-
    moi laisse-moi parler encore de la belle nageuse que avait peur du
    corail
Ne tyrannise plus ce séduisant sujet de mes rêves
La belle nageuse reposait dans un lit de dentelles et d'oiseaux
Les vêtements sur une chaise au pied du lit étaient illuminés par les
    lueurs les dernières lueurs du charbon
Celui-ci venu des profondeurs du ciel de la terre et de la mer était fier
    de son bec de corail et de ses grandes ailes de crêpe
Il avait toute la nuit suivi des enterrements divergents vers des
    cimetières suburbains
Il avait assisté à des bals dans les ambassades marqué de son empreinte
    une feuille de fougère des robes de satin blanc
Il s'était dressé terrible à l'avant des navires et les navires n'étaient pas
    revenus
Maintenant tapi dans la cheminée il guettait le réveil de l'écume et le
    chant des bouilloires
Son pas retentissant avait troublé le silence des nuits dans les rues aux
    pavés sonores
Charbon sonore charbon maître du rêve charbon
Ah dis-moi où est-elle cette belle nageuse cette nageuse qui avait peur
    du corail?
Mais la nageuse elle-même s'est rendormie

# XVI. Identity of images

Furiously I fight with animals and bottles
In a short space of time perhaps ten hours have passed one after
    the other
The lovely swimmer who feared the coral this morning awakes
The coral crowned with holly knocks at her door
Ah, the coal again always the coal
I beg you coal tutelary genius of the dream and of my solitude let
    me let me speak again of the lovely swimmer who feared the coal
Tyrannize this seductive subject of my dreams no longer
The lovely swimmer rested in a bed of lace and birds
Her clothes on a chair at the foot of the bed were lit by the glimmers
    the last glimmers of coal
Come from the depths of the sky and of the earth and of the sea
    the coal took pride in its coral beak and in its great crepe wings
All night long it had followed divergent funerals toward
    suburban cemeteries
Attended balls in embassies marked with its fern imprint
    white satin dresses
Had risen terrible before the ships and the ships had not returned
Now crouched in the chimney it awaited the awakening of foam and the
    song of teakettles
Its reverberating step had troubled the silence of nights in the streets
    with resounding paving stones
Coal resounding coal master of the dream coal
Ah tell me where is she this lovely swimmer this swimmer who feared
    the coral?
But the swimmer herself has gone back to sleep

Et je reste face à face avec le feu et je resterai la nuit durant à interroger
le charbon aux ailes de ténèbres qui persiste à projeter sur mon
chemin monotone l'ombre de sis fumées et le reflet terrible de ses
braises.
Charbon sonore charbon impitoyable charbon.

And I remain face to face with the fire and I shall remain the night long
    questioning the coal with shadow wings who persists in casting over
    my monotonous path the shade of its smoke and the terrible
    reflection of its embers
Coal resounding coal merciless coal

# XVII. Au petit jour

Le schiste éclairera-t-il la nuit blanche du liège?
Nous nous perdrons dans le corridor de minuit avec la calme horreur du
    sanglot qui meurt
Accourez tous lézards fameux depuis l'antiquité plantes grimpantes
    carnivores digitales
Accourez lianes
Sifflet des révoltes
Accourez girafes
Je vous convie à un grand festin
Tel que la lumière des verres sera pareille à l'aurore boréale
Les ongles des femmes seront des cygnes étranglés
Pas très loin d'ici une herbe sèche sur le bord du chemin.

# XVII. At daybreak

Will the schist brighten the white night of cork?
We'll be lost in midnight's corridor with the calm horror of
    the dying sob
Come all you ever-famous lizards climbing plants
    digital flesheaters
Come vines
Whistle of revolts
Come giraffes
I invite you to a feast
So grand the light of the glasses will equal the aurora borealis
Womens' nails will be strangled swans
Not far from here a grass is drying by the roadside.

# XVIII. Ténèbres! ô ténèbres!

Sycomore effréné fameuse division du temps fleur du silence animal
ô rouge rouge et bleu rouge et jaune silice surgie du creux des
    mains des nuits et des plaines en de féroces exclamations du
    regard prune éclat de vitre et d'aisselle acrobate ou des tours
    dressées du fin fond des abîmes à la voix qui dit je l'adore.
Salut c'est plus dur que le marbre et plus éclatant que la terre meuble et
    plus majestueux ô nuage que le rossignol du palissandre et de
    l'effroi.
Orgie du métal et des cloques de crapaud je parle et du ciel je l'entends
    et du soleil je l'imagine.
Taisons-nous mes amis devant les grands abîmes du clos de la veuve en
    crêpe de chine. Si tu veux lui obéir en fin de mer et de nuit par
    les draps de lin blanc que j'atteste et nous avons connu nos
    draps blancs les premiers.
Féroce et lui de dire à la cigogne et au serpent: «Surgissez à
    minuit juste dans le lait et dans les yeux»
Si tu l'abandonnes auprès d'un réverbère que les fleurs seront belles en
    cornets de bonbons.
Je désire et tu ordonnes et meurent les cricris sauvages dans les colliers
    d'ambre avec une pluie d'étincelles et de flottement d'étoffe à
    peine tu l'as su mais tu l'as deviné.
Litre brisé fleur pliante et comme elle avait de beaux yeux et de belles
    mains du volcan qui le coulisse ah! crevez donc un homard de
    lentille microscopique évoluant dans un ciel sans nuage ne
    rencontrera-t-il jamais une comète ni un corbeau?
Tes yeux tes yeux si beaux sont les voraces de l'obscurité du silence et
    de l'oubli.

# XVIII. Shadows! Oh shadows!

Frightened sycamore famous division of time flower of animal silence

Oh red red and blue red and yellow silex surging forth from the hollow
    of the hands of nights and plains in ferocious exclamations of the
    gaze plumburst of glass shine and acrobatic armpit or towers raised
    from the very depths of the abyss to the voice that says I adore it.

Greetings harder than marble and more dazzling than the movable earth
    and more majestic oh cloud than the nightingale of Brazilian
    rosewood and fright.

Metal orgy and I'm speaking of the bumps of toads and I mean
    of the sky and I imagine of the sun .

Friends, let's fall silent before the great enclosed abysses of the widow
    in crepe de chine. If you want to obey her finally in sea and
    night through the sheets of white linen I bear witness to and
    we were the first to know our white sheets.

Ferocious and he says to stork and snake: "Come forth just at
    midnight in milk and eyes."

If you leave him near a gaslight how beautiful the flowers will be in
    cups of candy.

I want and you command and wild chirping in the amber necklaces
    die with a rain of sparks and flapping cloth you scarcely knew it
    but you guessed it.

Shattered bottle folding flower and how beautiful were her eyes
    and hands of the volcano which grooves it ah! So then burst apart
    some lobster of a microscopic lens evolving in a cloudless sky
    won't he ever meet a comet or a crow?

Your eyes your lovely eyes devour the obscurity of silence
    and forgetting.

## XIX. Paroles des rochers

La reine de l'azur et le fou du vide passent dans un cab
À chaque fenêtre s'accoudent les chevelures
Et les chevelures disent: «À bientôt!»
«À bientôt!» disent les méduses
«À bientôt!» disent les soies
Disent les nacres disent les perles disent les diamants
À bientôt une nuit des nuits sans lune et sans étoile
Une nuit de tous les littorals et de toutes les forêts
Une nuit de tout amour et de toute éternité
Une vitre se fend à la fenêtre guettée
Une étoffe claque sur la campagne tragique
Tu seras seul
Parmi les débris de nacre et les diamants carbonisés
Les perles mortes
Seul parmi les soies qui auront été des robes vidées à ton approche
Parmi les sillages de méduses enfuies quand ton regard s'est levé
Seules peut-être les chevelures ne fuiront pas
T'obéiront
Fléchiront dans tes doigts comme d'irrévocables condamnations
Chevelures courtes des filles qui m'aimèrent
Chevelures longues des femmes qui m'aimèrent
Et que je n'aimai pas
Restez longtemps aux fenêtres chevelures!
Une nuit de toutes les nuits du littoral
Une nuit de lustre et de funérailles
Un escalier se déroule sous mes pas et la nuit et le jour ne révèlent à
      mon destin que ténèbres et échecs
L'immense colonne de marbre le doute soutient seule le ciel sur ma tête
Les bouteilles vides dont j'écrase le verre en tessons éclatants
Le parfum du liège abandonné par la mer

# XIX. Words of the rocks

The queen of the azure and the fool of emptiness pass in a cab
At each window manes of hair lean out
Calling "See you soon!"
"See you soon!" say the jellyfish
"See you soon!" say the silks
Says mother-of-pearl say the pearls say the diamonds
Soon a night of nights without moon or star
A night of all the littorals and of all forests
A night of all love and of all eternity
A pane shatters in the watched window
A rag is clacking over the tragic countryside
You will be alone
Among the mother-of-pearl dust and the carbonized diamonds
The dead pearls
Alone among the silks like dresses emptied at your approaching
Among the tracks of jellyfish fleeing when you lifted your gaze
Alone perhaps the manes of hair will not flee
Will obey you
They will bend in your fingers like irrevocable condemnations
Long hair of girls who loved me
Long hair of women who loved me
And whom I did not love
Remain at the windows oh manes of hair!
A night of all the littoral nights
A night of luster and of funerals
A staircase unwinds under my feet and the night and day reveal to
    my fate only shadows and failure
The immense column of marble doubt alone sustains the sky above my head
The empty bottles whose glass I shatter into dazzling splinters
The smell of cork abandoned by the sea

Les filets des bateaux imaginés par les petites filles
Les débris de la nacre qui se pulvérise lentement
Un soir de tous les soirs d'amour et d'éternité
L'infini profond douleur désir poésie amour révélation miracle
    révolution amour l'infini profond m'enveloppe de ténèbres bavardes
Les infinis éternels se brisent en tessons ô chevelure!
C'était ce sera une nuit des nuits sans lune ni perle
Sans même de bouteilles brisées.

The nets of boats imagined by little girls
The debris of mother-of-pearl slowly powdering
An evening of all the evenings of love and eternity
The infinite profound pain desire poetry love revelation miracle
    revolution love the profound infinite envelops me with talkative
    shadows
The eternal infinites shatter in splinters oh manes of hair!
It will be a night of nights without moon or pearl
Without even broken bottles.

## XX. Dans bien longtemps

Dans bien longtemps je suis passé par le château des feuilles
Elles jaunissaient lentement dans la mousse
Et loin les coquillages s'accrochaient désespérément aux rochers de la
     mer
Ton souvenir ou plutôt ta tendre présence était à la même place
Présence transparente et la mienne
Rien n'avait changé mais tout avait vieilli en même temps que mes
     tempes et mes yeux
N'aimez-vous pas ce lieu commun? laissez-moi laissez-moi c'est si rare
     cette ironique satisfaction
Tout avait vieilli sauf ta présence
Dans bien longtemps je suis passé par la marée du jour solitaire
Les flots étaient toujours illusoires
La carcasse du navire naufragé que tu connais—tu te rappelles cette nuit
     de tempête et de baisers? —était-ce un navire naufragé ou un
     délicat chapeau de femme roulé par le vent dans la pluie du
     printemps était à la même place
Et puis foutaise larirette dansons parmi les prunelliers!
Les apéritifs avaient changé de nom et de couleur
Les arcs-en-ciel qui servent de cadre aux glaces
Dans bien longtemps tu m'as aimé.

# XX. In long ago

In long ago I passed by the castle of leaves
They were slowly turning yellow in the moss
And far off the seashells were hanging on hard to the rocks in the sea
Your memory or rather your tender presence was in the same place
Transparent presence and mine
Nothing had changed but everything had aged at the same time as my
    temples and my eyes
Don't you love this commonplace? let me be let me be this ironic
    satisfaction is so rare
Everything had aged but your presence
In long ago I passed by the pond of the single day
The waves were still illusory
The hulk of the shipwrecked vessel you know—you remember that night
    of tempest and of kisses? —was it a shipwrecked vessel or a
    delicate woman's hat rolled by the wind into the springtime rain
    that was in the same place
And then phooey la-la-la let's dance in the blackthorns!
The aperitifs had changed their names and color
The rainbows framing the mirrors
In long ago you loved me.

## XXI. Jamais d'autre que toi

Jamais d'autre que toi en dépit des étoiles et des solitudes
En dépit des mutilations d'arbre à la tombée de la nuit
Jamais d'autre que toi ne poursuivra son chemin qui est le mien
Plus tu t'éloignes et plus ton ombre s'agrandit
Jamais d'autre que toi ne saluera la mer à l'aube quand fatigué d'errer
    moi sorti des forêts ténébreuses et des buissons d'orties je marcherai
    vers l'écume
Jamais d'autre que toi ne posera sa main sur mon front et mes yeux
Jamais d'autre que toi et je nie le mensonge et l'infidélité
Ce navire à l'ancre tu peux couper sa corde
Jamais d'autre que toi
L'aigle prisonnier dans une cage ronge lentement les barreaux de cuivre
    vert-de-grisés
Quelle évasion!
C'est le dimanche marqué par le chant des rossignols dans les bois d'un
    vert tendre l'ennui des petites filles en présence d'une cage où
    s'agite un serin, tandis que dans la rue solitaire le soleil lentement
    déplace sa ligne mince sur le trottoir chaud
Nous passerons d'autres lignes
Jamais jamais d'autre que toi
Et moi seul seul seul comme le lierre fané des jardins de banlieue seul
    comme le verre
Et toi jamais d'autre que toi.

# Never anyone but you

Never anyone but you in spite of stars and solitudes
In spite of mutilated trees at nightfall
Never anyone but you will follow a path which is mine also
The farther you go away the greater your shadow grows
Never anyone but you will salute the sea at dawn when tired of
    wandering having left the tenebral forests and thistle bushes
I shall walk toward the foam
Never anyone but you will place her hand on my forehead and my
    eyes
Never anyone but you and I deny falsehood and infidelity
This anchored boat you may cut its rope
Never anyone but you
The eagle prisoner in a cage pecks slowly at the copper bars
    turned green
What an escape!
It's Sunday marked by the song of nightingales in the woods of a
    tender green the tedium felt by little girls before a cage where a
    canary flies about while in the solitary street the sun slowly moves
    its narrow line across the heated sidewalk
We shall pass other lines
Never never anyone but you
And I alone like the faded ivy of suburban gardens alone like glass
And you never anyone but you

## XXII. Passé le pont

La porte se ferme sur l'idole de plomb
Rien désormais ne peut signaler à l'attention publique cette maison
    isolée
Seule l'eau peut-être se doutera de quelque chose
Les clairs matins d'automne la corde au cou plongent dans la rivière
Le myosotis petit chien de Syracuse n'appellera jamais plus la fermière
    aux yeux pers de son cri de mauvais augure
De temps de Philippe le Bel à travers les forêts de cristal un grand cri
    vient battre les murs recouverts de lierre
Le porte se ferme
Taisez-vous ah taisez-vous laisser dormir l'eau froide au bas de son
    sommeil
Laissez les poissons s'enfoncer vers les étoiles
Le vent du canapé géant sur lequel reposent les murmures le vent
    sinistre des métamorphoses se lève
Mort aux dents mort à la voile blanche mort à la cime éternelle
Laissez-la dormir dis-je laissez-la dormir ou bien j'affirme que des
    abîmes se creuseront
Que tout sera désormais fini entre la mousse et le cercueil
Je n'ai pas dit cela
Je n'ai rien dit
Qu'ai-je dit?
Laissez laissez-la dormir
Laissez les grands chênes autour de son lit
Ne chassez pas de sa chambre cette humble pâquerette à demi effacée
Laissez laissez-la dormir.

# XXII. Past the bridge

The door is closing on the idol of lead
Nothing from now on can draw attention to this isolated house
Only water will perhaps suspect something
The bright fall mornings a cord around their neck will plunge into
    the river
Forget-me-not little dog of Syracuse will never call again the farmerwoman
    with the seagreen eyes with its bad-omen yelp
In the time of Philippe le Bel through the crystal forests a great cry
    batters the ivy-covered walls
The door is closing
Keep quiet ah keep quiet let the cold water sleep in the depths of
    its slumber
Let the fish dive towers the stars
The wind of the giant sofa on which the murmurs of the sinister wind
    of metamorphoses rises up
Death to the teeth death to the white sail death to the eternal summit
Let it sleep I say let it sleep or else I swear abysses will be dug
All will be over between moss and coffin
I didn't say that
I said nothing
What did I say?
Let it let it sleep
Let be the great oaks around its bed
Don't chase this half-gone humble daisy from its room
Let it let it sleep.

## XXIII. En sursaut

Sur la route en revenant des sommets rencontré par les corbeaux et les
   châtaignes
Salué la jalousie et la pâle flatteuse
Le désastre. Enfin le désastre annoncé
Pourquoi pâlir, pourquoi frémir?
Salué la jalousie et le règne animal avec la fatigue avec le désordre avec
   la jalousie
Un voile qui se déploie au-dessus des têtes nues
Je n'ai jamais parlé de mon rêve de paille
Mais où sont partis les arbres solitaires du théâtre
Je ne sais où je vais j'ai des feuilles dans les mains, j'ai des feuilles dans
   la bouche
Je ne sais si mes yeux se sont clos cette nuit sur les ténèbres précieuses
   ou sur un fleuve d'or et de flamme
Est-il le jour des rencontres et des poursuites
J'ai des feuilles dans les mains j'ai des feuilles dans la bouche.

# XXIII. Startled

On the road returning from the summits met by the crows and the
  chestnuts
Jealousy hailed and the pale flatterer
Disaster finally disaster announced
Why turn pale? why shiver?
Jealousy hailed and the animal reign with fatigue disorder jealousy
A sail unfolding above bare heads
I have never spoken of my dream of straw
But where have they gone the solitary trees of theater
I don't know where I'm going I have leaves in my hands leaves in
  my mouth I don't know if my eyes closed last night on the
  precious shadows or on a river of gold and of flame
Is it the day of encounters and pursuings
I have leaves in my hands leaves in my mouth.

## XXIV. De la rose de marbre à la rose de fer

La rose de marbre immense et blanche était seule sur la place déserte
où les ombres se prolongeaient à l'infini. Et la rose de marbre seule
sous le soleil et les étoiles était reine de la solitude. Et sans parfum
la rose de marbre sur sa tige rigide au sommet du piédestal de granit
ruisselait de tous les flots du ciel. La lune s'arrêtait pensive en son
cœur glacial et les déesses des jardins les déesses de marbre à ses
pétales venaient éprouver leurs seins froids.

La rose de verre résonnait à tous les bruits du littoral. Il n'était pas un
sanglot de vague brisée qui ne la fît vibrer. Autour de sa tige fragile
et de son cœur transparent des arcs-en-ciel tournaient avec les
astres. La pluie glissait en boules délicates sur ses feuilles que
parfois le vent faisait gémir à l'effroi des ruisseaux et des vers
luisants.

La rose de charbon était un phénix nègre que la poudre transformait en
rose de feu. Mais sans cesse issue des corridors ténébreux de la mine
où les mineurs la recueillaient avec respect pour la transporter au
jour dans sa gangue d'anthracite la rose de charbon veillait aux
portes du désert.

La rose de papier buvard saignait parfois au crépuscule quand le soir à
son pied venait s'agenouiller. La rose de buvard gardienne de tous
les secrets et mauvaise conseillère saignait un sang plus épais qui
l'écume de mer et qui n'était pas le sien.

La rose de nuages apparaissait sur les villes maudites à l'heure des
éruptions de volcans à l'heure des incendies à l'heure des émeutes
et au-dessus de Paris quand la commune y mêla les veines irisées du
pétrole et l'odeur de la poudre elle fut belle belle au 21 janvier belle
au mois d'octobre dans le vent froid des steppes belle en 1905 à
l'heure des miracles à l'heure de l'amour.

## XXIV. From the marble rose to the iron rose

The marble rose immense and white was alone on the deserted
   square where the shadow stretched out to infinity. And the
   marble rose alone under the sun and the stars was queen of
   the solitude. And odorless the marble rose on her rigid stalk at
   the summit of the granite pedestal was streaming with all the
   floods of the sky. The moon paused pensive in her glacial heart
   and the goddesses of the gardens the goddesses of marble came
   to try their cold breasts against her petals.
The glass rose resounded with all the sounds of the littoral. There
   was not one sob of a broken wave which didn't make her tremble.
   About her fragile stalk and her transparent heart rainbows were
   turning with the planets. The rain slid in delicate globes down
   her leaves set moaning by the wind sometimes with fear of
   streams and glow worms.
The coal rose was a black phoenix which the powder transformed to
   a fire rose. But ceaselessly come forth from the shadowy corridors
   of the mine where the miners gathered her respectfully to take her
   to daylight in her vein of anthracite the coal rose kept watch at
   the portals of the desert.
The blotting paper rose used to bleed sometimes at twilight when
   the evening came to kneel at her feet. The blotting paper rose
   guardian of all secrets and a bad counselor bled with a thicker
   blood than seafoam and which was not her own.
The cloud rose appeared over the condemned cities at the hour of
   volcanic eruptions at the hour of fires at the hour of riots and
   above Paris when the commune mixed the irised beings of petrol
   and the smell of powder she was lovely on the twenty-first of
   January lovely in the month of October in the cold wind of the
   steppes lovely in 1905 at the hour of miracles at the hour of love.

La rose de bois présidait aux gibets. Elle fleurissait au plus haut de la guillotine puis dormait dans la mousse à l'ombre immense des champignons.

La rose de fer avait été battue durant des siècles par des forgerons d'éclairs. Chacune de ses feuilles était grande comme un ciel inconnu. Au moindre choc elle rendait le bruit du tonnerre. Mais qu'elle était douce aux amoureuses désespérées la rose de fer.

La rose de marbre la rose de verre la rose de charbon la rose de papier buvard la rose de nuages la rose de bois la rose de fer refleuriront toujours mais aujourd'hui elles sont effeuillées sur ton tapis.

Qui es-tu? toi qui écrases sous tes pieds nus les débris fugitifs de la rose de marbre de la rose de verre de la rose de charbon de la rose de papier buvard de la rose de nuages de la rose de bois de la rose de fer.

The wood rose presided at the gallows. She flowered at the top of
the guillotine then slept in the moss of the immense shadow of
mushrooms.

The iron rose had been hammered for centuries by forgers of sparks.
Each of her leaves was great like an unknown sky. At the slightest
shock she gave off the noise of thunder. But how gentle she was
to despairing girls in love the iron rose.

The marble rose the glass rose the coal rose the blotting-paper rose
the cloud rose the wood rose the iron rose will always flower
again but today they are depetaled on your carpet.

Who are you? you who crush under your naked feet the fugitive
debris of the marble rose the glass rose the coal rose the blotting-
paper rose the cloud rose the wood rose the iron rose.

1929
*Sirène-Anémone* (extracts)

. . .

C'était par un soir de printemps d'une des années perdues à l'amour
D'une des années gagnées à l'amour pour jamais
Souviens-toi de ce soir de pluie et de rosée où les étoiles
    devenues comètes tombaient vers la terre
La plus belle et la plus fatale la comète de destin de larmes et
d'éternels égarements
S'éloignait de mon ciel en se reflétant dans la mer
Tu naquis de ce mirage
Mais tu t'éloignas avec la comète et ta chanson s'éteignit parmi
    les échos
Devait-elle ta chanson s'éteindre pour jamais
Est-elle morte et dois-je la chercher dans le chœur tumultueux
    des vagues qui se brisent
Ou bien renaîtra-t-elle du fond des échos et des embruns
Quand à jamais la comète sera perdue dans les espaces
Surgiras-tu mirage de chair et d'os hors de ton désert de ténèbres
Souviens-toi de ce paysage de minuit de basalte et de granit
Où détachée du ciel une chevelure rayonnante s'abattit sur tes épaules
Quelle rayonnante chevelure de sillage et de lumière
Ce n'est pas en vain que tremblent dans la nuit les robes de soie
Elles échouent sur les rivages venant des profondeurs
Vestiges d'amours et de naufrages où l'anémone refuse de s'effeuiller
De céder à la volonté des flots et des destins végétaux
À petits pas la solitaire gagne alors un refuge de haut parage
Et dit qu'il est mille regrets à l'horloge
Non ce n'est pas en vain que palpitent ces robes mouillées
Le sel s'y cristallise en fleurs de givre
Vidées des corps des amoureuses
Et des mains qui les enlaçaient

. . .

It was a spring evening of one of the years lost to love
One of the years won to love forever
Remember that evening of rain and of dew when the stars became
    comets hurtling earthwards
Most beautiful and fatal the comet of destiny of tears and of eternal
    wanderings
Departed from my sky to be reflected in the sea
You were born from that mirage
But you departed with the comet and your song died out among echoes
Was your song to die out forever
Did it die and must I seek it in the tumultuous choir of waves breaking
Or will it rise again from the depth of echoes and spray
When the comets are lost forever in space
Will you rise mirage of flesh and bones from out your desert of shadows
Remember this landscape of midnight of basalt and granite
Where detached from the sky a mane of radiant hair flowed upon
    your shoulders
What radiant hair of shipmate and light
Not in vain do the silk dresses tremble in the night
As coming from the depths they are washed ashore on the banks
Vestiges of loves and shipwrecks where the anemone will not shed
    its petals
To cede to the wish of waters and of vegetal fates
With small steps the lonely one reaches then a refuge of high station
And says that it is a thousand regrets by the clock
No not in vain do these damp dresses tremble
Salt crystals of frost flowers form there
Emptied from lovers' bodies
And from the hands which held them

Elles s'enfuient des gouffres tubéreuses
Laissant aux mains malhabiles qui les laçaient
Les cuirasses d'acier et les corsets de satin
N'ont-elles pas senti la rayonnante chevelure d'astres
Qui par une nuit de rosée tomba en cataractes sur tes épaules
Je l'ai vue tomber
Tu te transfiguras
Reviendras-tu jamais des ténèbres
Nue et plus triomphante au retour de ton voyage
Que l'enveloppe scellée par cinq plaies de cire sanglante
Ô les mille regrets n'en finiront jamais
D'occuper cette horloge dans la clairière voisine
Tes cheveux de sargasses se perdent
Dans la pluie immense des rendez-vous manqués


. . .


Adieu déjà parmi les heures de porcelaine
Regardez le jour noircit au feu qui s'allume dans l'âtre
Regardez encore s'éloigner les herbes vivantes
Et les femmes effeuillant la marguerite du silence
Adieu dans la boue noire des gares
Dans les empreintes de mains sur les murs
Chaque fois qu'une marche d'escalier s'écroule un timide enfant paraît
à la fenêtre mansardée
Ce n'est plus dit-il le temps des parcs feuillus
J'écrase sans cesse des larves sous mes pas
Adieu dans le claquement des voiles
Adieu dans le bruit monotone des moteurs
Adieu ô papillons écrasés dans les portes
Adieu vêtements souillés par les jours à trotte-menu

They flee tuberous abysses
Leaving in the awkward hands which used to lace them
Breastplates of steel and satin corsets
Did they not feel the bright comet hair
Which on a night of dew cascaded over your shoulders
I saw it fall
You were transfigured
Will you ever reappear from the shadows
Naked and more triumphant on returning from your travels
Than the envelope sealed with five wounds of bleeding wax
Oh a thousand regrets will never cease
Filling this clock in the nearby clearing
Your gulf-weed hair is lost
In the immense plain of meetings missed


. . .


Farewell so soon among the porcelain hours
Look the day is darkening by the fire beginning in the hearth
Look again at the living grasses departing
And the women plucking petals from the daisy of silence
Farewell in the black mud of stations
In the imprints of hands on the walls
Each time a stairstep collapses a timid child appears at a garret window
It is no longer he says the time of the leafy parks
Endlessly I crush larvae under my feet
Farewell in the flapping sails
Farewell in the motors' monotonous roar
Farewell oh butterflies crushed in the doors
Farewell garments soiled by scampering days

Perdus à jamais dans les ombres des corridors
Nous t'appelons du fond des échos de la terre,
Sinistre bienfaiteur anémone de lumière et d'or
Et que brisé en mille volutes de mercure
Éclate en braises nouvelles à jamais incandescentes
L'amour miroir qui sept ans fleurit dans ses fêlures
Et cire l'escalier de la sinistre descente
Abîme nous t'appelons du fond des échos de la terre
Maîtresse généreuse de la lumière de l'or et de la chute
Dans l'écume de la mort et celle des Finistères
Balançant le corps souple des amoureuses
Dans les courants marqués d'initiales illisibles
Maîtresse sinistre et bienfaisante de la perte éternelle
Ange d'anthracite et de bitume
Claire profondeur des rades mythologie des tempêtes
eau purulente des fleuves eau lustrale des pluies et des rosées
Créature sanglante et végétale des marées

Du marteau sur l'enclume au couteau de l'assassin
Tout ce que tu brises est étoile et diamant
Ange d'anthracite et de bitume
Éclat du noir orfraie des vitrines
Des fumées lourdes te pavoisent quand tu poses les pieds
Sur les cristaux de neige qui recouvrent les toits

Haletants de mille journaux flambant après une nuit d'encre fraîche
Les grands mannequins écorchés par l'orage
nous montrent ce chemin par où nul n'est venu

. . .

Lost forever in the shadows of corridors
We summon you from the depths of earthly echoes
Sinister benefactor anemone of light and gold
And which broken into a thousand twirls of mercury
Bursts forth in new embers forever incandescent
This love this mirror which for seven years flowered in its cracks
And waxes the staircase of the sinister descent
Abyss we summon you from the depths of earthly echoes
Generous mistress of light of gold and of falling
In the foam of death and rocky coast
Balancing the supple body of lovers
In the currents marked with illegible initials
Sinister and benevolent mistress of eternal loss
Angel of anthracite and coal
Clear depth of roadsteads mythology of tempests
Purulent water of rivers shining water of rains and dews
Bleeding and vegetal creature of swamps

From the hammer on the anvil to the assassin's knife
Everything you shatter is star and diamond
Angel of anthracite and coal
Gleam of the darkness osprey of display
Heavy smokes drape you when you place your feet
On the snow crystals covering the roofs

Gasping with a thousand papers flaming after a night of fresh ink
The tall mannequins flayed by the storm
Show us this path by which no one has come

. . .

Je suis marqué par mes amours et pour la vie
Comme un cheval sauvage échappé aux gauchos
Qui retrouvant la liberté de la prairie
Montre aux juments ses poils brûlés par le fer chaud

Tandis qu'au large avec de grands gestes virils
La sirène chantant vers un ciel de carbone
au milieu des récifs éventreurs de barils,
au cœur des tourbillons fait surgir l'anémone.

*1929*

I am marked by my loves and for life
Like a wild horse escaped from the gauchos
Who, finding once more the prairies' freedom
Shows the mares his hair burned by branding

While on the deep sea with great virile gestures
The mermaid, singing toward a carbon sky
Amid reefs murderous to vessels,
In the heart of whirlwinds, makes the anemone flower.

*1929*

# 1930–31
## *Siramour* (extracts)

*Il est minuit au pied du château qui n'est ni celui de la belle au bois dormant, ni le seul en Espagne, ni le roi des nuages mais celui dont les murailles dressées au sommet d'une montagne dominent la mer et la plaine et maints autres châteaux dont les tours blanchissent au loin comme les voiles perdues sur la mer. Il est minuit dans la plaine et sur la mer, il est minuit dans les constellations vues d'ici et voici que l'étoile, la tantôt noire, la tantôt bleue, surgit au-delà de l'écume éclatée comme un orage bas dans les ténèbres liquides. À ses rayons, la bouteille abandonnée dans l'herbe et les ajoncs s'illumine des voies lactées qu'elle paraît contenir et ne contient pas car, bien bouchée, elle recèle en ses flancs la sirène masquée, la captive et redoutable sirène masquée, celle qu'on nomme l'Inouïe dans les mers où jamais elle ne daigne chanter et la Fantômas dans les rêves. Et, vrai, vêtue du frac et du haut de forme, on l'imagine parcourant un bois de mauvais augure tandis que musiques d'une fête lointaine somment vainement les échos de ramener à elles ce charmant travesti. On l'imagine encore, amazone, dans ce même bois, à l'automne, serrant contre elle un bouquet de roses trop épanouies dont les pétales s'envolent sous les efforts combinés du vent et du trot de son cheval.*

*Pour l'instant captive elle attend la délivrance dans sa prison bien bouchée par une main amoureuse, tandis qu'une lettre, non remise à son destinataire, moisit sur le sol. C'est l'heure où les dés et les horloges font des bruits singuliers qui étonnent les veilleurs. C'est l'heure où l'amant qui déshabille sa maîtresse s'étonne du crissement musical et inaccoutumé de la soie et du linge. Pâles et rêveurs tous écoutent ces manifestations de l'invisible qui n'est que leurs pensées et leurs rêves et, ceux-là, sur les chiffres fatidiques et, ceux-ci, sur l'heure qui marqua jadis le rendez-vous manqué et, les derniers, sur l'éclat de la chair admirable éternisent quelques secondes leurs regards qui, soudain, voient loin, très loin au-delà des enjeux et des changements de date, au-delà des caresses et des serments, au-delà même des chants indéchiffrables des sirènes. Il est minuit sur le château, sur la plaine et sur la mer.*

*It is midnight at the foot of the castle which is neither Sleeping Beauty's,
nor the only one in Spain, nor is it the king of clouds but rather the one whose
walls rising on the mountaintop overlook the sea and plain and other castles
whose towers are white in the distance like sails lost upon the deep. It is mid-
night in the plain and on the sea it is midnight in the constellations visible
from here and now the star, partly black and partly blue. rises beyond the foam
burst like a low cloud in the liquid shadows. In its light, the bottle abandoned
in the grass and jonquils is lit with the Milky Ways it seems to hold but does
not, for tightly corked, it conceals within its sides the masked mermaid, the
captive and awesome masked mermaid, called the Unheard in the sea where
she never deigns to sing and called Fantomas in dreams. And in truth she
should be imagined dressed in frock coat and top hat striding through an ill-
omened forest while the music from a far off celebration vainly commands the
echoes to bring back this charming transvestite. Or again she can be imagined
sidesaddle on a horse in this same forest in autumn, clutching against her a
bouquet of roses too full-blown, whose petals fly off in the combined effort of
the wind and the horses' trotting.*

*A prisoner for the moment she awaits deliverance in her prison tightly
corked by a loving hand while a letter, never delivered to its intended owner,
lies molding on the ground. It is the hour where the dice and clocks make
strange noises that surprise the watchmen. It is the hour when the lover un-
dressing his mistress is astonished by the musical and unaccustomed rustling of
silk and undergarments. Pale and dreaming, all are listening to these signals of
the invisible which is only their own thoughts and dreams and some of them
let their gaze linger a few seconds on the fateful numbers, and some on the
hour which once marked the missed meeting, and yet others, let their gaze
linger some seconds on the gleam of handsome flesh suddenly seeing far, far off
beyond the stakes and changes of calendar, beyond caresses and vows, beyond
even the indecipherable songs of mermaids. It is midnight on the castle, on the
plain, and on the sea.*

Il est minuit sur les jeux et les enjeux.

Il est minuit au cadran des horloges.

Il est minuit sur l'amour et sur les lettres égarées et la sirène chante, mais sa voix ne dépasse pas les parois de verre, mais le buveur survient et boit la chanson et libère la sirène, celle qu'on nomme l'Inouïe et qu'on nomme aussi la Fantômas.

. . .

Que le buveur, ivre de la chanson, parte sur un chemin biscornu bordé d'arbres effrayants au bruit de la mer hurlant et gueulant et montant la plus formidable marée de tous les temps, non hors de son lit géographique, mais coulant d'un flux rapide hors de la bouteille renversée tandis que, libre, la sirène étendue sur le sol non loin de cette cataracte, considère l'étoile, la tantôt noire, la tantôt bleue, et s'imagine la reconnaître et la reconnaît en effet.

*Ceci se passe ne l'oublions pas dans une véritable plaine, sur un véritable rivage, sous un véritable ciel. Et il s'agit d'une véritable bouteille et d'une véritable sirène, tandis que s'écoule une mer véritable qui emporte la lettre et monte à l'assaut du château.*

. . .

*Ô sirène ! je te suivrai partout. En dépit de tes crimes, compte tenu de la légitime défense, tu es séduisante à mon cœur et je pénètre par ton regard dans un univers sentimental où n'atteignent pas les médiocres préoccupations de la vie.*

*Je te suivrai partout. Si je te perds, je te retrouverai, sois-en sûre et, bien qu'il y ait quelque courage à t'affronter, je t'affronterai car il ne s'agit de souhaiter ici ni victoire ni défaite tant est beau l'éclat de tes armes et celui de tes yeux quand tu combats.*

It is midnight on the games and gambling.

It is midnight on the face of clocks.

It is midnight on love and lost letters and the mermaid sings, but her voice does not penetrate the glass walls, but the drinker comes and imbibes the song to free the mermaid, called the Unheard and called also Fantomas.

. . .

Let the drinker, drunk on the song, depart on an irregular path bordered with frightening trees with the sound of the sea howling and roaring and raising the greatest tide of all time, flowing not from its real bed, but flowing rapidly from the bottle overturned while the mermaid freed and stretched out on the ground not far from this waterfall, gazes at the star, black and blue in turn, thinks she recognizes her and does recognize her.

*This takes place, let's not forget, in a real plain, on a real riverbank, under a real sky. And it's really a matter of a real bottle and a real mermaid, while the flux of a real sea carries away the letter and rises in assault against the castle.*

. . .

*Oh mermaid? I shall follow you everywhere. Despite your crimes (considering the right of self-defense), you are seductive to my heart and by your look I enter a universe of feeling where the mediocre preoccupations of life never reach.*

*I shall follow you everywhere. If I lose you, I shall find you again, rest assured of it, and even though it takes courage to approach you, I shall do so, for I could wish neither for victory nor defeat, in view of the splendor of your weapons and of your eyes when you are in battle.*

*Marche dans ce château désert. Ton ombre surprend, c'est sûr, les marches des escaliers. Ta queue fourchue se prolonge longuement d'étage en étage.*
*Tu étais tout à l'heure au plus profond des souterrains.*
*Te voici maintenant au sommet du donjon. Soudain tu t'élèves, tu montes, tu t'éloignes en plein ciel. Ton ombre, d'abord immense, a diminué rapidement et ta minuscule silhouette se découpe maintenant sur la surface de la lune. Sirène tu deviens flame et tu incendies si violemment la nuit qu'il n'est pas une lumière à subsister près de toi dans des parterres de fleurs inconnues hantées pas les lucioles.*

. . .

Nous voici vieux déjà tous deux.
Nous avons trente ans de plus qu'aujourd'hui,
nous pouvons parler de jadis sans regret, sinon sans désir.
Tout de même nous aurions pu être heureux,
s'il était dit qu'on puisse l'être
et que les choses s'arrangent dans la vie.
Mais du malheur même naquit notre insatiable, notre funeste, notre étonnant amour

Et de cet amour le seul bonheur que puissent connaître deux cœurs insatiables comme les nôtres.

Écoute, écoute monter les grandes images vulgaires que nous transfigurons.
Voici l'Océan qui gronde et chante et sur lequel le ciel se tourmente et s'apaise semblable à ton lit.
Voici l'Océan semblable à notre cœur.
Voici le ciel où naufragent les nuages dans l'éclat triste d'un fanal promené à tour de rôle par les étoiles.
Voici le ciel semblable à nos deux cœurs.

*Walk along in this deserted castle. Your shadow is bound to surprise the staircases. Your forked tail stretches out lengthily from floor to floor.*

*A short while ago you were in the deepest of underground passages.*

*Now you are at the dungeon's summit. Suddenly you rise, climb, depart into the sky itself. Your shadow, immense at first, disappeared rapidly and your tiny silhouette stands out now on the moon's surface. Mermaid you become a flame burning the night so violently that no light subsists near you in the terraces of unknown flowers haunted by fireflies.*

. . .

Here we are old already both of us.

We are thirty years older than today,

We can speak of former times without regret, if not without desire.

All the same we could have been happy,

If it was said that one could be so

and that things work themselves out in life.

But from unhappiness itself our insatiable, our fateful, our astonishing love was born.

And from this love the only happiness which two insatiable hearts like ours can know.

Listen, listen to the great vulgar images which we transfigure as they rise.

Here is the sea rumbling and singing over which the sky worries and settles down like your bed.

Here is the sea like our heart.

Here is the sky where the clouds are shipwrecked in the sad flashing of a lighthouse beam sent out by each star in its turn.

Here is the sky like our two hearts.

Et puis voici les champs, les fleurs, les steppes, les déserts, les plaines, les sources, les fleuves, les abîmes, les montagnes,
Et tout cela peut se comparer à nos deux cœurs.
Mais ce soir je ne veux dire qu'une chose:
Deux montagnes étaient semblables de forme et de dimensions
Tu es sur l'une
Et moi sur l'autre.
Est-ce que nous nous reconnaissons ?
Quels signes nous faisons-nous ?
Nous devons nous entendre et nous aimer.
Peut-être m'aimes-tu ?
Je t'aime déjà.
Mais ces étendues entre nous, qui les franchira ?
Tu ne dis rien mais tu me regardes
Et, pour ce regard,
Il n'y a ni jour ni étendue.
Ma seule amie mon amour.

Je n'ai pas fini de te dire tout.
Mais à quoi bon . . .
L'indifférence en toi monte comme un rosier vorace qui, détruisant les murailles, se tord et grandit,
Étouffe l'ivrogne de son parfum . . .
Et puis est-ce que cela meurt ? Un clair refrain retentit dans la ruelle lavée par le matin, la nuit et le printemps.
Le géranium à la fenêtre fermée semble deviner l'avenir.
C'est alors que surgit le héros du drame.
Je ne te conte cette histoire qui ne tient pas debout que parce que je n'ose pas continuer comme j'ai commencé.
Car je crois à la vertu des mots et des choses formulées.

. . .

And now here are the fields, the flowers, the steppes, the deserts, the plains, the springs, the rivers, the abysses, the mountains
And that all can be compared to our two hearts.
But tonight I wish to say one thing only:
Two mountains were alike in form and dimension.
You are on one
And I on the other.
Do we recognize each other?
What signs do we make to each other?
Perhaps you love me?
I love you already.
But these distances between us, who will traverse them?
You say nothing but you look at me
And, for this look,
There is neither day nor distance
My only friend my love.

I have not finished telling you everything.
But what good is it...
Indifference in you rises like a voracious rosebush destroying the walls, twisting and growing,
Stifling the drunkard with its smell...
And then, does it die?
In the street washed by the morning, the night and springtime, there sounds a clear refrain.
The geranium at the closed window seems to guess the future.
It is then that the hero of the drama comes forth.
I am only telling you this story with no sense because I dare not continue as I began.
For I believe in the power of words and formulated things.

. . .

*La sirène rencontre son double et lui sourit*
*Elle s'endort alors du sommeil adorable dont elle ne s'éveillera pas.*
*Elle rêve peut-être. Elle rêve certainement. Nous sommes au matin d'un*
*jour de moissons lumineuses et de tremblements de terre et de marées de dia-*
*mants, les premières retombant sur tes cheveux et surgissant de tes jeux,*
*les seconds signalant ta promenade et les troisièmes montant à l'assaut de*
*ton cœur.*
*Il est cinq heures du matin dans la forêt de pins où se dresse le château*
*de la sirène, mais la sirène ne s'éveillera plus car elle a vu son double, elle*
*t'a vu.*
*Désormais ton empire est immense.*
*D'un sentier sort un bûcheron sur lequel la rosée tremble et s'étoile*
*Au premier arbre qu'il abat surgit un grand nombre de libellules !*
*Elles s'éparpillent dans des territoires de brindilles.*
*Au second arbre se brisent les premières vagues.*
*Au troisième arbre tu m'as dit:*
*«Dors dans mes bras.»*

. . .

Mais je connais une chanson bien plus belle
Celle d'une aube dans la rue ou parmi les champs prêts à la moisson
ou sur un lit désert
On a brûlé ce début de printemps les dernières bûches de l'hiver
De vieilles douleurs deviennent douces au souvenir
Des yeux plus jeunes s'ouvrent sur un univers lavé.
J'ai connu cette aube grâce à toi.
Mais se lèvera-t-elle jamais
Sur les douleurs que tu provoques ?

*The mermaid meets her double and smiles at her.*

*She goes to sleep then to the adorable sleep from which she will not waken.*

*Perhaps she dreams. She certainly dreams. We are in the morning of a day of luminous harvests and of earthquakes and of diamond tides, the first falling on your hair and spilling forth from your eyes, the second marking your going out and the third rising to assault your heart.*

*It is five in the morning in the pine forest where the mermaid's castle rises, but the mermaid will awake no more for she has seen her double, she has seen you. From now on your empire is immense.*

*From a path a woodchopper comes forth on whom the dew trembles and shines like a star.*

*At the first tree he chops down a horde of dragonflies comes forth!*

*They scatter in territories of twigs.*

*At the second tree the first waves break*

*At the third tree you said to me:*

*"Sleep in my arms."*


. . .


But I know a far lovelier song

That of a dawn in the street or among the fields ready for harvest or on a deserted bed

At this start of spring they have burned the last logs of winter

Old griefs become sweet in the memory

Younger eyes are opened on a universe freshly washed

I have known this dawn thanks to you

But will it ever rise

On the griefs you cause?

Tu sais de quelle apparition je parle,
et de quelle réincarnation
Coulez, coulez larmes et fleuves
Et vins dans les verres.

Le temps n'est plus où nous riions
quand nous étions ivres.

. . .

Fougères, rasoirs, baisers perdus, tout s'écroule et renaît par une belle
matinée tandis que, par un sentier désert, délaissant sur l'herbe les cartes
d'une réussite certaine, la sirène s'éloigne vers la plage d'où elle partit au
début de cette histoire décousue.

Regagne la plage au pied du château fort
La mer a regagné son lit
L'étoile ne brille plus mais sa place décolorée comme une vieille robe
luit sinistrement.
Regagne la plage.
Regagne la bouteille
S'y couche
L'ivrogne remet le bouchon
Le ciel est calme.
Tout va s'endormir au bruit du flux blanchi d'écume.

You know of what apparition I speak
And of what reincarnation
Flow flow tears and rivers
And wines into glasses.

It is not as it used to be, when we laughed
Intoxicated.

. . .

Ferns, razors, lost embraces, all crumbles and is born once more on a lovely morning while, down a deserted path, leaving behind on the grass the cards of a certain success, the mermaid departs in the distance toward the beach that she left at the outset of this disjointed story.

Goes back to the beach at the foot of the fortress
The sea has gone back to her bed
The star shines no longer but its place discolored like an old dress gleams with a sinister light.
Goes back to the beach.
Goes back to the bottle
Lies down in it.
The drunkard replaces the cork
The sky is calm.
All will fall asleep in the sound of the whitened rush of foam.

Ô rien ne peut séparer la sirène de l'hippocampe.

Rien ne peut défaire cette union

Rien

C'est la nuit

Tout dort ou fait semblant de dormir

dormons, dormons,

ou faisons semblant de dormir.

Ne manie pas ce livre à la légère

à la légère à la légère à la légère à la légère.

Je sais ce qu'il veut dire mieux que personne.

Je sais où je vais,

Ce ne sera pas toujours gai.

Mais l'amour et moi

l'aurons voulu ainsi.

Oh nothing can separate the mermaid from the seahorse!
Nothing can undo this union
Nothing
It is night
Everything sleeps or seems to
Let's sleep, let's sleep.
Or let's seem to sleep.
Don't handle this book lightly
Lightly lightly lightly lightly.
I know what it means better than anyone
I know where I am going,
It won't always be good.
But love and I
Will have wished it so.

1930–31
from *The Night of Loveless Nights* (extracts)

*J'habite quand il me plaît un ravin ténébreux au-dessus duquel le ciel se découpe en un losange déchiqueté par l'ombre des sapins des mélèzes et des rochers qui couvrent les pentes escarpées.*

*Dans l'herbe du ravin poussent d'étranges tubéreuses des ancolies et des colchiques survolées par des libellules et des mantes religieuses et si pareils sans cesse le ciel la flore et la faune où succèdent aux insectes les corneilles moroses et les rats musqués que je ne sais quelle immuable saison s'est abattue sur ce toujours nocturne ravin avec son dais en losange constellé que ne traverse aucun nuage.*

*Sur les troncs des arbres deux initiales toujours les mêmes sont gravées. Par quel couteau par quelle main pour quel cœur?*

*Le vallon était désert quand j'y vins pour la première fois. Nul n'y était venu avant moi. Nul autre que moi ne l'a parcouru.*

*La mare où les grenouilles nagent dans l'ombre avec des mouvements réguliers reflète des étoiles immobiles et le marais que les crapauds peuplent de leur cri sonore et triste possède un feu follet toujours le même.*

*La saison de l'amour triste et immobile plane en cette solitude.*

*Je l'aimerai toujours et sans doute ne pourrai-je jamais franchir l'orée des mélèzes et des sapins escalader les rochers baroques pour atteindre la route blanche où elle passe à certaines heures. La route où les ombres n'ont pas toujours la même direction.*

*Parfois il me semble que la nuit vient seulement de s'abattre. Des chasseurs passent sur la route que je ne vois pas. Le chant des cors de chasse résonne sous les mélèzes. La journée a été longue parmi les terres de labour à la poursuite du renard du blaireau ou du chevreuil. Le naseau des chevaux fume blanc dans la nuit.*

*I inhabit when I choose to a shadowy ravine above which the sky is cut out in a diamond shape nicked on the edges by the shadow of firs, larch trees and rocks covering the abrupt slopes.*

*In the grass of the ravine strange tuberoses grow, and ancoly, and poppies over which swoop dragonflies and praying mantises and so alike are the sky the flora and the fauna where morose crows and muskrats follow closely on the insects, that I do not know what immutable season has fallen on this always nocturnal ravine with its canopy of a constellated diamond traversed by no cloud.*

*On the tree trunks two initials, always the same, are inscribed. By what knife, by what hand, for what heart?*

*The valley was deserted when I came there for the first time. No one had come there before me. No one other than myself has traversed it.*

*In the swamp where the frogs swim about in the shadow with regular movements reflect immobile stars and the marsh peopled by the sad and sonorous cry of toads there is a firefly, always the same.*

*The season of sad and immobile love hangs over this solitude.*

*I shall always love her and shall probably never be able to cross the boundary of the larch trees and the firs, or climb the baroque rocks to reach the white road where at certain hours she passes. The road where the shadows lie not always in the same direction.*

*Sometimes it seems to me that night has just fallen. On the road pass hunters whom I do not see. The song of hunting horns resounds under the larch trees. The day has been long, among the lands of ploughing, in pursuit of the fox, of the badger or the roe. The nostrils of the horses smoke white in the night air.*

*Les airs de chasse s'éteignent. Et je déchiffre difficilement les initiales iden-*
*tiques sur le tronc des mélèzes qui bornent le ravin.*


. . .


Églantines flétries parmi les herbiers
Ô feuilles jaunes
Tout craque dans cette chambre
Comme dans l'allée nocturne les herbes sous le pied
De grandes ailes invisibles immobilisent mes bras et le retentissement
d'une mer lointaine parvient jusqu'à moi
Le lit roule jusqu'à l'aube sa bordure d'écume et l'aube ne paraît pas
Ne paraîtra jamais
Verre pilé, boiseries pourries, rêves interminables, fleurs flétries,
Une main se pose à travers les ténèbres toutes blanche sur mon front,
Et j'écouterai jusqu'au jour improbable
Voler en se heurtant aux murailles et aux meubles l'oiseau de paradis
l'oiseau que j'ai enfermé par mégarde
Rien qu'en fermant les yeux.

*The hunting songs die out. And I decipher with difficulty the identical initials on the larch trees' trunks on bordering the ravine.*

. . .

Sweetbriars withered among the lofts
O yellow leaves
Everything creaks in this room
As in the nocturnal alley grasses crunch under the foot.
Invisible great wings pin down my arms and the pounding of a distant sea reaches my ears.
The bed rolls to the dawn its edge of foam and the dawn does not appear.
Will never appear.
Shattered glass, rotted woodwork, interminable dreams, withered flowers,
A hand completely white touches my forehead through the darkness
And I shall listen until the improbable day
To the bird of paradise as it bumps against the walls and the furniture the bird I carelessly shut in
By merely closing my eyes.

1930–39
*Bagatelle: Destinée arbitraire*

# La chambre close

La chambre est fermée et vide, bien vide
Seul, le soleil, à certaines heures, déplace sa ligne sur les couvertures
    en désordre et sur l'oreiller froissé;
Une robe, sur une chaise, palpite par instants au souffle d'un mystérieux
    courant d'air
Un cheveu frémit aussi sur le drap replié,
Et l'horloge qui bat encore et ne tardera pas à s'arrêter, chante
    dans le désert.
Colibri du soir, colibri du matin,
Mon beau colibri entre dans la chambre,
Bat des ailes,
Éclate en couleurs vives sur l'oreiller.
L'arc-en-ciel pâlit dans le ciel autour des parterres d'étoiles.
Mon beau colibri, colibri du soir et du matin,
Vole.
Heurte ta tête fine à ton double dans la glace dont le tain s'écaille.
Saigne.
Meurs.
Mon beau colibri du soir et du matin.
Ventre gonflé,
Bec sanglant,
Ailes ouvertes,
Pattes raidies,
Meurs


Afin que dans la chambre vide le soleil déplace sa ligne autour
    de ton cadavre
Où la fenêtre se reflète dans le sang qui poisse ton duvet.

# The airtight room

The room is closed and empty, quite empty
The sun alone, at certain hours, shifts its line over the bedclothes in
    disorder and the wrinkled pillow;
A dress on a chair shudders at moments in the breath of a
    mysterious draft One hair trembles also on the sheet folded back,
And the clock still ticking will stop soon, sounding in the desert.
Hummingbird of evening, hummingbird of morn,
My lovely hummingbird comes in the room,
Beating its wings,
Bursting in lively colors on the pillow.
The rainbow pales in the sky around the flowerbeds of stars.
My lovely hummingbird, hummingbird of evening and of morn,
Fly off.
Dash your delicate head against the images of your double in the
    mirror whose silvering flakes off.
Bleed.
Die
My lovely hummingbird, hummingbird of evening and of morn
With a swollen stomach,
A bleeding beak,
Open wings,
Stiffened feet
Die


So that in the empty room the sun may shift its line about your corpse
Where the window is reflected in the blood spotting your down,

Pour un chant identique, pour un vol égal,
Paré des mêmes couleurs,
Colibri du soir, colibri du matin,
Tu renaîtras.
Et dans la chambre vide, l'horloge à nouveau chantera
Colibri, colibri,
Colibri du soir, colibri du matin.


L'oiseau qui vole vers la côte
n'est pas près du bord où, tendant les lèvres,
Le ciel de terre, au ciel de mer
offre un baiser d'écume.


n'a pas tort de voler, l'oiseau perdu en mer,
n'a pas tort, le marin qui fixe à l'avant du navire,
figure de proue, figure de rêve,
L'image même de celle qu'il aime.


Ceci se passe loin de tous les continents,
Loin des continents herbus où courent les taureaux sauvages,
Loin des continents mouillés où le lamantin et l'hippopotame
Barbotent grassement dans la boue qui luit et sèche et craque,


Loin des continents de ville et d'amour,
Loin des continents d'éternelle jalousie,
Loin des continents de steppe et de neige et de sable,
Loin des continents de soleil

For an identical song, for an equal flight,
Bedecked with the same colors,
Hummingbird of evening, hummingbird of morn,
You will be reborn.
And in the empty room, the clock will sound once more
Hummingbird, hummingbird,
Hummingbird of evening, hummingbird of morn,


The bird flying toward the coast
Is not near the edge where, stretching out its lips,
The sky of earth offers to the sky of sea
a kiss of foam.

The bird lost at sea is not wrong to fly off,
he is not wrong, the sailor affixing to the aft of his ship,
a figurehead, figure of dream,
the very image of the one he loves.

This happens far from all continents,
Far from the grassy continents where wild bulls run,
Far from the humid continents where the manatees and the
    hippopotamus
Splatter lazily in the mud shimmering, drying and cracking,

Far from the continents of town and love,
Far from the continents of eternal jealousy,
Far from the continents of steppe and snow and sand,
Far from the continents of sun

Ceci se passe où je veux,
Au pays des sirènes et des typhons,
au pays des roulements de tonnerre
Près du continent du ciel aride,
Dans l'archipel éternel des nuages.

Roulez, roulez, nuages, tandis que l'oiseau vole.
Non loin de là,
Une fiancée reçoit pour sa fête
La carte postale d'éternel serment

La colombe, au bec, tient la lettre cachetée:
«Je vous jure un amour de toujours.»
Roulez, roulez, nuages, archipel de nuages,
Océan, aride océan.

Les fontaines se lamentent loin des oiseaux
Loin du murmure du vent dans les platanes.
À pleine gueule, le poisson que tient la sirène
Crache l'eau dans la lueur des réverbères et les reflets du macadam

Et toute cette histoire s'achève,
Loin des yeux, loin du cœur,
Près de l'éternel serment.
À Paris, place de la Concorde
Une femme la plus belle et la plus touchante passe
Seule, à pied, triste.

This happens where I want it to,
In the country of mermaids and typhoons,
In the country of thunderclaps
Near the continent of the arid sky,
In the eternal archipelago of clouds.

Roll, roll, clouds, while the bird flies.
Not far off,
A fiancée receives for her birthday
The postcard of eternal promise.

The dove holds the sealed letter in his beak;
"I swear to you an eternal love."
Roll, roll, clouds, archipelago of clouds,
Sea, arid sea.

The fountains are lamenting far away from the birds
Far from the wind's murmur in the plane-trees.
His mouth wide open, the fish held by the mermaid
Spits water in the gleam of the gas lamps and the reflections of asphalt

And this whole story ends,
Far from the eyes, far from the heart,
Near the eternal oath.
In Paris, Place de la Concorde
A most beautiful and touching woman passes by
Alone, sad, on foot.

Et, loin d'elle, au-dessus de la mer vole un oiseau
Et jamais la femme ne verra le vol de cet oiseau jamais, de son ombre,
le vol de cet oiseau ne rayera
Le chemin suivi par cette femme.
Jamais? Est-ce bien sûr?
ô, rencontres—
ô, fontaines gémissantes au cœur des villes
ô, cœurs gémissants par le monde.


Vive la vie!


L'oiseau terrible, menaçant,
Est sur une branche de l'arbre épouvantable
Et la mort est cachée dans un couteau.
Le rire des furieuses
T'ouvre la bouche en vain.
Je te sais condamnée,
Je refuse de te sauver.

L'arbre est en feu
Et la mort est inscrite en lettres majuscules,

Pendue à tes cheveux,
Reliée à ta nuque par des fleurs souterraines,
Mêlée à tes regards.

Ton front est une injure
Une pierre dans un gouffre,
Ma langue dans ma bouche.

Je sais qu'il n'est jamais plus temps.

And, far from her, above the sea a bird flies
And never will the woman see the flight of this bird, never with his
    shadow will this bird's flight mark
The path the woman follows.
Never? Is that certain?
oh, meetings—
oh, fountains sighing in the heart of towns,
oh, hearts sighing throughout the world.


Long live life!


The terrible, menacing bird
Perches on the branch of a frightening tree
And death is hidden in a knife.
The laughter of the furies
Opens your mouth in vain.
I know you to be condemned,
I refuse to save you.

The tree is aflame
Death inscribed in capitals,

Hanging from your hair,
Tied to your nape by underground flowers,
Mingled with your glances.

Your forehead is an insult,
A stone in an abyss,
My tongue in my mouth.

I know there's never time any more

**1931**
From *Le Livre secret pour Youki*

## Lumière de mes nuits Youki

Te souviens-tu des nuits où tu apparaissais
Sur le rectangle clair des vitres de ma porte?
Où tu surgissais dans les ténèbres de ma maison
Où tu t'abattais sur mon lit comme un grand oiseau
Fatigué de passer les océans et les plaines et les forêts.
Te souviens-tu de tes paroles de salut
Te souviens-tu de mes paroles de bienvenue
de mes paroles d'amour?
Non, il ne t'en souvient pas,
On ne se souvient pas du présent, personne . . .
Or, il est nuit,
Tu surviens, tu arrives, tu t'abats sur mon lit
Je suis ton serviteur et ton défenseur soumis à ta loi
et toi soumise à mon amour.
Il est minuit il est midi
Il est minuit et quart
Il est minuit et demie
Il est minuit à venir ou midi passé
Il est midi sonnant
Il est toujours midi sonnant pour mon amour
Pour notre amour
Tout sonne tout frémit et tes lèvres
Et sur mon lit tu t'abats entre minuit et quatre heures du matin
comme un grand albatros
Échappé des tempêtes.

*27-11-32*

# Light of my nights Youki

Do you remember appearing those nights
Through the clear panes of my door?
When you came forth in the shadows of my house
When you sank down on my bed like a great bird
Tired of passing over seas and plains and woods.
Do you remember your greeting words
My welcoming words
my words of love?
No, you don't remember,
We remember nothing of the present, no one . . .
But, it is night,
Tu come forth, you arrive, you sink down on my bed
I am your servant your knight subject to your lwaw
and you subject to my love.
It is midnight it is noon
It is midnight and a quarter
It is midnight and a half
It is midnight to come or past noon
It is just sounding noon
It is always noon sounding for my love
For our love
Everything is sounding trembling and your lips
And on my bed you sink down between midnight and four a.m.
like a great bird
Escaped from the storm.

*27-11-32*

1932
*Tattoos*
In *Vu*, No 203, Feburary 5, 1932

The Costume Museum, that they are trying to set up somewhere in France, as just one section of anthropology, is bound to be incomplete, since it won't be able to present a series, even an incomplete one, of the art of tattooing. Just as men and woman have felt the need to ornament themselves with jewels, they have felt, during various stages of civilization, the need to paint themselves and to tattoo their body. Ethnography, overlooked for so long in France, and which finds a worthy asylum in the Trocadero Museum, would surely profit greatly from a collection of human skins painted or tattooed according to the circumstances of their lives. I would like above all for there to be no attention paid to any esthetic criteria of beauty except for excluding the arbitrary notion of the beautiful and the ugly and that this practice be deemed legitimate once and for all just as fashion dictates that a tie be knotted in such or such a way. A state of mind perhaps difficult in an epoch which still lives in the respect of Greek law, systematically overlooking everything magical there might be in this civilization more oriental than Mediterranean, if there ever was a Mediterranean civilization in the proper sense of the word. For a tattoo is not only a jewel, and so not a costume, it is still, and more even than any jewel, a fetish, a lucky charm. It isn't only by chance that the convict had tattooed on this forehead "Child of unhappy fate". Perhaps without his knowing it, he expects this formula to entreat his fate, just as he will expect other attributes to keep the heart of his mistress, or give him back his freedom. The tattoos presented here belong strictly to the naive esthetics of fantasy post cards, and so belong to a popular modern symbolism, and thus to a degenerate form of sorcery. Certain of these motives are purely allegorical in the very style of the billboard of the barber-tattoo. But the charm of the presentation is exceptionally heightened by an almost nude mannequin seen through a window pane, wearing on her body a sample of what it is possible to embed in flesh. Also the domain of the artist is extremely varied, from the humorous face of the sailor to this mermaid that you sense in the shadow like a fish in the obscure transparency of the submarine depths. But it is to be noted that only the working class uses the tattoo artist with the aim of embellishing itself, while it is the fashion in the upper classes to resort to its services only because of snobism, because a few lords, for example the prince of Wales, have brought back from their trips one of these ornaments. And yet one can see in this snobism itself a desire of ennoblement like the fondness for decorations. Touching like an inscription on the wall of a cell, tattoos will always bear the mark of depressions and sentimental enthusiasms, and, like the initials engraved on the trunk of a tree, the commemoration of a moment of grief or of tenderness. Like this boy from Picardy I knew in Morocco. He came from a certain disciplinary community. Two days before returning to France, definitively freed, he had himself tattooed on this forehead the fateful "No luck" which, in civilian life, must have aroused the disapproval of his family, the horror of his companions, and have terribly complicated his social life. There, as in all the attempts of spellbinding, the spellcaster is captivated just as much as the spellbound person, and unhappiness is a fearsome adversary who has nothing to lose in such games. There is a particular love of the abyss, a taste for the worst, which takes over the ambitious, the heroes and the pitiful dark melancholics. Also society has a taste for masks and, as in all rituals, however ancient they are, there comes the moment when the faithful throw stones at the kindly demon, when the sacrificer cuts the throat of the scapegoat.

1934
*Les Sans cou*
translator, Martin Sorrell

# Apparition

Né de la boue, jailli au ciel, plus flottant qu'un nuage, plus dur que le
    marbre,
Né de la joie, jailli du sommeil, plus flottant qu'une épave, plus dur
    qu'un cœur,
Né de son cœur, jailli du ciel, plus flottant que le sommeil, plus dur que
    le ciel,
Né, jailli, flottant plus dur et plus ciel, et plus cœur et plus marbre,
Et plus de sommeil et plus de nuage et plus d'épave, et tant et plus,
Mais du sommeil flottant au cœur des marbres dispersés comme des
    épaves,
Au long du ciel d'un pauvre paysage jaillissant et flottant comme un
    cœur . . .
Et saignant, oh saignant, saignant tellement
Que tant de marbres, abandonnés, alignés, dressés comme jaillis,
Finiront bien par flotter comme des épaves.
Mais il ne s'agit plus de flotter, ne de jaillir, ni de durcir,
Mais, de toute boue,
Faire un ciment, un marbre, un ciel, un nuage et une joie et une épave
Et un cœur, cela va de soi, et tout ce qui est dit plus haut
Et un sommeil, un beau sommeil, un bon sommeil,
Un bon sommeil de boue
Né du café et de la nuit et du charbon et de l'encre et du crêpe des
    veuves
Et de cent millions de nègres
Et de l'étreinte de deux nègres dans une ombre de sapins
Et de l'ébène et des multitudes de corbeaux sur les carnages . . .
Tel qu'enfin s'épanouisse, recouvrant l'univers,
Un bouquet, un immense bouquet de roses rouges.

# Apparition

Born from mud, sprung heavenwards, more floating than a cloud,
    harder than marble,
Born of joy, sprung from sleep, more floating than flotsam, harder
    than a heart,
Born of its heart, sprung from the skies, more floating than sleep,
    harder than the heavens,
Born, sprung, floating more hard and more sky, more heart and
    more marble,
And no more of sleep, no more of clouds and no more of flotsam,
    and so much so more,
But from floating sleep to heart of marble scattered like flotsam,
Down a meagre landscape sky springing and floating like a heart . . .
And bleeding, oh bleeding, bleeding so much
That so much marble, abandoned, laid out, standing as it sprang,
Will finish up floating like flotsam.
But it's no more about floating or springing or hardening,
But, from pure mud,
Making cement, marble, sky, cloud, joy and flotsam
And a heart, it goes without saying, and everything said thus far
And sleep, lovely sleep, good sleep,
A good sleep of mud
Born of coffee and night and coal and ink and widow's weeds
And a hundred million blacks
And the embrace of two blacks beneath the shade of pine trees
And ebony and multitudes of crows perched on carnage . . .
So that at last, recovering the universe,
There may blaze
A bouquet, an immense bouquet of red roses.

# Fête-diable

La dernière goutte de vin s'allume au fond du verre
Où vient d'apparaître un château.
Les arbres noueux du bord de la route s'inclinent vers le voyageur.
Il vient du village proche,
Il vient de la ville lointaine,
Il ne fait que passer au pied des clochers.
Il aperçoit à la fenêtre une étoile rouge qui bouge,
Qui descend, qui se promène en vacillant
Sur la route blanche, dans la campagne noire.
Elle se dirige vers le voyageur qui la regarde venir.
Un instant elle brille dans chacun de ses yeux,
Elle se fixe sur son front.
Étonné de cette lueur glaciale qui l'illumine,
Il essuie son front.
Une goutte de vin perle à son doigt.
Maintenant l'homme s'éloigne et s'amoindrit
Dans la nuit.
Il est passé près de cette source où vous venez au matin cueillir le
    cresson frais,
Il est passé près de la maison abandonnée.
C'est l'homme à la goutte de vin sur le front.
Il danse à l'heure actuelle dans une salle immense,
Une salle brillamment éclairée,
Resplendissante de son parquet ciré
Profond comme un miroir.
Il est seul avec sa danseuse
Dans cette salle immense, et il danse
Au son d'un orchestre de verre pilé.
Et les créatures de la nuit
Contemplent ce couple solitaire et qui danse

# Feast of corpus diaboli

The last droplet of wine catches fire in the bottom of the glass
Where a château has just appeared.
The gnarled trees that line the route bow down before the traveller.
He comes from the nearest village,
He comes from a far-distant town,
Just passing by the base of the bell-towers.
At the window he sees a red star stir,
Descend, shaking as it moves
Down the white road, the black countryside.
It heads for the traveller, who watches it arrive.
For an instant it shines in each of his eyes,
Then alights on his forehead.
Startled by this glacial glow illuminating him,
He wipes his brow.
A bubble of wine forms on his finger.
Now the man moves away, getting smaller
In the night.
He has passed close to that spring where you come in the morning
To gather fresh cress,
He has passed close by the abandoned house.
It's the man with the drop of wine on his brow.
At this moment he's dancing in an immense room,
A brilliantly lit room,
Its burnished parquet floor
Deep as a mirror flashing light.
He and the woman he dances with are alone
In this immense room, and he dances
To the sound of a powdered glass orchestra.
And the creatures of the night
Contemplate this solitary couple dancing

Et la plus belle d'entre les créatures de la nuit
Essuie machinalement une goutte de vin à son front,
La remet dans un verre,
Et le dormeur s'éveille,
Voit la goutte briller de cent mille rubis dans le verre
Qui était vide lorsqu'il s'endormit.
La contemple.
L'univers oscille durant une seconde de silence
Et le sommeil reprend ses droits,
Et l'univers reprend son cours
Par les milliers de routes blanches tracées par le monde
À travers les campagnes ténébreuses.

And the most beautiful of the creatures of the night
Without thinking wipes a drop of wine from his brow,
Puts it back in a glass,
And the sleeper awakes,
Sees in the glass the drop bright with a hundred thousand rubies,
Empty when he fell asleep.
Contemplates it.
The universe sways for a silent second
And sleep reclaims its due,
The universe follows its course
Among the thousand thousand white roads the world has mapped
Across the countryside cast in shadow.

# Le bœuf et la rose

De connivence avec le salpêtre et les montagnes, le bœuf noir à l'œil
   clos par une rose entreprend la conquête de la vallée, de la forêt et
   de la lande.

Là où les fleurs de pissenlit s'étoilent gauchement dans le firmament
   vert d'une herbe rare,

Là où resplendissent les bouses grasses et éclatante, les soleils de
   mauvaise grâce et les genêts précieux,

Là où les blés sont mûrs, là où l'argile taillée en branches et fendillée
   offre des ravines aux ébats des scarabées,

Là où le scorpion jaune aime et meurt de son amour et s'allonge tout
   raide,

Là où le sable en poudre d'or aveugle le chemineau.

D'un pas lourd, balançant sa tête géante sur une encolure fourrée, et de
   sa queue battant à intervalles égaux sa croupe charrue,

Le bœuf noir comme l'encre surgit, passe et disparaît.

Il écrase et paraphe de sa tache le paysage éclatant

Et ses cornes attendent qu'il choisisse la bonne orientation

Pour porter un soleil à sa mort dans leur orbite ouverte sur le vide,

Mettant plus d'un reflet sur ses poils luisants et projetant, tache
   issue d'une tache,

Son ombre fabuleuse sur la terre avide d'une pluie prochaine

Et du vol incertain des papillons,

Ou peut-être une rose éclatante issue de la seule atmosphère et
   grandissant entre les branches de leur croissant comme un
   fantôme de fleur.

# The ox and the rose

Colluding with saltpetre and mountains, the black ox
    its eye covered over by a rose attempts the conquest
    of the valley, the forest and the plain.
There where dandelions clumsily switch on their lights in the green
    firmament of scant grass,
Where thick dung shines, the churlish suns and precious broom,
Where wheat is ripe, where clay sculpted like branches
Cracks and offers ravines for the battle of beetles,
Where the yellow scorpion loves and dies of love and stretches out
    stiffly,
Where gold-dust sand blinds the vagrant.
With lumbering step, huge head rocking on thick-coated neck, tail
    hitting fleshy flanks with regular slaps,
The ox as black as ink appears, passes by, and disappears.
His toil crushes and marks with his stamp the bursting countryside
And his horns wait until he's chosen the proper direction
Before lifting a sun to its death in their orbit opened onto emptiness,
Throwing more than one reflection onto gleaming hairs, and projecting,
    stain issuing from stain,
His fabled shadow onto the earth eager for imminent rain
And the hesitating flight of butterflies,
Or perhaps a radiant rose sprung from pure atmosphere and
    growing between the branches of its crescent
    like the phantom of a flower.

# Comme

Come, dit l'Anglais à l'Anglais, et l'Anglais vient.

Côme, dit le chef de gare, et le voyageur qui vient dans cette ville
descend du train sa valise à la main.

Come, dit l'autre, et il mange.

Comme, je dis comme et tout se métamorphose, le marbre en eau,
le ciel en orange, le vin en plaine, le fil en six, le cœur en peine,
le peur en seine.

Mais si l'Anglais dit as c'est son tour de voir le monde changer de forme
à sa convenance

Et moi je ne vois plus qu'un signe unique sur une carte:

L'as de cœur si c'est en février,

L'as de carreau et l'as de trèfle, misère en Flandre,

L'as de pique aux mains des aventuriers.

Et si cela me plaît à moi de vous dire machin,

Pot à eau, mousseline et potiron.

Que l'Anglais dise machin,

Que machin dise le chef de gare,

Machin dise l'autre,

Et moi aussi.

Machin.

Et même machin chose.

Il est vrai que vous vous en foutez.

Que vous ne comprenez pas la raison de ce poème.

Moi non plus d'ailleurs.

Poème, je vous demande un peu?

Poème? je vous demande un peu de confiture,

Encore un peu de gigot,

Encore un petit verre de vin

Pour nous mettre en train . . .

# Like

Laïque, says the Frenchman, and the Frenchman is civil.

Lake? Says the pleasure-boat captain, and the tripper trips up the
    gangplank.

Leica, explains the tourist snap-happily.

Like, I say like and everything is metamorphosed, marble into water,
    the sky into orange ribbons, wine into new bottles, three into
    two, the heart into little pieces, one's back into it, laughter into tears.

But when the Englishman says as, it's his turn to see the world change
    shape to his liking.

As for me, I see only a single aspect, one sign on a playing-card,

The ace of hearts if it's astringent February,

The ace of diamonds and the ace of clubs, penury in Asturias.

The ace of spades ready for the assault.

What if it pleases me to say "whatsit" to you,

Pitcher, mashed potato, pumpkin,

Let the English say whatsit,

Whatsit the stationmaster,

Whatsit what's his name,

And me as well.

Whatsit.

Even whatsit thingummy.

It's true you don't give a toss

Whether you get the point of this poem.

Me neither for that matter.

Poem, I've one or two favours to ask you.

Poem, could you give me a little more jam,

A little more lamb,

Another little glass of wine

To get us going properly . . .

Poème, je ne vous demande pas l'heure qu'il est.
Poème, je ne vous demande pas si votre beau-père est poilu comme un
    sapeur.
Poème, je vous demande un peu . . . ?
Poème, je ne vous demande pas l'aumône,
Je vous la fais.
Poème, je ne vous demande pas l'heure qu'il est,
Je vous la donne.
Poème, je ne vous demande pas si vous allez bien,
Cela se devine.
Poème, poème, je vous demande un peu . . .
Je vous demande un peu d'or pour être heureux avec celle que j'aime.

Poem, I'm not asking you what time it is.

Poem, I'm not asking if your father-in-law's as hairy as a
     champion weight-lifter.

Poem, can I ask you a favor . . . ?

Poem, I'm not asking you to give me charity,

I'm giving it to you.

Poem, I'm not asking you to tell me the time,

I'm telling you.

Poem, I'm not asking you if you are well,

It's easy to guess.

Poem, poem, I'm asking you a favor . . .

I'm asking you for the odd gold nugget so I can live happily with the
     one I love.

1942
from *Les Sans-Cou* in *Fortunes*
translator, Bill Zavatsky

# Mi-route

Il y a un moment précis dans le temps
Où l'homme atteint le milieu exact de sa vie,
Un fragment de seconde,
Une fugitive parcelle de temps plus rapide qu'un regard,
Plus rapide que le sommet des pâmoisons amoureuses,
Plus rapide que la lumière.
Et l'homme est sensible à ce moment.
De longues avenues entre des frondaisons
S'allongent vers la tour où sommeille une dame
Dont la beauté résiste aux baisers, aux saisons,
Comme une étoile au vent, comme un rocher aux lames.
Un bateau frémissant s'enfonce et gueule.
Au sommet d'un arbre claque un drapeau.
Une femme bien peignée, mais dont les bas tombent sur les souliers
Apparaît au coin d'une rue,
Exaltée, frémissante,
Protégeant de sa main une lampe surannée et qui fume.

Et encore un débardeur ivre chante au coin d'un pont,
Et encore une amante mord les lèvres de son amant,
Et encore un pétale de rose tombe sur un lit vide,
Et encore trois pendules sonnent la même heure
À quelques minutes d'intervalle,
Et encore un homme qui passe dans une rue se retourne
Parce que l'on a crié son prénom,
Mais ce n'est pas lui que cette femme appelle,
Et encore, un ministre en grande tenue,
Désagréablement gêné par le pan de sa chemise coincé entre son
    pantalon et son caleçon,

# Half way

There's a precise moment in time
When a man reaches the exact middle of his life,
A fraction of a second,
A flitting atom of time faster than a glance,
Faster than the peak of blackout in love,
Faster than light.
And a man can feel this moment happening.
Long avenues between foliage
Stretch toward the tower where a lady sleeps
Whose beauty withstands kisses, seasons,
Like a star the wind, like a rock the waves.
A trembling boat plunges and hollers.
A flag flaps atop a tree.
A well-groomed woman, though her stockings are falling down around
    her shoes,
Appears at the corner of a street,
Hot-headed, trembling,
Shielding a smoky antique lamp with her hand.

And a drunken stevedore still sings at the corner of a bridge,
And a woman still bites the lips of her lover,
And a rose-petal still falls on an empty bed,
And three clocks still chime the same hour
A few minutes apart,
And a man walking down a street still turns around
Because someone shouted his name,
But he's not the one the woman's calling,
And still, a secretary of state in formal attire,
Uncomfortably hindered by his shirttail jammed between his
    trousers and his drawers,

Inaugure un orphelinat,

Et encore d'un camion lancé à toute vitesse

Dans les rues vides de la nuit

Tombe une tomate merveilleuse qui roule dans le ruisseau

Et qui sera balayée plus tard,

Et encore un incendie s'allume au sixième étage d'une maison

Qui flambe au cœur de la ville silencieuse et indifférente,

Et encore un homme entend une chanson

Oubliée depuis longtemps, et l'oubliera de nouveau,

Et encore maintes choses,

Maintes autres choses que l'homme voit à l'instant précis du milieu de
    sa vie,

Maintes autres choses se déroulent longuement dans le plus court des
    courts instants de la terre.

Il pressent le mystère de cette seconde, de ce fragment de seconde,

Mais il dit «Chassons ces idées noires»,

Et il chasse ces idées noires.

Et que pourrait-il dire,

Et que pourrait-il faire

De mieux?

Inaugurates an orphanage.
And from a truck moving at full speed
In the empty streets of night
A marvelous tomato still falls rolling into the gutter
To be swept up later,
And a fire still breaks out on the sixth floor of a house
Blazing in the heart of the silent, indifferent city,
And a man still hears a song
Forgotten a long time, will forget it again,
And still more things,
Many more things that the man sees at the precise moment at the
middle of his life
Many more things unfold deliberately in the briefest of earth's brief
moments.
He squeezes the mystery from that second, that fraction of a second.
But he says, "Let's chase those blues away,"
And what could he say,
And what could he do
That's better?

tr. Bill Zavatsky

## Couchée

A droite, le ciel, à gauche, la mer.
Et devant les yeux, l'herbe et ses fleurs.
Un nuage, c'est la route, suit son chemin vertical
Parallèlement à l'horizon de fil à plomb,
Parallèlement au cavalier.
Le cheval court vers sa chute imminente
Et cet autre monte interminablement.
Comme tout est simple et étrange.
Couchée sur le côté gauche,
Je me désintéresse du paysage
Et je ne pense qu'à des choses très vagues,
Très vagues et très heureuses,
Comme le regard las que l'on promène
Par ce bel après-midi d'été
A droite, à gauche,
De-ci, de-là,
Dans le délire de l'inutile.

# Lying down

To the right, the sky, to the left, the sea.
And before your eyes, the grass and its flowers.
A cloud, the road, follows its vertical way
Parallel to the plumbline of the horizon,
Parallel to the rider.
The horse races toward its imminent fall
And the other climbs interminable.
How simple and strange everything is.
Lying on my left side
I take no interest in the landscape
And I think only of things that are very vague,
Very vague and very pleasant,
Like the tired look you walk around with
Through this beautiful summer afternoon
To the right, to the left,
Here, there,
In the delirium of uselessness.

tr. Bill Zavatsky

1944
*Contrée*

# Crépuscule d'été

Crépuscule d'été baigné de brouillard rose
Déchiré par le bleu des ardoises des toits,
Le bleu du ciel, le bleu de l'asphalte et, parfois
Saignant sur une vitre où les reflets s'opposent

Reflet de la rivière en le feuillage enclose
Reflet du son, reflet du lit en désarroi,
Vibrations des carreaux au fracas des convois,
Tout ici se rencontre et se métamorphose.

Le soleil lourdement roulée sur les maisons,
Dans la rumeur du soir et l'écho des chansons:
La nuit effacera cet univers fragile,
Le fantôme du lit quitté par les amants
Et le défaut du verre imitant le diamant.
Mais la vitre longtemps vibrera sur la ville.

# Summer twilight

Summer twilight bathed in rose mist
Torn by the blue of the roof slates
The blue of the sky, the blue of the asphalt and, sometimes
Bleeding onto a windowpane where reflections oppose one another

Reflection of the river enclosed by leaves
Reflection of sound, reflection of the bed in disarray,
Vibrations of the panes at the roar of the convoys,
Everything here meets and is metamorphosed.

The sun rolls heavily over the houses,
In the stirrings of the evenings and the echo of songs:
The night will erase this fragile universe,
The ghost of the bed left by the lovers
And the flaw of the glass making it look like a diamond.
But the pane will vibrate for a long time over the city.

tr. Katharine Conley

# La cascade

Quelle flèche a percé le ciel et le rocher?
Elle vibre. Elle étale, ainsi qu'un paon, sa queue
Ou, comme la comète à minuit vient nicher,
Le brouillard de sa tige et ses pennes sans nœuds.

Que surgisse le sang de la chair entr'ouverte,
Lèvres taisant déjà le murmure et le cri,
Un doigt posé suspend le temps et déconcerte
Le témoin dans les yeux duquel le fait s'inscrit.

Silence? nous savons pourtant les mots de passe,
Sentinelles perdues loin des feux de bivouac
Nous sentirons monter dans les ténèbres basses
L'odeur du chèvrefeuille et celle du ressac.

Qu'enfin l'aube jaillisse à travers tes abîmes,
Distance, et qu'un rayon dessine sur les eaux,
Présage du retour de l'archer et des hymnes,
Un arc-en-ciel et son carquois plein de roseaux.

# Cascade

What sort of arrow split the sky and this rock?
It quivers, spreading like a peacock's fan
Like the mist around the shaft and knotless feathers
Of a comet come to nest at midnight.

How blood surges from the gaping wound,
Lips already silencing the murmur and the cry,
One solemn finger holds back time, confusing
The witness of the eyes where the deed is written.

Silence? We still know the passwords.
Lost sentinels far from the watch fires
We smell the odor of honeysuckle and surf
Rising in the dark shadows.

Distance, let dawn leap the void at last,
And a single beam of light make a rainbow on the water
Its quiver full of reeds,
Sign of the return of archers and patriotic songs.

tr. Katharine Conley

# Printemps

Tu, Rrose Sélavy, hors de ces bornes erres
Dans un printemps en proie aux sueurs de l'amour,
Aux parfums de la rose éclose aux murs des tours,
à la fermentation des eaux et de la terre.

Sanglant, la rose au flanc, le danseur, corps de pierre
Paraît sur le théâtre au milieu des labours.
Un peuple de muets d'aveugles et de sourds
applaudira sa danse et sa mort printanière.

C'est dit. Mais la parole inscrite dans la suie
S'efface au gré des vents sous les doigts de la pluie
Pourtant nous l'entendons et lui obéissons.

Au lavoir où l'eau coule un nuage simule
À la fois le savon, la tempête et recule
l'instant où le soleil fleurira les buissons.

*Desnos*
*6.4.44*
*19, rue Mazarine*
*Paris VI*

# Spring

You, Rrose Selavy, wander out of reach
In the spring caught up in love's sweat,
In the scent of the rose budding on tower walls,
in the ferment of waters and earth.

Bleeding, a rose in his side, the dancer's stone body
Appears in the theatre in the midst of ploughing
A mute, blind, and deaf people
will applaud his dance and his spring death.

It is said. But the word written in soot
Is erased by the whims of the winds under fingers of rain
though we hear and obey it.

At the wash house, where the water runs,
a cloud pretends to be the soap and the storm as it pushes back
the moment when the sun will break the bushes into flower.

tr. Katharine Conley

# Le paysage

J'avais rêvé d'aimer. J'aime encor mais l'amour
Ce n'est plus ce bouquet de lilas et de roses
Chargeant de leurs parfums la forêt où repose
Une flamme à l'issue de sentiers sans détour.

J'avais rêvé d'aimer. J'aime encor mais l'amour
Ce n'est plus cet orage où l'éclair superpose
Ses bûchers aux châteaux, déroute, décompose,
Illumine en fuyant l'adieu du carrefour.

C'est le silex en feu sous mon pas dans la nuit,
Le mot qu'aucun lexique au monde n'a traduit
L'écume sur la mer, dans le ciel ce nuage.

À vieillir tout devient rigide et lumineux,
Des boulevards sans noms et des cordes sans nœuds.
Je me sens me roidir avec le paysage.

## The landscape

I had dreamed of loving. I love still but love
Is no longer that bouquet of lilacs and roses
Drenching with perfume the forest holding
A flame at the end of unswerving paths.

I had dreamed of loving. I love still but love
Is no longer that storm where the lightning
Builds bonfires on castles, confuses; unsettles,
Illuminates fleeing the crossroad farewell.

It's the flint afire under my step in the night,
The word that no lexicon contained,
The foam on the sea, in the sky this cloud.

As one ages all becomes bright and hard,
Nameless boulevards and knotless cords.
I feel myself growing rigid with the landscape.

tr. Stephen Romer

## L'epitaphe

J'ai vécu dans ces temps et depuis mille années
Je suis mort. Je vivais, non déchu mais traqué.
Toute noblesse humaine étant emprisonnée
J'étais libre parmi les esclaves masqués.

J'ai vécu dans ces temps et pourtant j'étais libre.
Je regardais le fleuve et la terre et le ciel
Tourner autour de moi, garder leur équilibre
Et les saisons fournir leurs oiseaux et leur miel.

Vous qui vivez qu'avez-vous fait de ces fortunes?
Regrettez-vous les temps où je me débattais?
Avez-vous cultivé pour des moissons communes?
Avez-vous enrichi la ville où j'habitais?

Vivants, ne craignez rien de moi, car je suis mort.
Rien ne survit de mon esprit ni de mon corps.

# Epitaph

I lived in those times and for a thousand years
I have been dead. I lived, not fallen but haunted.
All human nobility being imprisoned
I was free among masked slaves.

I lived in those times and still I was free.
I watched the river and the earth and the sky
Turn about me, keeping their balance
And the seasons bearing their birds and their honey.

You who are living what have you made of these fortunes?
Do you regret the times when I struggled?
Have you farmed the land for common harvests?
Have you enriched the town where I lived?

O living men, fear nothing from me, for I am dead.
Nothing survives of my mind or my body.

tr. Stephen Romer

## La Rivière

D'un bord à l'autre bord j'ai passé la rivière,
Suivant à pied le point qui la franchit d'un jet
Et mêle dans les eaux son ombre et son reflet
Au fil bleu par le savon des lavandières.

J'ai marché dans le gué qui chante à sa manière.
Etoiles et cailloux sous mes pas le jonchaient.
J'allais vers le gazon, j'allais vers la forêt
Où le vent frissonnait dans sa robe légère.

J'ai nagé. J'ai passé, mieux vêtu par cette eau
Que par ma propre chair et par ma propre peau.
C'était hier. Déjà l'aube et le ciel s'épousent.

Et voici que mes yeux et mon corps sont pesants,
Il fait clair et j'ai soif et je cherche à présent
La fontaine qui chante au coeur d'une pelouse.

# The river

I walked to where the river can be crossed—
A jutting point: from bank to bank I passed.
Its shadow and reflection merge their hue;
Laundresses turn the stream a soapy blue.

I trudged the ford, that sings to suit its mood,
Strewn underfoot with stars and bits of rock.
I headed for the greensward and the wood
Where the wind shivered in its flimsy frock.

I swam, I got across, clothed better in
That water than in my own flesh and skin.
A night has passed. Now, sky has married dawn.

And see, my eyes and limbs are faltering,
It's bright, I'm thirsty, looking for the spring
Whose song regales the middle of a lawn.

tr. Timothy Adès

# La nuit d'été

Aux rosiers remontants ta robe déchirée
Accroche des lambeaux, les vapeurs du matin.
Tu mêles en marchant les lilas et le thym
Aux fleurs d'autres saisons et d'une autre contrée.

Tu te diriges vers le bois, là où l'orée
Ouvre un chemin retentissant de cris lointains.
Le feu de la Saint-Jean dans le vallon s'éteint.
La nuit, la courte nuit, déjà s'est égarée.

Jeune fille aux beaux seins, au regard sans lumière,
J'ai déjà vu tes soeurs. Tu n'es pas la première
A te perdre en courant les jardins et les champs.

Quand, à travers la haie, tu te fis un passage
La ronce t'a griffé la cuisse et le visage
Et le ciel a pâli au bruit de nouveaux chants.

# The summer night

Roses go rambling up. Your dress is torn,
Snagging the bush with scraps of misty morn.
Perfumes from other days, another clime,
Blend, as you walk, with lilac and with thyme.

You move towards the wood, whose boundaries
Open a path that's loud with distant cries.
Fires of midsummer in the vale die back;
The night, so short, has soon strayed off the track.
Fine-bosomed girl, no light shines in your gaze.
I've seen your sisters. You are not the first
To run through fields and gardens and be lost.

You scrambled through the hedge and, as you passed,
The bramble-bushes scratched your thigh and face;
New songs were heard; the sky turned pale at last.

tr. Timothy Adès

## La voix

Une voix, une voix qui vient de si loin
Qu'elle ne fait plus tinter les oreilles,
Une voix, comme un tambour, voilée
Parvient pourtant, distinctement, jusqu'à nous.
Bien qu'elle semble sortir d'un tombeau
Elle ne parle que d'été et de printemps,
Elle emplit le corps de joie,
Elle allume aux lèvres le sourire.

Je l'écoute. Ce n'est qu'une voix humaine
Qui traverse les fracas de la vie et des batailles,
L'écroulement du tonnerre et le murmure des bavardages.

Et vous? Ne l'entendez-vous pas?
Elle dit "La peine sera de peu de durée."
Elle dit "La belle saison est proche."

Ne l'entendez-vous pas?

# The voice

A voice, a voice coming from so far away
That it no longer rings in the ears,
A voice, like a drumbeat, muffled
Reaches us even so, distinctly.
Though it seems to issue from a tomb
It speaks only of summer and spring,
It fills the body with joy,
It kindles a smile on the lips.

I'm listening. It's only a human voice
Coming across the din of life and of battles,
The crash of thunder and the babble of talk.

What about you? Don't you hear it?
It says "The pain will be short-lived"
It says "The beautiful season is near".

Don't you hear it?

tr. Timothy Adès

**1943**
*Ce Coeur qui haïssait la guerre*

## Ce cœur qui haïssait la guerre . . .

Ce cœur qui haïssait la guerre voilà qu'il bat pour le combat et la
   bataille!
Ce cœur qui ne battait qu'au rythme des marées, à celui des saisons, à
   celui des heures du jour et de la nuit,
Voilà qu'il se gonfle et qu'il envoie dans les veines un sang brûlant de
   salpêtre et de haine
Et qu'il mène un tel bruit dans la cervelle que les oreilles en sifflent
Et qu'il n'est pas possible que ce bruit ne se répande pas dans la ville et
   la campagne
Comme le son d'une cloche appelant à l'émeute et au combat.
Écoutez, je l'entends qui me revient renvoyé par les échos.
Mais non, c'est le bruit d'autres cœurs, de millions d'autres cœurs
   battant comme le mien à travers la France.
Ils battent au même rythme pour la même besogne tous ces cœurs
Leur bruit est celui de la mer à l'assaut des falaises
Et tout ce sang porte dans des millions de cervelles un même mot
   d'ordre:
Révolte contre Hitler et mort à ses partisans!
Pourtant ce cœur haïssait la guerre et battait au rythme des saisons,
Mais un seul mot: Liberté a suffi à réveiller les vieilles colères
Et des millions de Français se préparent dans l'ombre à la besogne que
   l'aube proche leur imposera.
Car ces cœurs qui haïssaient la guerre battaient pour la liberté
   au rythme même des saisons et des marées, du jour et de la nuit.

# This heart that hated war

This heart that hated war here it is beating for combat and battle!
This heart that only beat at the rhythm of tides, seasons, hours of the
    day and night,
Here it is swelling  sending to the veins a blood burning with
    saltpeter and hatred
And making such a noise in the brain that the ears whistle
And this noise spreads in city and country
Like the sound of a bell calling for revolt and combat.
Listen, I heard it coming to me sent echoing back.
But no, it's the sound of other hearts, millions of other hearts
beating like mine throughout France.
They are beating at the same rhythm for the same task all these hearts,
Their noise is that of the sea breaking against cliffs
And all this blood bears in the millions of brains one motto:
Revolt against Hitler death to his partisans!
Yet this heart used to hate war and beat to the rhythm of the seaons,
But a single word: Freedom was enough to waken the old anger  .
And millions of Frenchmen are getting ready in the shadows for the
    duty that the next dawn will imposed on them.
On these hearts that hated war beat for freedom at the same rhythm
    of the seasons and seas, of day and of night.

# POSTFACE

# POSTFACE

## Desnos Surrealist and Later

The situation of Robert Desnos within the surrealist movement must be taken into account in any discussion of his work. Even after Breton's attacks on him, even after his supposed formal separation from the movement, which he had "betrayed" by his writing of formal alexandrines, his occasional mockery of the sacreds of surrealism, and, finally, his journalism, Desnos never ceased to call himself a surrealist. He used the term "in its most open sense," as he explains in his own *Troisième manifeste* (Breton wrote prolegomena for a third manifesto, but never the manifesto itself).

The remarkable powers of Desnos in regard to automatic writing were alluded to frequently by the other members of the group, especially Breton, who was generous in his praise. Desnos' talent was first recognized in the era of "hypnotized slumbers": these experiments with sleep-writing were intended to liberate the unconscious and give it free creative rein. In *Une Vague de rêves*, Louis Aragon describes the heady exaltation of this period in which Desnos' particular prowess became evident: "Their slumbers are lengthier and lengthier. . . . They fall asleep just from watching each other sleep, and then they carry on dialogues like persons from a blind and distant world, they quarrel and occasionally you have to snatch the knives out of their hands. Real physical ravages, difficulty on several occasions of pulling them out of a cataleptic sleep where a hint of death seems to pass. . . . "[1]

Aragon describes Desnos' particular talent thus:

> In a café, amid the sound of voices, the bright light, the
> jostlings, Robert Desnos need only close his eyes, and he
> talks, and among the steins, the saucers, the whole ocean
> collapses with its prophetic racket and its vapors
> decorated with long banners. However little those
> who interrogate this amazing sleeper incite him,
> prophecy, the tone of magic, of revelation, of revolution,
> the tone of the fanatic and the apostle, immediately
> appear. Under other conditions, Desnos, were he to cling
> to this delirium, would become the leader of a religion,
> the founder of a city, the tribune of a people in revolt.[2]

Either through some extraordinary effort of the will or through some even more extraordinary chance, Desnos demonstrated an incredible fertility of imagination, dictating, writing or drawing feverishly, answering questions with a sustained lyric power at first impressive to Breton and the others but finally discouraging to them. As Desnos points out, Breton, who bent for hours over a manuscript, was not likely to accept with good grace this spectacle of facility. Perhaps Desnos exaggerated this dramatic side of the experiments precisely to impress the leader of the group—Breton had on repeated occasions to force Desnos to awaken—but perhaps also it was in the long run exactly this drama and this facility which served to turn Breton against the poet who had been more impressive than the others.

The rift between the two men, far apart in temperament, is apparent as early as 1926–27 and Desnos' expulsion from the surrealist "chapel" in 1929 is hardly surprising. He had already left that chapel of his own volition, declaring its dogma too narrow and too "mystical," its claims to freedom unjustified, and its total rejection of traditional forms too limiting. The separation culminated in a fiery message he sent to a meeting on the rue du Château in March, 1929: "Absolute scorn for all activity, whether it be literary or artistic or anti-literary or anti-artistic, an absolute pessimism concerning social activity."[3] He did not at this point reject any possibility of further collaboration, but he firmly refused what seemed to him too arbitrary a discipline. In the "Second Manifesto," Breton condemned him for not choosing between "marxism and anti-marxism," and Desnos, insisting always on the absolute freedom of the poet, condemned in his turn what he called the obscurantism of Breton. Thus his "Third Manifesto," included in this volume.

Claiming that Breton's lofty exaltations of the illogical, and diatribes against the heretical, "paved the road for God," Desnos turned to interests of a sort which seemed to him more genuinely liberating. Breton always considered *journalism* a pejorative term, indicating a concern with the lesser and the trivial at the expense of the essential and the poetic. Desnos, on the other hand, considered the *journalier* or the daily affairs of life including the most trivial, to be the possible matter of the poetic. Surrealism, as Katharine Conley points out, "was a way of life. Surrealism was a way of walking down the streets of Paris and seeing the marvelous in the everyday." [4]And Desnos exemplified this in the strongest sense.

A comparison may be made here with Blaise Cendrars' eulogies on the poetics of advertising (in *Modernités*, 1927, the essay called "Publicité = Poésie"). It is, he says, an affirmation of optimism and pleasure, a proof of vigor and art, a triumph of lyricism. Desnos' attitude is similar. Nothing farther from the strict surrealist principles can be imagined, however, and it is not hard to see why, from that point of view, Desnos' comportment was shocking. What was to him openness was to Breton non-revolutionary and therefore non-poetic: it was commercialism.

But it is not in fact the themes of Desnos' work or its subjects that the most revealing in the context of his separation from the surrealist group. It is true that these become more "realistic," that the images of mermaid and dream make way for other images and for the eventual condemnation of dream and dream-inducing drugs in his late novel *Le Vin est tiré*. It is true that in many cases these latter images are more expected, more trite. It is true that his resistance poetry is far more simplistic than his surrealist poetry and therefore less interesting to the critic. More germane, however,

Yvonne George
Vers 1925
(Collection Marie-
Claire Dumas)

to the basic split between the surrealist way of seeing and expressing and
Desnos' own vision and expression is the problem of traditional and novel
style.

Desnos, always an experimenter, tried out a variety of styles: he wrote
simple verses and much intricate prose poetry, some meditations on the
dream adventure, extremely complicated in structure, and then alexandrines,
and sonnets in a classical form. One of the main points of Breton's public at-
tack on Desnos in the *Second manifeste* was the latter's fondness for quoting
alexandrines and composing them (see, for example, the pseudo-Rimbaud
at the beginning of *La Liberté ou l'amour!*). In the surrealist code, a liber-
ated or novel form must bear witness to the new vision; more precisely, a
traditional form, however brilliant, betrays that vision. But Desnos was not
content to experiment in present and future forms, and constantly experi-
mented in the forms of the past as well.

Some of his last poems, in *Contrée*, are in fact written in sonnet form:

Youki Desnos
(Collection
Marie-Claire Dumas)

we might interpret this as a regression toward fixity, voluntary or involuntary. "Je me sens me roidir avec le paysage," he says in "Le Paysage," one of his last poems, lamenting his growing rigidity along with what he sees around him, his landscape.[5] Or again we may see them as a further experiment in openness to all forms, or as a simple statement that any form is as viable as any other to a poet of the modern consciousness. Desnos always wanted to combine one thing with its opposite: poetry with mathematics and dreams with logic, as in the postface to *Fortunes*; the delirious and the lucid, the mind and the senses. These poems might then, in the very fixity of their form and landscape, be a deliberate contrast to an expression of freedom, just as the poems published with *Contrée* and given a title reminiscent of mythological culture, *Calixto*, might be seen as using the traditional landscape of myth and the traditional alternations of light and dark images for a statement of what seemed to Desnos a "present" reality.

## Landscape of Surrealism

The major adventure of these early years is an inner one, of dream, also identified with poetry. The predominant landscape is that of darkness. For the possible and always awaited perception of the marvelous which is the stated goal of all the poets who adopted the surrealist attitude, the fixed landmarks of logic and the "normal" or daytime vision must be abandoned in favor of the contraries, in which daylight was interpenetrated with darkness, sunlight with night. Whether Desnos was or was not in the habit of *simulating* a sleeping condition for his friends:"Dormons, dormons, / Ou faisons semblant de dormer"(Let's sleep, let's sleep, / Or let's pretend to sleep) does not affect the importance to his poetry of his constant evocation of night, which furnishes this poetry with its most striking themes. In these years the intermingling was what mattered, so that lyric intoxication predominated over the logical and the clear. The marvelous of the everyday—never forgotten—was precisely that because of its interpenetration with what opposed it.

The surrealist marvelous can be read on many levels: image and style so interpenetrate each other, like night and day, that the reading can start anywhere and end where it started, or then far beyond. As with Breton's summoning of the mermaid and water imagery to render the hard and linear landscape of the male imagination at once more fertile and more malleable, in Desnos's poetry and prose, liquid imagery prevails, enabling the rapid transformations of figures and visions. Three passages from the long and important poem "Siramour," a bottle is invoked—to signal the intoxication of the poetry and the love of the star and mermaid therein (Yvonne George as the star, Youki as the mermaid). Now the bottle, we are assured, is a real bottle, no figment of the imagination, and the remnants of wax sticking to it might imply a past flame, from a candle whose light endures: "C'était pourtant une bouteille comme les autres et elle ne devait pas contenir plus de 80 centilitres et, pourtant, voilà que l'océan tout entier jaillit de son goulot où adhèrent encore des fragments de cire" (O,893). (It was however a bottle like other bottles, and it wasn't supposed to hold more than 80 centilitres, and yet here was the whole ocean pouring forth from its mouth to which some fragments of wax still adhered.) This is one of the clearest affirmations of the *merveilleux* contained in this ordinary vessel, a bottle sent out to sea, communicating as it does with the totality of the universe.

In the second passage, the chain of transforming and transformed images is openly stated in a paradoxical presence and absence, this contrast present in many of the early poems of the poet. The star rises:

> ... au-delà de l'écume éclatée comme un orage bas dans les
> ténèbres liquides. A ses rayons, la bouteille abandonnée dans
> l'herbe et les ajoncs s'illumine des voies lactées qu'elle paraît
> contenir et ne contient pas car, bien bouchée, elle recèle en ses
> flancs la sirène marquée, la captive et redoutable sirèn masquées.
> ... Pour l'instant captive elle attend la délivrance dans sa prison
> bien bouchée par une main amoureuse, tandis qu'une lettre,
> non remise à son destinataire, moisit sur le sol. (O, 891-2)

> ( ... beyond the foam burst open like a deep storm in the liquid
> shadows. In its rays, the bottle abandoned in the grass and the
> rushes is illuminated by the milky way that it seems to contain
> and does not, for it is firmly corked and contains in its depths
> the masked mermaid, the captive and awesome mermaid. ...
> ... Captive for the moment, she awaits her deliverance in her
> prison tightly closed by a loving hand, while a letter,
> undelivered to its addressee, lies moldy on the ground.)

The corked bottle here can be associated with another possible reading of the wax remnants in the preceding quotation—that is, the closing of the bottle related to the eventual illumination it may provide. The "liquid shadows" are at once the source of Desnos' surrealist vision and of the darkness distinguishing that vision from everyday sight. The milk bottle seems (falsely) to contain the Milky Way, by a series of suggestions, first homonymic, and then conceptual *mer* (sea) ➙ *mère* (mother) ➙ *voies lactées* (mother's milk): Milky Way), lending this text its particular density. Whether or not its message reaches us or rots upon the ground seems never to have been the particular concern of the poet. The extent to which any surrealist text demands to be, or can be, shared is a very moot point indeed.

The third passage pours out in one lengthy sentence like a drunken song, spilling forth not from the mouth of the poetic drunkard but from the bottle itself, overturned. It is from the few objects recurring again and again in these texts that all the illumination comes, if we know how to look at them:

Que le buveur, *ivre de la chanson*, parte sur un chemin biscornu
bordé d'arbres effrayants au bruit de la mer hurlant et *gueulant* et
montant la plus    formidable marée de tous les temps, non hors
de son *lit géographique*, mais *coulant d'un flux rapide* hors de
la bouteille renversée tandis que, libre, la sirène *étendue* sur le
sol non loin de cette *cataracte*, considère l'étoile, la tantôt noire,
la tantôt bleue, et s'imagine la reconnaître et la reconnaît
en effet. (O, 893)

(Let the drinker, *drunk on the song*, set out on a misshapen path
bordered with frightening trees with the sound of the sea
roaring and *bellowing* and swelling in the most astonishing tide
of all time, not outside of its geographic *bed*, but *flowing*
*rapidly* from the bottle overturned while the mermaid free and
*stretched* out on the ground not far from this *rushing water*,
stares at the star, now black, now blue, and thinks she
recognizes her, and recognizes her in fact.)

I have italicized here the possible references to the textual production in its own spreading or stretching out, in a rapid course across the page, dependent on the oral impact and on the reaction of the reader. It is clear that this is no ordinary drinker, since he is drunk on his song rather than singing because he is drunk: at this point the intoxication can be seen as structuring the poem.

Rather than an overall perspective, Desnos frequently forces our attention to the minute detail or an unexpected angle of vision, not as a passing variation from the large to the small but rather as if his obsession must become ours. The recurrence of certain objects, which gradually take on all the resonances of myth, the narrowing of focus as if in a dazed state, is at once curious and effective, linking as it does the apparently disconnected parts of discourse or vision each to the other by a rapid transfer of close attention.[6] There is a parallel breaking-down of the logical patterns and habits of looking, so that even the shapes of letters can take on a profile of primary importance regardless of content. Everything is visual: in one of his cinematic scenarios, Desnos endlessly repeats the injunction, implicit and explicit, to focus on an eye, a coin, a hoop, a ball, a circle in the water—the accumulation of circular elements as the center of our gaze, controlled as it is by his own, is as obsessive as it is cohesive. In both his early novels, certain figures repeatedly attract the writer's attention and thus ours. Nor can they be said to have any predictable place in the text; rather, they appear and reappear, fixing our gaze, their presence unpremeditated and seemingly unmotivated: thus the billboards and calendars are not seen from different angle but always from the same one, their iteration hypnotic and obsessive.

In the poems of *A la mystérieuse*, the repetition is often present in its simplest form of exact restatement or alternation. In contrast to the axiom of information theory, according to which the message weakens in communicative content as it is repeated—unless the context changes—this particular process of poetic obsession acquires an accumulated value, enhanced by the number of instances in which the obsession is recognized and verbally accounted for: "O douleurs de l'amour/O douleurs de l'amour" (O pangs of love/O pangs of love). The same factor of repetition marks many of Desnos's most effective poems. Parallel to the obsessed staring at an object,

absent or present, or the fixation on a particular angle, is the series of struc-
tures caused by the repetition of phrases—exact or altered—almost as if the
poet were stammering. These repetitions and accumulations which serve as
a focus here on several occasions take different forms: sometimes a repeat-
ed series of lines or images serves as a warming-up exercise, as in Desnos'
recommendation for automatic texts and automatic drawings started by any
random lines scratched on the surface.

The obsession can be hidden as is the image of a mermaid within the
poem "Identité des images," where it nonetheless controls the poem, each
of its images, and its final path, as if the poet were staring into space, absent
from the surface or the sober covering of the poem. Or it can be apparent,
as in "L'Idée fixe," a fixed idea like Paul Valéry's text of the same name,
the poet points to the arrangement of a woman's hair that so obsesses him:
"Mais tes cheveux si bien nattés/Mais tes cheveux si bien nattés ont la
forme d'une main." (But your hair so neatly braided/But your hair so neatly
braided has the form of a hand.) Even the initial "but" calls our immediate
attention to the unprepared quality of the image. Although it has no logi-
cal place in the poem, it surges forth from the flow of words to control the
subsequent direction, arresting the vision and concluding the poem, which
it turns into an avowal of obsession. This obsessive repetition marks, unfor-
gettably, the celebrated poem, called "the last poem" even as it was writ-
ten far before Desnos's death (and retranscribed by the Czech Josef Stuna,
who found the poet as he was dying of typhoid fever). Here the mysterious
nature of the beloved addressed, first Yvonne and then Youki, is stressed by
the repetition of the pronoun "toi" and the balance of contrasting pronouns
"je / toi / je / toi," as well as the repeated lines: "J'ai tant rêvé de toi/J'ai tant
rêvé de toi." The poetic effectiveness reaches the level of legend: this is the
poem by which Desnos is best known.

The focus can then be deflected, as the poet turns away from the origi-
nal obsessive image. In the poem "About the Flower of Love and the
Migrating Horses," which according to the title is presumably focused on
a flower, all the interest built up about this object of obsession is finally
turned away, as the last four lines show, in their exact repetition, a band

of migrating horses capturing the spectacle and galloping on beyond the space of the poem. So the initial direction is changed, suddenly and drastically. The poet stares out at the horses just as he is about to speak of himself, or so he has said; is he no more in control of his text than is the reader?

Famouly, given the so frequent reference to "La Voix de Robert Desnos" (The Voice of Robert Desnos), the poem by this title begins its meditation on metaphoric discourse in a halting manner: "Si semblable à . . . / et au . . . / au . . . / . . . aux . . . / au . . . / si semblable à . . . / et à la . . . " (so like . . . like . . . like). The elements are here of less importance than their combined weight. This momentum becomes, then, the source of the poem's "flux" or progression or of its final self-destruction. The poet, drunk on his own poem, betrays his intoxication with his words. And ironically, the successive phrases built up about the woman loved—as elements of the universe effectively summoned—are shown at last to be useless: she neither listens nor responds. The tragic end can be read as plaintive, the poet having lost control of his voice, his poetic power, and of the text itself.

The poem begins with a comparison to fleeting and flowing images: flower, breeze and water, and then continues with a peremptory summons:

> I summon to me all those lost in the countryside
> tornadoes and hurricanes
> I summon to me volcano smoke..
> before a trinitarian insistence at the very center:
> summon the one I love:
> I summon the one I love
> I summon the one I love

No response is given yet: will she or will she not hear him? Somehow, Desnos has managed to involve all of us in the narration, in which all the elements rush obedient to him, at his slightest command. Power is invoked and shared. Things resuscitate because of him, and his word is efficacious, except, of course, in love. For the triple denial of the ending, picks back up the triple invocation of love and summons. The reader listens, in place of the beloved, because of whose non-reception, the entire poem falls away into silence, with no ear to hear and no tongue to answer. The "appel" and "appeal" or summons proffered by Desnos must be answered individually. This discourse is the inheritor of that long tradition of Romanticism as it replaces the Enlightenment faith in rational speech allied with knowledge. Here, what can be said is precisely that which is not true. So silence is preferred over speech, and judged to escape the inauthenticity that speech brings with it.

As opposed to straight-line patterns, where the poem is clearly directed toward an end prepared by its development, the texts of Desnos are prone to sudden veerings, swerves, and deviations. The pathetic lament in "En Sursaut" (Startled) is symptomatic of the tone of many of these poems: "Je ne sais pas où je vais . . . " (I don't know where I'm going. . . . ) For instance, "Vieille clameur" (Old Clamor), still in *Les Ténèbres*, is built on the repeated and jovial toast, "Here's to you!" But it is suddenly transformed into a poem of lamentation, as the joviality turns to the negation of possible continuity, a negation stressed by the number of preceding affirmations:

> Early morning greetings when drunkenness is shared . . .
>     . . .
> Early morning greetings to the flower of coal the generous virgin who
>     will put me to sleep tonight
> and so on. But then comes the denial:
> But never again alas! will we be able to say again
> Early morning greetings everyone! crocodiles crystal eyes thistles
>     virgin flower of coal generous virgin.)

The accumulation thus denied, precisely by the repetition of the identical phrase used originally to build up the effect, has the effect of canceling out the text itself, here only a drunken song.

In certain cases, the cessation of poetic power appears to come from

without, from some universal menace. But on occasion, and more charac-
teristically, Desnos testily denies what he himself has said, as if one had
challenged him. In "Passé le pont" (Past the Bridge) after proffering a men-
ace, he takes it back hurriedly, acknowledging that he was out of control:

> I did not say that.
> I said nothing
> What did I say?

Now, for a surrealist to be out of control suggests, one would have
thought, an ideal situation, as if here the automatic power of the poem itself
were at last to overrule the conscious hand. But the denial of speech itself
entails in every case the denial of the poem: for it is in the mouth that the
latter originates, as an oral text coming forth from the unconscious.

Later, when Desnos goes beyond the early intoxication with speech to
a more prosaic landscape of sober realism, obsession and obsessive repeti-
tion are consciously absent, as is his unique and complicated lyricism, in its
statement and its self-denials. The irony of this progression is implicit: with
the disappearance of the poet's own symptoms of verbal intoxication there
disappears also one of the most valuable sources for his most engaging po-
etic technique. The poet who "ventured further than any other," in Breton's
words, was also to discover the temptation of silence and, worse, of banality,
once the persuasive facility of sleep-writing had been transcended.

> The tide will be high, and the star has faltered.
> ("The Night of Loveless Nights")

Occasionally the ground for the poem seems to be composed of the space
stretched taut between the elements in opposition, in intense alternation or
conversation. "Les Espaces du sommeil" (Sleep Spaces) and "Si tu savais"
(If You Knew) are both sufficiently long to give full play to this ground: the
two poems can be seen as mirror images of each other. In the former poem
the two elements "Dans la nuit" and Il y a toi" (In the night and You are

there) begin in rapid alternation *ABAB* and are given a gradual amplitude
as the poem slows down and expands on each element. Does the daytime
presence undercut or underline the marvelous (mysterious, as in the title)
nature of the woman? The ambiguity of meaning depends completely upon
the complex structure.

On the other hand, the famous poem "Si tu savais" begins the alterna-
tion of its two elements slowly, in an expanded form, then in a more rapid
alternation. So the dynamic structures of the poems vary, even as a fixed
element generally stresses the outline of the poem, making the *architexture*
visible. This fixed element might be a repeated image or phrase, such as in
the poem "Désespoir du soleil" (Despair of the Sun), where the fixed ele-
ments of "coal-master-of-the-dream" and "poem-of-the-day-beginning" are
not placed in a rigid framework, but serve simply as incantations and focus
within the body of the poem. Or then the unifying image is carefully posi-
tioned, as in "Le vendredi du crime" (The Friday of the Crime), where the
phrase "passez cascades" occurs at regular intervals, or in the tragic "Per-
sonne d'autre que toi" (No One but You), where the transformation of a
seemingly banal statement of love into a striking admission of loneliness is
brought about through the positioning of the repeated line which gives the
poem its title: it begins the poem, functions as its center, and ends it.

In the poem "Trois Etoiles" (Three Stars), the image first presented
seems to change its direction during the course of the poem, from losing to
winning, and yet it does not: it was an illusion.We might have thought the
losing to stand in direct contradiction to the middle section of the poem,
about domination. But in fact, the loss is first of regret, then of a glory de-
spised, so that there is an implied negation of this negation. He has finally
lost all *except* his love, with the result that this losing is seen as equated with
winning, and on the same side of the fence, as it were, with mastery. So, in
this next reading, the line carries through from the beginning positive (un-
der the guise of negative) to the next positive element, or the mastery. But
in fact at the center, the preceding refrain—"De tout hormis l'amour de sa
belle" (All except the love of his lady)—is picked up and, this time, reversed
in implication:

Maître de tout enfin hormis l'amour de sa belle
Master of everything finally except the love of his lovely one.

So if, in the beginning, we had read that the losing was negated by the keeping, then here we have to read that the mastery is negated by the losing. Now the triple repetition of this tragic refrain stresses the beginning irony of the three seemingly negative or "losing" terms against the seemingly positive term "winning": now master of the wind and the pebbles only, he has lost what he most cared about. A typical Desnos move.

At times, an image is suspended while we wait for it to recur, as in the poem entitled "Infinitif" (Infinitive), in which the entire ten-line sequence (spelling out the name Yvonne) depends on the expectancy created by the initial negation, "to die" and "not to die yet":

y *mourir* ô belle flammêche y *mourir*

. . .

*ne pas mourir* encore . . .
naître avec le feu et *ne pas mourir*
(my italics)

(to die there oh most beautiful flame to die there

. . .

not to die yet . . .
to be born with the fire and not to die)

The poem, made only of infinitive forms ("étreindre," "embrasser," "gagner," "découvrir," "omettre de transmettre," "rire") is sustained and suspended—as the infinitive is precisely a verbal suspension of situation— until the final line:

et mourir ce que j'aime au bord des flammes.

(and die what I love at the edge of the flames.)

Another favored structure, wherein repeated elements are compressed and massed together, creates sufficient energy for the later occurrences of those same elements or parts of them in isolation from each other still transmit the dynamism thus built up. In the epic poem "De la fleur d'amour et des chevaux migrateurs," the initial appearance of the flower is strengthened by the amassed comparatives ("more radiant than," "paler than," "sadder than"), so that the poet's abandoning all else in the universe including his own love to speak only of her is formally justified:

> Je parle de la fleur de la forêt et non des tours
> Je parle de la fleur de la forêt et non de mon amour

Later, having built up this paradigm, he can repeat it in a more diffuse version, stretched out the length of the poem, until a slight reversal occurs. For this object he has built up by comparison and by speech is now left aside and the poet returns to his own concerns, which he was not to speak of before. Finally, however, the entire scene, flower, poet, and the poet's love or recounting of it is swept away by the exterior or migrating element, a physical interruption, repeated four times for stress. Everything has gone by.

This poem exemplifies the most characteristic process in all the poems of Desnos dependent on the technique of repetition: that is, the concentration of sentiment or energy about a central focus, and then its undoing. The momentum built up about this flower spoken of by the narrating poet is then denied, so that the energy for speech is transferred to the poet, then that energy in its turn is transferred to the migrating horses, so that poet speaking is denied by the passing spectacle, while the poem itself is canceled out in favor of the surrounding scene.

The most famous and most tragic poems of the cycle *Les Ténèbres* show this structure. The very first poem, "La Voix de Robert Desnos," begins with a formal stressing of comparison as the basis of poetry: "So like . . ." It then continues with the comparative, extended here in fifteen lines of quantitative accumulation: "I summon . . . ", and then widens the scope of poetic summons to the woman loved, a challenge totally different, even in its exact repetition: "I summon the one I love." Everything in nature responds to his summons, in thirty-four separate but connected answerings, and yet the most crucial summons is to no avail.

The accumulations in "Avec le cœur de chêne" (With Oaken Heart) are of a different sort altogether, not massive and quantitatively important; rather one unit is added at a time, as in children's songs. The tone is therefore light, in spite of the underlying negation ("I love another")—as always, it is the structure of the repetitions which controls the tone. The pattern is simple: after the initial question, how much of this and that does it take to produce such a result, and then the alternating responses add one element each time to the refrain. The form is plainly meant to be accented over the words themselves. In the middle of the poem, the mention of death and varnished leaves (thus, nature denatured) turns the direction of the poem, so that the accumulation is negated and the poem begins afresh; this time, however, the accumulation is not prepared by the help of an intervening refrain. The final explanation, "J'en aime une autre qu'Isabelle la vague" (I love another than Isabelle the Vague), takes place before the final summing up, which is therefore determined only by form, certainly not by any cumulative optimism as in the first part.

"De la rose de marbre à la rose de fer" (From the Marble Rose to the Iron Rose) is again simple in structure like a child's poem. The seven roses, each placed in a long verse according to their different material (marble, glass, coal, etc) have accreted around them a series of appropriate descriptive phrases so that the accumulation in each line is self-contained, all the linguistic energy being absorbed by the initial element. Then all these elements, assured of eventual rebirth, are negated, their petals strewn on the rug like so many adjectival phrases dispersed, the whole series of descriptions reduced to the prime element. And this ultimate negation is the mysterious definition of the one who has undone all the preceding elements.

Elsewhere, a ten-line stanza of the same light tone as "Avec le cœur de chêne" and, like it, interesting mainly for its form, "Chant du ciel" (Sky Song), demonstrates the technique of advancing and receding elements, toward and away from the center. Each element (the sky, the waves, etc.)

speaks to the second element of its virtues, then the second speaks to a third until the poet at the center is addressed; he, of course, speaks only of his love. The other speakers, after speaking of her also, then withdraw, and he is left to speak of her alone. Here, all the weight of the preceding conversation is absorbed in the final exclamation, as the poet speaks either to himself or to us.

Typically, the denial of the substance of the poem and of its structure is brought about by the denial of speech itself when the speaking may refer by implication to the poem. Thus in "Vieille clameur" (Ancient Clamor), the concluding section, based on the repeated greeting "Salut de bon matin" (four times) is suddenly cut off by the next to the last line, "Mais hélas ne pourrons-nous dire encore" (But alas shall we never again be able to say), placed before the final repetition.

In "Passé le pont" (Past the Bridge), the entire structure, built upon the closing of the door and the plea for quiet, with its implied menace ("Taisez-vous. . . . Laissez-la dormir ou bien j'affirme que des abîmes se creuseront" (Be still. . . . Let it sleep or else I say that abysses will be dug), is challenged by a middle section in which speech or the act of speech just performed by the poet is canceled out. The end, which repeats the beginning, is placed in an ambiguous situation. Was the menace denied or just the plea?

In all these cases, the repetition underlines and stresses the structure as well as the theme of a love lost and haunting. The techniques of accumulation, deflection, reversal, denial, dispersion can all be seen as relating to that love, to those shadows, or seen alone, on the surface of the text itself, in their profundity and textural complexity.

## A Poetry of Shadows

*Les Ténèbres* contains some of the most complex surrealist poetry ever written. The twenty-four poems demonstrate a wide range of forms, from the several dense circular poems of ten or eleven lines in which the end joins on to the beginning, to far longer poems where the brief conclusion is

occasionally set apart from the main body of the poem in a formal echo to
the isolation felt within the poem itself. The length of the lines ranges from
a single word (for example, "Crie") to an uninterrupted flow of a hundred
words; there are prose poems with as many as six sentences included in the
space of one indentation, others with shorter and evenly spaced divisions
and of a repetitive form, while a few poems show an extremely various and
complex texture, where for instance among sixteen short lines there sudden-
ly appears a very long one, completely distinct in tone. Within these poems
of description, of statement, of lamentation, an extensive series of questions:
"Eh quoi?" (What then?), threats: "Mort à la voile blanche" (Death to the
white sail,) exclamations: "Quelle evasion!" (What an escape!), break up the
interior rhythm. Yet the latter may be balanced by an equally extensive series
of appositions whose links are assured, if not made explicit, so that the sur-
face jerkiness overlies a genuine continuity, in the language the poet ascribes
at times to the things surrounding him, as in these "Paroles des rochers" or
words of the rocks:

> L'infini profond douleur désir poésie amour révélation miracle
> révolution amour l'infini profond m'enveloppe de ténèbres
> bavardes

> (The profound infinite sorrow desire poetry love revelation
> miracle revolution love the profound infinite surrounds me
> with talkative shadows) .

The strength of the passage is such that the elements in apposition tend
to fuse with one another, without the daylight banality of connectives which
would, ironically, weaken the sense of enveloping shadows and the unmarked
interior cohesion they surround.

Now Desnos, like the baroque poet he partly is, chooses images of light
to play against dark, of flowering and fire to play against the depths. In
particular, the star, the crystal bottle, and the sea are paralleled by and op-
posed to coal, anemone, abyss within the imaginative focus of his writings,

which he considered to be the individual and visible parts of one long poem "elaborated from birth to death." These images and the works containing them are all closely linked, as around the central focus of a star various ideas spread partial illuminations. Now the star suggests to Desnos the starfish— that is the mermaid also, the captivating singer of sailor songs or Yvonne George—and thus the starfish of the "anti-poem" *La Place de l'étoile*, written in 1927 and revised in 1944, is at once connected with the sky and the sea: she reappears in Man Ray's film *L'Etoile de mer*, based on Desnos' poem or anti-poem. In the long poems "Sirène-Anémone" and "Siramour," the mermaid and the star are sisters and rivals, the star vies with coal too as a giver of equal light, thus the fire and the sea are joined, and opposed to the shadows, darkness, and ashes which are their doubles. Just so, desert and town, sea and sand, voyage and shipwreck, forest and road are seen as inseparable complementaries, each leading to the other, so that the notion of crossroads or conjunction remains primary in the imagination for the reader as for the poet. A theoretical and metaphoric basis for this reliance on opposites juxtaposed can be found in all the images of communicating vessels and conducting wires common to the theories of surrealism. The violence of the illumination depends often on the unexpectedness of the opposed elements, but in Desnos it depends rather on the repetitions of a small number of images in their interconnections.

Desnos makes a frequent and complex use of interpenetrations of images and of their mutual definition. In a typical poem of these years, the convergence of imagery is so marked as to make possible the suppression of one central image, all the while pointing implicitly to that image as the location of the original impulse for the poetic statement. If the image said to be suppressed in one poem appears frequently as the clearly predominant element of other texts, the initial perception of its centrality receives additional support.

Often within a particular poetic universe of great cohesiveness, constructed about a constantly recurring small number of images each of equal importance, a central poem can be found whose elements and their interrelations may serve as paradigms for all the other poems, whatever their date. Each poem of the given set may point in some way, explicitly or implicitly, to this particular key poem. Rather than discussing abstracted components of the poet's sensibility, style or his images, readers may choose the text which appears central, distinguish in that text the salient factors, explaining how they are marked as high points (set off from the others by the poet), and what other elements in the text justify or determine them. Then those stressed elements should be matched to those same elements stressed elsewhere in order to sketch a precise or post-text profile of the particular poetic imagination in question. Any poem and any series of poems can be read in both directions, so that an image may be justified by one following it, and vice versa. A text written before another can be retrospectively clarified by the later one; these parallel readings stress the continuity of a particular language, of the chain of obsessive imagery over the discontinuity of chronological points taken separately.

It is within *Les Ténèbres* that the most significant clues to Desnos' evolution are to be found. This collection contains twenty-four connected aspects of tenebral vision, corresponding, perhaps, to the hours of the night and day seen as the temporal space of the continuing surrealist dream, as in Breton's image of the communicating vessels. (*Les vases communicants*). The alternations of night / day, language / silence, faith / doubt, or love / loneliness often perceived in the other surrealist poets are arranged in more difficult patterns than is customary in the poetry of Tzara, Eluard, Péret, or even Breton. Sometimes apparent, and sometimes hidden within the poem, are various complicated and disturbing oppositions of involvement and separation between the poet and the poem, between the poet and the language or vision, between the poet and the reader. The overall force of the poems seems to deny the power of poetic language and the marvelous vision by the disintegration of elements within the poem, while the poet seems to pursue his adventure beyond the space of the poem, thus denying us any participation in it.

At least three possible interpretations can be given of this poetic attitude: first, that Desnos' experience necessarily bars any observer. This might be true, but no more so for him than for any of the other surrealists;

consequently, it would not be sufficient to explain the peculiar nature of his poetry. Second, that Desnos is here predicting, implicitly his final journey beyond the surrealist experience of the shadows to the more open poem of the day ("*poème du jour*") which he mentions in two of these texts. Finally, that these poems are a confirmation of Desnos' own statement that beyond all free poetry there is the free poet. This seems preferable to me: even if the experiments with language and with dream had proved to be endlessly rewarding, even if he had felt no constriction within their framework, Desnos would have chosen to move beyond them. Since he always maintained, and to a far greater extent than any of his companions, the absolute separation of every second from the next, it is probably his constant rejection, in principle and in fact, of all the experiments already undertaken which finally determines his evolution beyond the limits of the shadows. *The Night of Loveless Nights*, published three years later than *Les Ténèbres*, begins with an invocation of night (closely resembling Tzara's texts of darkness in *L'Antitête* called "Avant que la nuit"):

> Nuit putride et glaciale, épouvantable nuit
> Nuit du fantôme infirme et des plantes pourries,
> Incandescente nuit, flamme et feu dans les puits
> Ténèbres sans éclairs, mensonges et roueries.

(O, 904)

> Putrid and glacial night, terrifying night
> Night of the sick phantom and of rotted plants,
> Incandescent night, flames and fire in the wells,
> Shadows, without flashes, lies and knaveries.

It ends by another simple evocation calling for the overthrow even of the realm of poetic darkness just created: "Tais-toi, pose la plume / . . . / O Révolte! Quiet! put down your pen / . . . / O Revolt!" (O, 921) This whole realm of shadows is itself an exploration of the language and the goal of the poetic adventure, centered about the themes of love and dream, alternating with recurrent strains of loneliness and suffering, as well as more violent references to suicide, strangling, and murder. The poems of speech and poetic metamorphosis are countered by those of silence and despair, the images of the marvelous by those of bareness, negation, and destruction. Now, according to surrealist theory, this negation of language and love can be considered an exemplification of the necessary contraries and their resolution. For each element is always juxtaposed with its polar opposite, the resulting and marvelous union approximating, on the metaphysical level, a *point sublime*, and on the human level, poetry. In this light, such a collection represents, even at the point where it denies its own language, an unsurpassed creation of polarity and ambiguity.

## Day and Night

Even in the period of *Les Ténèbres*, Desnos writes a few poems of relative simplicity, and some of them read like exact poetic transcriptions of certain theoretical attitudes already discussed. In the poem entitled "Désespoir du soleil" (Despair of the Sun) which appears in a series directly after four titles alluding to day and night, "Le Suicidé de nuit," "Pour un rêve du jour," "Il fait nuit," and "Nuit d'ébène" (Night Suicide, For a Day Dream, It is Night, Ebony Night), the two poles of optimism and pessimism meet. However, the general tone seems to deny the despairing element, in keeping with the positive direction of surrealism.

> Quel bruit étrange glissait le long de la rampe d'escalier au bas
> de laquelle rêvait la pomme transparente.
> . . .
> L'escalier s'enfoncera-t-il toujours plus avant?
> montera-t-il toujours plus haut?
> Rêvons acceptons de rêver c'est le poème du jour qui commence.

(What strange noise was gliding along the banister at whose base
the transparent apple dreamed?

. . .

Will the staircase always sink lower?
will it always mount higher?
Let us dream be willing to dream it's the poem of day beginning.)

The theme is thus as simple as the implied dualities: a sphinx who leaves
the desert to investigate the mysterious sound is contrasted with a man to-
tally devoid of mystery, calmly cleaning the steps in a banal routine gesture.
The invocation of dream coincides oddly with the beginning of daytime real-
ity, and the central image of the staircase obviously suggests both upward
and downward motion, made explicit in the verbs "s'enfoncer" and "mont-
er." The entire mood is optimistic, with the accent falling on the question
of widened range: "L'escalier s'enfoncera-t-il . . . " and on the indirect but
definitely positive answer about the fresh beginning of the dream and of the
day. The smaller elements are also positive, such as the transparent apple (or
round banister knob)[5] at the bottom of the staircase; of course, in the sur-
realist universe, temptation is the greatest good, and the highest compliment
the poet can address to an object is to see it as crystalline. This poem is of a
simple clarity consonant with the subject.

As one would expect, however, it is not the poem of the day which
forms the center of this or any surrealist collection of texts. Although Breton
alludes, at the conclusion of Les Vases communicants, to the eventual pos-
sibility of carrying on the poetic or alchemical work in daylight, our atten-
tion is usually focused on the irrational and inexplicable. The image of the
communicating vessels of day and night or of reality and dream—an image
which we perceive as transparent because of Breton's many references to the
crystal and the diamantine clarity he desires in his life and work—is, like the
crystal itself, an image typical of the 1930 decade of surrealism. In the early
years of the movement, when obscurity was valued for its ambiguous power
to illumine, Desnos' favorite image of coal was perhaps more appropriate, as
he describes it in the passages from "Sirène-Anémone" already quoted, and

in the litanic and impressively monotonous central poem "Identité des images." As the mentor of his dreams and of his solitude, coal or the nocturnal fire it represents serves as the basic image for all the texts from this period. Since they can best be seen from his particular starting point, it is essential to study that image / source as it is simultaneously revealed and suppressed, in order to show the ambiguous character of a typical Desnos text, marked by multiple signals pointing only to an absence strongly felt.

A paradigmatic indicator of Desnos' poetic universe of 1926–27 and of the great series of testimonials to mystery and to the power of shadow, to which the titles *A la mystérieuse* and *Les Ténèbres* bear witness, is the central or key poem called "Identité des images," from the latter collection. As the title already indicates, the poet here refuses—as, in fact, he always does—to make traditional categorical separations between elements, real or imaginary. All the elements mentioned within this poem are equivalent to each other; they are also equivalent paths leading finally to the center of the labyrinth hidden inside the obvious fabric of the text.

In this poem, itself the center of the poems clustered about it, the central image, implicit but suppressed, the real underlying support for a series of other images and developments of thought, is that of the mermaid.

> Ma sirène est bleue comme les veines où elle nage
> Pour l'instant elle dort sur la nacre
>
> . . .
>
> Mais le ciel de ma sirène n'est pas un ciel ordinaire
> (*DA*. p. 97)

> (My mermaid is blue as the veins in which she swims
> For the moment she is asleep on mother-of-pearl
>
> . . .
>
> But my mermaid's sky isn't an ordinary sky)

As the heroine of Desnos' novels and of his poems, the mythical incarnation of the "mystérieuse" herself, and the sole permanent resident of *Les*

*Ténèbres*, the mermaid, who is also and simultaneously the star, Melusina, and the soror of the alchemists, serves both as guide and as temptress. Her presence is here so strongly felt that any specific mention, however trivial, of her noble and awful role is a metonymic indication of the whole series of forces with which she is associated; thus, the mention of a "belle nageuse" or a lovely swimmer is already, for the initiated, an incantation of the power of dream.

But without a preliminary understanding of this role and these forces, of the substitution or suppression of the central idea and its open acknowledgement by the reader, the poem feels hollow, its deliberate incantatory quality seems an exaggerated formal play, undertaken to no emotional end. Once the hidden center is exposed in its formal absence, the true identity of bottle and fragments—form a whole of which the single identity is finally apparent, as well as the identification of each image with every other. "Identité des images" (Identity of Images) then, stands out among the other poems as an enigma capable of resolution, as a clue to the lyric labyrinth, a clue which has at its own center another labyrinth, whose Minotaur is a mermaid. It begins with a desperate struggle and a waking of the swimmer, while the ubiquitous coal illuminates the scene with its pitiless and eternal fire:

> Je me bats avec fureur contre des animaux et des bouteilles
> Depuis peu de temps peut-être dix heures sont passées l'une après l'autre
> La belle nageuse qui avait peur du corail ce matin s'éveille
> Le corail couronné de houx frappe à sa porte
> Ah! encore le charbon toujours le charbon
> . . .
> Et je reste face à face avec le feu et je resterai la nuit durant à
> interroger le charbon aux ailes de ténèbres qui persiste à projeter
> sur mon chemin monotone l'ombre de ses fumées et le reflet terrible
> de ses braises
> Charbon sonore charbon impitoyable charbon
>
> (Furiously I fight with animals and bottles

In a short space of time perhaps ten hours have passed one after the other
The lovely swimmer who feared the coral this morning awakes
The coral crowned with holly knocks at her door
Ah, the coal again always the coal

. . .

And I remain face to face with the fire and I shall remain the night
long questioning the coal with shadow wings which persists in casting
over my monotonous path the shade of its smoke and the terrible
reflection of its embers
Coal resounding coal merciless coal)

The world of fire and shadow, the flickering opposite of the static and
seemingly certain daytime world, does not require or even permit the fixed
categorical relations essential to the formal and descriptive balance of "nor-
mal" linguistic construction. In the latter, for example, following the initial
fight with "animals" in the first line, one would have expected a general
balancing expression such as "men" or "things" or "myths." But here both
a linguistic and a thematic emphasis are placed on the unbalancing of the
terms, as in this juxtaposition of the animate with the inanimate.

Furthermore, in this poem, the specific and banal term "bottles" might
seem only realistic to the reader unaware of the profusion of crystalline im-
ages in this period, of the crystal mountains and glass corridors in the essays
of Tristan Tzara, of Breton's salt cubes in his "éloge du crystal" (praise of
the crystal), of Benjamin Péret's images of fountains and windows, of the
mirrors of Aragon and Eluard. When this bottle shatters into glass splinters,
these "tessons" haunting all the early work of Desnos, the darkest moments
of consciousness are at hand, that the disintegration of the brilliant dream is
an imminent reality. When, on the other hand, as in some of Desnos's work,
it contains a message, we may read that as the definite indication of the pos-
sible link between the world of adventure and the world of the poet's work.

The legendary marvelous power of the mermaid who enchants is here
altered in direction. The swimmer, beautiful as ever but less powerful, is
herself afraid: neither she nor the poet have any control over their sleep,

their dream, or their waking life. And so, the seduction is double. As the mermaid seduces the poet, albeit in the guise of a simple swimmer, she is in turn seduced by the image of coal which casts light upon her discarded clothing and is seen, retrospectively, to have furnished the luxurious elements for the bed where she reposes. The latter is made of lace and also of feathers or down, these latter images only hinted at by the actual term birds, "oiseaux," The coral-red protruding beak of the coal is the visual support for the image of the bird with its black crepe wings: as the substance of the coal burns away, the charred and paper-thin shell which remains flutters in the hot air. The tissue suggested, crepe-like, is seen as the possible determination of the lace on the bed, the latter now doubly connected to the image of the bird and, by extension, to its flight. Crepe and lace, feathers, beak, and wings, nighttime repose and fire, the red of coral and of burning coal, in glaring contrast to the black of mourning—all these interconnections tie the fire to the dream. The elements of water ("la belle nageuse") and fire ("charbon sonore") meet in a rarefied atmosphere of sonority and silence, hope and threat: it is this "bec de corail" and these mourning wings of black crepe which predetermine, in the context of the poem, the mermaid's fear.

After this preliminary warning of the risk incurred in dream, the poet elaborates on the images of mourning ("enterrements divergents"), the signs of death even in the midst of splendor ("marque de son empreinte . . . des robes de satin blanc")—the latter image of luxury corresponding to the lace and feathers of the bed—and of shipwreck, where the coal takes upon itself the traditional role of the mermaid, enchanting the sailors whose ships will never return.

This development of imagery should be compared with two other passages on shipwreck which are as stationary in form as the trapped vessels. In the first example, from *Liberty or Love!*, static spectacle and certain knowledge ("je sais," "je connais") replace action; in the second, memory and uncertainty interrupt a statement which technically affirms, in its lengthened form and retarded rhythm, its own non-moving character.

Ebony ship departed for the North Pole, now death appears in
the form of a glacial bay of circular form, without penguins,
without seals, without bears. I know the agony of a ship caught
in the ice-floes, I recognize the cold death rattle, the pharaoh's
death met by Arctic and Antarctic explorers. . . . ( LA, 49)

In the second passage, from the poem "Dans bien longtemps," the hulk
of the ship lends its own mystery to the setting:

The carcass of the shipwrecked vessel which you know—do you
remember that night of storm and embraces? Was it a shipwrecked
vessel or a woman's delicate hat tossed along by the wind in the
spring rain? Was in the same place. (DP, 144))

Elsewhere the poet says plainly that he longs for this shipwreck, that it
has been the object of all his surrealist adventure, hidden within the poem's
more apparent language. Here menace and adoration are identified, forming
the parallel leitmotifs of the voyage. The sailor trapped and consciously im-
mobile is one in the poetic imagination with the dreamer as he wakes from
an unmoving position, physically still in spite of his nocturnal adventures
now evaporated. They are seen to have led nowhere, except back once more
to the fireplace beside which he dreams.

For a poet so devoted to mental adventure as Desnos, the ambivalence
of the line in "Identity of Images," about the coal stoked in the fireplace,
waiting, and listening, is both ironic and moving:

Maintenant tapi dans la cheminée il guettait le réveil de l'écume
et le chant des bouilloires

(Now crouched in the fireplace it awaited the waking of foam
and the song of kettles)

For here, in the rhythm of elation and deception characteristic of Desnos, the coal is suddenly placed in a humble position of discrete watchfulness—no longer guide, genius, tyrant, but spy—as it hides, watches, awaits the sad contrast of the waking sea foam, an image of freedom, with the kettle it causes to sing, pathetic image of a sedentary existence of comfort at the close of adventure. And yet the coal keeps within itself the memory of the mermaid's song, sufficiently potent to override the banal singing of a teakettle. Here the dominating image of the seductive mermaid, suppressed as it is in the written texts, makes itself known through the echo of song.

The explicit image of the sleeping swimmer replaces the implicit image of the mermaid as the poet's ideal companion for his dream; she eventually abandons the poet to his lonely vigil by the fire whose double spectacle of flickering illumination and fearful blackness, of terrible brightness (thus the fear of coral expressed by the mermaid) and equally terrible shadows (its songs of darkness, the shadow of its smoke), absorbs within it the singing of the mermaid together with her own pitiless nature. The intricate transferrals and shiftings of imagery reflect the flickering form of the light here illuminating the dream.

This poem in its desperate and understated loneliness prefigures the final and complete desertion of the poet by the mermaid, described most vividly in the long poem about the mermaid and the anenome: "Sirène-Anémone," where her presence is plainly announced in the title. This central preoccupation appears as clearly in the tone of the text, written in the year of the poet's actual separation from surrealism, as in any of his invocations to shipwreck. The farewell here is at once a farewell to the guiding image of his work, and to a particular form of that work over which the mermaid as muse presided, explicitly or implicitly. Here the former understatement gives way to open regret, as the hidden source becomes apparent at the very moment of departure.

Adieu déjà parmi les heures de porcelaine
Regardez le jour noircit au feu qui s'allume dans l'âtre

Adieu dans la boue noire des gares
Dans les empreintes des mains sur les murs
. . .
Adieu dans le claquement des voiles
Adieu dans le bruit monotone des moteurs
Adieu ô papillons écrasés dans les portes
. . .
Tandis qu'au large avec de grands gestes virils
La sirène chantant vers un ciel de carbone
Au milieu des récifs éventreurs de barils
Au cœur des tourbillons fait surgir l'anémone.

(O, 572-4)


(Farewell already among the porcelain hours
See how the day darkens at the fire lit in the hearth

Farewell in the black mud of stations
In the imprints of hands on the walls
. . .
Farewell in the snapping of sails
Farewell in the monotone roar of motors
Farewell butterflies crushed in the doors
. . .
While on the deep with great virile gestures
The mermaid departs singing toward a carbon sky
Who at the center of the murderous reefs
In the heart of whirlwinds makes the anemone flower.)


The mark first made by the coal of death on the majestic white
ball dresses is made now by human hands on simple walls. All the
once noble images of bird flight and sailing and shipwreck are trans-
formed now into the more banal and less legendary snapping of sails
or the monotonous roar of motorboats. No longer is the door of

beauty decorated with a wreath; rather the most delicate and frag-
ile insect is crushed in the closing door. The clothing is no longer
illuminated by the firelight or placed in implicit correspondence with
the luxurious covering of a bed; it is only soiled by daily and trivial
cares. And the poet who once dreamed of adventure by the fireside
is now lost with his fellow poets in a subterranean labyrinth.

But the fire itself, taking its source in the depths of the earth like the
poem drawing its strength from its hidden center, sings the way toward a
sinister fall which is now adventure enough.

> Maîtresse généreuse de la lumière de l'or et de la chute
> . . .
> Maîtresse sinistre et bienfaisante de la chute éternelle
>
> (O, 572)

> (Generous mistress of light of gold and of the fall
> . . .
> Sinister and benevolent mistress of the eternal fall)

At last the coral of fire, the anemone of light, and the mermaid of po-
etry merge in a final luminous identification of all the guiding images of the
unified and difficult universe of Desnos. As the mermaid swims out to sea,
beyond the reach of the poet's voice or vision, as the living images in their
turn depart or are destroyed, all the texts converge in this integral, central,
and ultimately tragic perception.

Unlike the preceding collection, *A la mystérieuse*, where the dreams in-
cluded the presence, however illusory, of a woman—'J'ai tant rêvé de toi,"
(I Have So Often Dreamed of You) "Dans la nuit il y a toi," (In the Night
You Are There)—in *Les Ténèbres*, the dreams of both the waking and the
sleeping hours of night seem to be associated with the poet's inevitable soli-
tude, with his "monotonous path" along which he moves alone. He was the
mermaid's companion neither in the water, for him the supreme image of
adventure, nor in her dream, which he cannot make his. At the conclusion

of the poem "Il fait nuit" (It Is Night), the poet goes to sleep beside the extinguished lamp, having accepted his solitude from the beginning, as if it were the necessary prior condition for the advent of the marvelous dream. As in the "Journal of an Apparition," the atmosphere of love is fated to be tragic in its isolation.[8]

> Tu t'en iras quand tu voudras
> Le lit se ferme . . .
>
> (You will go away when you wish to
> The bed closes up . . . )

All these poems having the bed of the dreamer for their scene are illuminated, from another perspective, by the poem "La Chambre close," included in *Destinée arbitraire*. In particular, "L'Identité des images" is reflected in it like a mirror image so that many of the basic elements are reversed. In place of the firelight flickering over the clothes by the bed, as in the nocturnal scene of the poem previously discussed, the sunlight comes here to play on the bedclothes and the pillow, while a dress on the chair alongside the bed is agitated "by the breath of a strange breeze." The single hair said to be trembling on the sheet folded back seems, in the context of this accentuated emptiness, the discarded dress, and the mysterious draft, less absurd than touching, a possible indication of the memory of past love, or then a mocking of present beauty soon to be reduced. They are the substitutes for the beloved who should be resting there, the counterpart of the mermaid. The feeling of desertion is stressed by the desolate ticking of a clock, "about to stop." The room, closed and empty, "quite empty," is a convincing scene of life almost arrested, of diminished action until the arrival of a humming-bird, whose wings beat feverishly and in vivid colors on the pillow, like a lively corresponding image to contrast with the very slight motion of the single hair: this technique of doubling by contraries is typical of the surreal-ists in general, and of Desnos in particular. But in a characteristic evolution from drama to tragedy, the poet imagines the bird striking its head against its double in the mirror where the silver is flaking off, dying in a series of one-word lines, so that in the empty room the sun may move finally about the corpse and reflect itself in the blood on the pillow: (*DA*, 126) Yet from the static if remarkable reflection of the window in the blood comes an assurance of renewal, for the image of openness gives a new breathing space to the room. The humming-bird rises once more like a phoenix, resurrected this time from the red color of blood by analogy with fire:

> Pour un chant identique, pour un vol égal,
> Paré des mêmes couleurs,
> Colibri du soir, colibri du matin,
> Tu renaîtras.
> Et dans la chambre vide, l'horloge à nouveau chantera
> Colibri, colibri,
> Colibri du soir, colibri du matin
>
> (*DA*, p. 126)

> (For an identical song, an equal flight,
> Bedecked with the same colors,
> Humming-bird of evening, humming-bird of morn,
> You will be reborn.
> And in the empty room, the clock will sound once more
> Humming-bird, humming-bird,
> Humming-bird of evening, humming-bird of morn.)

Thus the expression "colibri" leads to the refrain of the same moving and repetitive sort as the "charbon" in the first poem, and summons—as did the image of coal in the other poem—the images of wing and flight, and the presence of song simultaneous with the renascence of love. In the second section of the long tripartite poem, the bird is seen flying toward the coast, and then lost at sea, setting the scene once more for sailors and for figureheads, for the event taking place in the "country of mermaids and typhoons, / in the country of thunderclaps" (*DA*, p. 127).

"All this takes place where I wish it to," claims the poet, and as in his novels and his poems, the marvelous convergence prevails finally over the doubt: "Oh, these encounters . . . Long live life!"(*DA*, p. 128) We are reminded of the poems which end by questioning their own vision, of the loneliness echoing throughout the early writing of Desnos —but in the second part of this poem, after the doubt as to the renascence of the phoenix of love, the exclamation is undeniably vital and positive:

> Vive la vie!
> (Long live life!)

Yet from the tree aflame, no phoenix rises. Rather, death is inscribed in capital letters, hanging from the hair of the woman addressed and linked to her glances, while images of insult, abyss, and subterranean fear conclude the poem. Furthermore, the reader may see the knife's cutting as implicit in the poet's own tongue ("Ma langue dans ma bouche / My tongue in my mouth") so that even at the source of poetry there lies the cruelty of the drama.

The final line of the poem denies explicitly the possibility of love, of encounter and renewal, of imagination and of future: we are familiar with the desperate conclusions of Desnos and each contributes to the intensity of all:

> Je sais qu'il n'est jamais plus temps.
>
> (*DA*, p. 429)

> (I know there's never time any more.)

So the three acts of the poem close on negation, as if this text were itself the dark double of that former "Identité des image," the mirror whose surface reflects—imperfectly, for the mirroring capacity is flaking away—not just that poem but all the others included in it.

In the subtle and tragic poem whose title "Paroles des rochers" (Words of the Rocks) is a further indication of Desnos' fascination with language, the solitude of the poet dreaming is intensified. It begins in apparent luxury, both qualitative (taxis, sill, mother-of-pearl, diamonds) and quantitative (at every window a mass of hair), and an abundance of trivial social communication to match: "A bientôt!" "A bientôt!" "A bientôt!" (See you soon!). But then, the all-inclusive landscape of night: "Une nuit de tous les littorals et de toutes les forêts / Une nuit de tout amour et de toute éternité" (A night of all the littorals and all the forests / A night of all love and all eternity) suddenly draws back to reveal catastrophe, loneliness, a desperate emptiness, and death. That the night predicted should be without exterior illumination of any kind—"A bientôt une nuit des nuits sans lune et sans étoile" / Soon a night of moonless and starless nights)—might have seemed positive, since it could have created a more propitious background for the more profound mental illumination of dream; but it turns out to be only a darkness filled with artificial light and death, "une nuit de lustre et de funérailles," where the poet is alone amid the debris of all the former signs of value:

> Une vitre se fend à la fenêtre guettée
> Une étoffe claque sur la campagne tragique
> Tu seras seul
> Parmi les débris de nacre et les diamants carbonizes
> Les perles mortes

> (A pane breaks at the watched window
> A cloth clacks over the tragic field
> You will be alone
> Among the pieces of mother-of-pearl and the carbonized diamonds
> The dead pearls)

The use of the present and future tenses intensifies the loneliness: the windowpane which shatters as it is watched, and the rag which flaps desolate in the wind of the "tragic countryside" prefigure the future separations and unhappiness. However, the presence of the poet even the action changes to the past, as if it were putting itself at a distance from his approach and removing itself as an object of his gaze. Immediately after this, the poem switches to an uncertain future, prefaced by the sign of doubt: "Seules peut-être les chevelures ne fuiront pas / T'obéiront" (Only the manes of hair will perhaps not flee from you / Will obey you), once more to a tragic, lonely past: "Chevelures longues des femmes qui m'aimèrent / Et que je n'aimai pas" (Long hair of women who loved me / And whom I did not love) and then to a present of absolute absence, darkness, and self-doubt. At this point the staircase, once the path toward surrealist undertakings, is transformed into the place of misfortune; and the sea, usually the privileged place for heroic adventure, now abandons even the cork of the bottle, the only remnant of the poet's chosen image of surrealist vision. This poem is at the opposite pole from the poem ruled by the mermaid, obeying only an inner tragic structure:

> Un escalier se déroule sous mes pas et la nuit et le jour ne révèlent à mon destin que ténèbres et échecs
> L'immense colonne de marbre le doute soutient seule le ciel sur ma tête
> Les bouteilles vidées dont j'écrase le verre en tessons éclatants
> Le parfum du liège abandonné par la mer . . .

> (A staircase winds under my feet and night and day reveal to my fortune only shadows and failure
> Doubt alone an immense marble column sustains the sky above my head
> The empty bottles whose glass I shatter to shining bits
> The smell of cork abandoned by the sea . . . )

The debris of mother-of-pearl further decomposes into a dull powdery substance, the infinite hope which Desnos had placed in the action of dream and in the world of shadows splinters like the windowpanes and the bottles, images of a crystalline faith deceived:

> Les infinis éternels se brisent en tessons ô chevelure!

> (Eternal infinites shatter to glass splinters o mane of hair!)

And in the final lines, as the night is banished from the present completely, and exiled either to the past or to the future, it is suddenly deprived not only of the images of light and luxury but even of those which show a potentiality destroyed:

> C'était ce sera une nuit des nuits sans lune ni perle
> Sans même de bouteilles brisées.

> (It was it will be a night of nights without moon or pearl
> Without even broken bottles.)

Poetic momentum comes to a halt. Now the poet's encounters have apparently no privileged place, his adventures have no apparent importance.


## Disposession and Deflection

Within the sleeping state, which Desnos regards as a part of surrealist research, like a scientific experiment: "Je conte et décris le sommeil / Je recueille les flacons de la nuit et je les range sur une étagère" (I count and describe sleep / I gather the flasks of night and arrange them on a shelf), adventures are to be pushed to their extreme limit, a ground for further ambiguity. His most significant observation on this point is at once a prideful statement of poetic risk, and a lament of poetic impotence:

> Le naufrage s'accentue sous la paupière.

> (Shipwreck is stressed under closed eyelids.)

One might imagine the poet always present in his adventures, participating entirely in whatever drama of metamorphosis they provoke. Parallel, however, to the personal separations occasioned by sleep or imagining is the distance between the adventures dreamed of by the poet and the poet's own "monotonous" path, which is only the shadow of the dream state. He is privileged to enter the world of dream and absolute shadow ("les ténèbres absolues"), but never to possess that world.

In a similar fashion, much of the action is deflected out beyond the poem, out of the reach of the poet as well as that of the reader. The longest and most complex poem of the collection, about the flower of love and the migrating horses ("De la fleur d'amour et des chevaux migrateurs"), a poem already analyzed, contrasts a splendid and flourishing chrysanthemum without spot or weakness to the yellowed and rotting fern of the poet's heart, to the stagnant waters and swamps which surround it, and to the other flowers losing their petals which are future predictions for the fate of even the most splendid flower.

Going beyond, in a formal and literally spatial *dépassement* of all the other elements, the final image of migrating horses, which has recurred several times and then is repeated in four lines of unadorned and rapid succession at the end ("les chevaux migrateurs, les chevaux migrateurs," etc.), deflects attention away from the simple descriptions within the poem, forcing the reader's gaze toward a place beyond the specific and limited formal boundaries. For these lines dominate all the preceding ones, in which they were predicted by fragmentary allusions. The initial pathos, the action developing gradually to the lyric summit where all the images of ripeness and loss, sharpness and softness contrast and mingle, all of this is swept away by the violence of the conclusion and the insistence on immediate departure. The verbal and visual subtleties of the color yellow played against the icy white of the ground, the hints of death juxtaposed with a natural luxury, the promise sensed in the sky and the open doors, is then cut off. This series of oppositions and parallel statements is finally reduced to the immobility of a flower, which is then in turn left behind when the attention is finally drawn to the road and the "real" adventure:

Je parle en vain de la fleur mais de moi

. . .

Le ciel n'est pas si clos

. . .

C'est de la fleur immobile que je parle et non des ports de l'aventure et de
la solitude

. . .

Et le givre craquant les fruits mûrs les fleurs effeuillées l'eau croupissante
le terrain mou des marécages qui se modèlent lentement
Voient passer les chevaux migrateurs

Les chevaux migrateurs
Les chevaux migrateurs
Les chevaux migrateurs
Les chevaux migrateurs.

(I speak in vain of the flower but of myself

The sky's not so closed

. . .

It's of the immobile flower that I speak and not of the ports of adventure
and solitude

And the frost splitting open the ripe fruits the depetaled flowers the
stagnant water the spongy land of marshes slowly forming
See the migrating horses passing

The migrating horses
The migrating horses
The migrating horses
The migrating horses.)

An especially oblique poem of the same final elusiveness, "Avec le cœur
de chêne," also already discussed, has as its apparent subject a lady called
"Isabelle the Vague," whose name is repeated in each refrain with traditional

accumulation of emphasis. Yet in the center of the poem Isabelle is suddenly described as unimportant for the poet, as if her vagueness were in fact a reflection of his genuine attitude toward her, of which the formal framework was a betrayal. She is, he says, only an image of dream; now one would have thought that alone sufficient to guarantee her permanent merit, considering the usual surrealist evaluation of dream and of the imaginative adventure. But here, on the contrary, this image of dream is scorned, in favor of the world beyond the dream. The poet claims that whatever approach Isabelle the Vague might make—whether to speak to him, kiss him, strip herself naked before him, kill him, walk on him, or die at his feet—will make no difference to him in reality:

> Car j'en aime une autre plus touchante qu'Isabelle la vague.
> Avec le cœur du chêne et l'écorce du bouleau, avec le ciel, avec les
> océans, avec les pantoufles.

> (For I love another more touching than Isabelle the vague.
> With oaken heart and birchbark, with the sky, with oceans, with slippers.)

All the attributes of the poem which have been successively repeated in a form typical of much surrealist love poetry are suddenly moved out of the poem to the space of the "real," as the poet's other sentiment is acknowledged; the poem itself counts no longer, nor does its heroine, nor does the dream of which she is nothing else but the embodiment.

Anyone who is already convinced, apart from the evidence of these particular texts, that Desnos was at this point disillusioned with the dream experiments is likely to interpret certain passages as indications of Desnos' gradual loss of interest in this period of the surrealist adventure. On the other hand, these passages might be interpreted as positive suggestions about the mingling of dream with reality, in a surrealising world. And the case becomes not less complicated, but more so, as one reads the work of Desnos more closely.

For instance, at the end of the title poem "Ténèbres! O Ténèbres!" there is a specific image or group of images seemingly referring to the marvelous possibilities of the dream—" ... un homard de lentille microscopique évoluant dans un ciel sans nuage ne rencontrera-t-il jamais une comète ni un corbeau?" (will a lobster of microscopic lens evolving in a cloudless sky never meet a comet or a crow?). Now that image is likely to add its own weight to another poem, whose title, "En sursaut" (With a Start), is more indicative of a ragtime awakening then of a nighttime invocation such as "Ténèbres! O Ténèbres!" The opening line of this second poem reads, "'Sur la route en revenant des sommets rencontré par les corbeaux et les châtaignes ... " (On the road returning from the summits met by crows and chestnuts): we do not know if the poet is here returning from the heights of dream with the hope of going there again, or if it is considered a unique venture. The poem then acknowledges the presence of disaster ("Le désastre enfin le désastre annoncé"), admitting to an ignorance of the particulars of his dream and of their significance, and to a doubt of his own success as a wanderer:

> Mais où sont partis les arbres solitaires du theatre?
> Je ne sais où je vais j'ai des feuilles dans les mains j'ai des feuilles
> dans la bouche

> (But where have they gone those solitary trees of the theatre
> I don't know where I'm going I have leaves in my hands I have
> leaves in my mouth

Here Desnos seems to value the shadows above the heat and brightness, as one would expect of him at this period, but that appearance may be as hard to fathom as the night with neither moon nor pearl. Was that darkness precious, or was its value illusory, empty as the bottles seem to become at the poet's approach? Are the leaves which remain from the spectacle, preventing him from action and from speech, simply disordered remnants akin to the debris and the *tessons*, or are they natural reminders, valuable within the system of recalls and echoes, of the green branches, the sycamores, the willows, oaks, and birches in at least five other poems of this collection as well as the solitary trees of this poem? Do all the trees of dream finally turn into the inconsequential images of themselves as the mother-of-pearl is finally transformed into just another dust? And, still within this one short poem, the poet says that he has never spoken of his "rêve de paille." In what sense can the "ténèbres précieuses" or a "fleuve d'or et de flame" conceivably be compared to the aridity and brittleness of a dream of straw? Are all the images finally doomed as in the withered objects like the faded fans ("les éventails flétris"), the things grown stale? Or was that particular vision, of which he cannot speak, opposed to his usual visions of growing, if solitary, trees?

In this case, at least the living spectacle, even in its fragmentation, leaves the poet with at least some matter for speech, whether the speech be comprehensible or not. Only the remnants of the dream crowd other language out of the mouth, and as in the poem of Isabelle, the vagueness of dream may be finally rejected for the world of the present.

In another instance, he entitles a poem "Passé le pont" (Past the Bridge), a title which forces us to acknowledge that, in a formal sense, the poem has gone past a boundary we knew nothing about, that the spectacle has changed its location before we were even conscious of the framing effect. Furthermore, since the text commences with a door closing, any reader familiar with all the surrealist images of doors left swinging and vessels communicating with each other will feel especially shut out from the text. The feeling is intensified by the poet's sudden demand for our silence to equal his own: "Taisez-vous, ah taisez-vous," threatening natural catastrophes and personal schisms unless his demands are met.

Subsequently, he refuses to us and to himself even the certainty of what he has said, when in a passage already quoted, he manifests a self-doubt touching on language and going past it, to the possibility of believing as of expressing:

> Je n'ai pas dit cela
> Je n'ai rien dit
> Qu'ai-je dit?

ESSENTIAL POEMS AND WRITINGS OF ROBERT DESNOS

(I didn't say that
I didn't say anything
What did I say?)

These self-critical elements are more frequent in Desnos than in any other surrealist of his time or after. It might be tempting to speculate that they reflect a repressed scepticism as to the surrealist adventure, as to his part in it, and so on, or his innate preference for other sorts of poetry already mentioned. In any case they give to all his early writing, poetry and prose, a complex and ambiguous texture that coincides with the equally ambiguous texture of fragmentary dream material, and its related images.

In the strange poem concerning time which is entitled "Dans bien long-temps" (For a Long Time Since), an image of a woman's transparent presence, appropriate to all the other crystalline images of surrealism and the preceding ones of Dada poetry makes a sharp contrast with a juxtaposed lament on the simultaneous aging of the poet's own body and of the universe. Desnos then breaks the sentimental flow of the poem by a sarcastic attack on the banal character of his own poetic language: "N'aimez-vous pas ce lieu commun? laissez-moi laissez-moi c'est si rare cette ironique satisfaction" (Don't you like this commonplace? leave me alone leave me alone, this ironic satisfaction is so rare). For the reader familiar with Desnos, there is a double irony, since the case is not rare at all. And, to such a reader, the illusory waters and the shipwrecked vessel are in no way happened upon at random, since ships and shipwreck and the associated images of mermaids and deserts pervade all the work of Desnos, and especially the novel *La Liberté ou l'amour!*, which appeared in the same year as these poems.

So that the passage can be read as another instance of self-doubt. The ideal and mysterious image of the wrecked vessel, which was once the agent of adventure, with all its suggestions of adventure condemned and its aura of nostalgia for the faith and passion of the days of adventure is no more in reality than an everyday object. The non-literary world of the present becomes the "real" opposite of the illusory passion, and of the purely literary images allied with it.

The way out from all the irony and doubt of language and of dreaming might have been the heroine of the dream. But the central poem, "Ténèbres! O ténèbres!" where the poet calls upon his friends to be silent with him before the great abyss of shadows ("devant les grands abîmes") and where he states with pride that they have been the first to know their white sheets (both the abyss and the sheets being apparent eulogies of the dream), ends with an invocation of woman as a broken bottle, her beauty only parasitic, always absorbing more than it offers, and herself bringing nothing to the poet or the dream: "Tes yeux tes yeux si beaux sont les voraces de l'obscurité du silence et de l'oubli." (Your eyes your beautiful eyes are hungry for darkness silence and forgetfulness.) She seems to desire not language but silence, not dream or the memory of the dream but the complete denial of the past. Either she deserts the poet at the moment of the dream: "Tu t'en iras" (You will go away) or she refuses to mediate between its experience (seen as illusory, like the water where the shipwreck takes place) and the daytime reality. The latter exists, and really exists, outside the closed doors and on the return road from the summits. She herself is perhaps an illusion—certainly she cannot be known.

The last poem of the collection is an extraordinary and mysterious portrait written in an intensely lyric prose, combining a strong sense of desolation with a sense just as strong of exaltation and even sublimation: Desnos creates a formal atmosphere of a complexity fitting to the complexities of concept it must embody. "De la rose de marbre à la rose de fer" is a series of separate elaborations on the rose as a traditional image of feminine beauty, the elements of the series then linked in one long sentence affirming their endless future regeneration and the negative splendor of their present destruction for the glorification of the woman on whose rug they lie scattered, by the same process as the pulverization of the preceding poems.

The mystery and importance of the possessor of the rug are amplified by the previous multiplication in quantity and species of the roses to be sacrificed and then by the restatement of the whole catalogue which is destroyed for her benefit; yet the fact that she is also herself a woman and therefore present by implication in their sacrifice is one more inversion to belie the apparent simplicity of the construction: "Qui es-tu? toi qui écrases sous tes pieds nus les débris fugitifs de la rose de marbre de la rose de verre de la rose de charbon de la rose de papier buvard de la rose de nuages de la rose de bois de la rose de fer." (Who are you? you who crush under your bare feet the fugitive debris of the marble rose the glass rose the coal rose the blotting paper rose the cloud rose the wood rose the iron rose.) The entire poem, and perhaps the entire collection of poems, has been written for her, and still she is not known to the poet. The fact that we know the name of the woman for whom these poems were written does not in the slightest alter, for us or for the poet, the sense of this final question. The absence of knowledge is felt as a more general absence in what might have been, or seemed to be, a poem of presence.

In the surrealist universe, the essential value of the perception is grasped instantly or not at all. Surrealism always emphasizes the moment in its constant novelty rather than traditional continuities and temporal developments. "Toujours pour la première fois" (Always for the first time), said Breton. Differing perceptions are linked to each other by the strength of a connecting wire, or a *fil conducteur*, as are distant elements of experience or imagination, but again these links do not imply any organic, logical, or chronological enchaining. Metamorphosis takes place chiefly within the observer's eye, and it is always rapid. Since instantaneous observation replaces structured unfolding, the most formal architectural framework of the sentence or the poem holds the perceptions together, and controls their transmission.

The overriding interest in communication, from the word play early poems through the late and formally-structured ones, is concretized in the great poem called "La Voix de Robert Desnos/The Voice of Robert Desnos," which begins with the poet summoning the world authoritatively and surely—powerful over tornadoes, tempests, storms, cyclones, tidal waves, earthquakes as well as over the more humble elements of the universe:

J'appelle à moi la fumée des volcans et celle des cigarettes

(I summon volcano smoke and that of cigarettes)

and ends with the uselessness of the summons in the face of love, despite the power of the summons on everything and everyone else: pilots, builders, architects, and criminals—even on the body itself. The final perception of impotence in the realm of love thus works a retrospective destruction on the rest of the poem and, through it, on the entirety of the poet's language:

> celle que j'aime ne m'écoute pas
> celle que j'aime ne m'entend pas
> celle que j'aime ne me répond pas.

> (the one I love does not listen to me
> the one I love does not hear me
> the one I love does not answer me.)

So, from a celebration of the poet's cosmic strength, this poem moves to an absolute denial of that strength in the one instance which counts; the closing triplet is a tragic testimony to silence and emptiness in the place of language and in the moment of love.

For the Desnos of these poems, as it is already evident, the idea of affection seems to be incompatible with that of adventure: "Il n'est plus temps il n'est plus temps d'aimer vous qui passez sur la route" (It is no longer time it is no longer time to love you who pass by on the road). The poet's language is based either on love or on dream, inspirations which are mutually exclusive, or appear to be. Within the world of the poems, the love is of uncertain duration, its object is always distant and unknown in nature, and so the love carrier with it certain loneliness and deception. The dream negates the possibility of knowledge and of action, and even of speech. At least within this world, therefore, the language will cease, as the poet's enthusiasm for a certain kind of adventure subsides.

"Pour un rêve du jour" (For a dream of day) is the ironic opposite of the other poem of daybreak, "le poème du jour qui commence" (the poem of day beginning). Here, the possibility of linguistic metamorphosis is initially announced and then abruptly canceled out by the reiteration of the word *silence*:

> Un cygne se couche sur l'herbe voici le poème des métamorphoses.
> Le cygne qui devient boîte d'allumettes et le phosphore en guise de
> cravate. Triste fin Métamorphose du silence en silence . . .

> (A swan lies down on the grass here is the poem of metamorphosis.
> The swan which becomes a matchbox and the phosphorus
> disguised as a tie. Sad end Metamorphosis of silence into
> silence . . . )

As the swan is a nostalgic reminder and inheritor of symbolist imagery—like the "cygne" of Mallarmé so importantly coincident in sound with the sign or "signe," the serious bearer of all the nobility of past poetry and the guarantee of possible change—its end in silence spells the doom of traditional poetic language, and of surrealist adventure as such, based on the surrealist hope in metamorphosis. The question at the end of this poem, "qui qui qui et qui?" (who who who and who?) has no answer, and could have none. The last admonition of the poet is in part the playful reminder of the traditional "carpe diem" juxtaposed with the genuine lesson expounded by the poet in the present. And it is also in part a sarcastic statement of the necessary replacement of the faith once founded in the adventures of language and of love by the creation of an artificial situation, the only possible source of permanence: from the time of Pierre Ronsard, French poetry has taken the rose as the symbol of life, love, and being, so that its appearance in a poem signals a whole history of poetic and practical faith in the ephemeral moment: "Cueille cueille la rose et ne t'occupe pas de ton destin cueille cueille la rose et la feuille de palmier et relève de paupières de la jeune fille pour qu'elle te regarde ETERNELLEMENT." (Pluck pluck the rose and don't worry about your fate pluck pluck the rose and the palm leaf and lift the eyelids of the girl so she will gaze at you ETERNALLY.)

Perhaps Desnos realized from the beginning that the essential condition for overcoming the limits of time and the monotony of the real in the timelessness of adventure is the serious and repeated acknowledgement of genuine separation, and the acceptance of an artifice, replacing the artifice of language.In one of the poems which ends by transcending poetry in an action removed beyond the formal place of the poem, Desnos deliberately retreats into an interior distance and offers a typically ambiguous warning, either to us or to himself:

> Je pense à très loin au plus profond de moi
> Les temps abolis sont pareils aux ongles brisés sur les portes closes . . .

> (I think of distance in my inner depths
> Abolished instants are like fingernails broken on closed doors. . . . )

It all depends on which side of the doors the adventure takes place. If the meditation and the dream provide sufficient and lasting vision, then the closed doors are a simple proof that the outsiders to surrealism are limited forever to their own framework of seasons and perceptions and actions. But if they are parallel in significance to the return road from the summits, then perhaps the voyage which Desnos eventually makes from the "closed" language of surrealism to that of journalism, and what he calls universal comprehension, is based on a prior and tragic silence or *closure*. Only he could have said whether the "ténèbres et échecs" (those shadows and failures) he envisioned for himself in the fate of his days and nights were ineluctably associated. Since Desnos closes his whole poetic system within itself, we cannot know if the closed doors represent only our own exclusion from knowledge and vision, or the poet's as well.

In the latter case, the escape beyond the individual poem and the individual dream was all along illusory, as the poet seems to indicate in his "Vieille clameur" ("Old noise"):

Au flanc de la montagne se flêtrit l'édelweiss
L'édelweiss qui fleurit dans mon rêve . . .

(On the side of the mountain the edelweiss withers
The edelweiss which flowers in my dream . . . )

This kind of withering casts doubt not only on the notion of companionship in his adventure, which he had done all along, but on the notion of the voyage itself. If it is only in the dream that the flower can bloom, what possible real link can be perceived between the sleeping and the waking worlds? Perhaps, in his earlier surrealist years, Desnos might not have asked to bring a proof out beyond the universe of the marvelous as would an ordinary traveler; perhaps that universe would have seemed then a sufficient ground of faith, its importance clearly visible from any point *within* itself. At this point, however, he is already reacting against the reliance on what he sees as purely immaterial, a reaction which was to culminate in his diatribe in the *Troisième manifeste* of 1930 against what he called Breton's too limited mysticism.

Now the adventure, formerly marked as the adventure of dream, becomes itself identified with the epic voyage of language while the poems focus endlessly on the question of their own poetic essence and poetic technique. Throughout the collection, the voyage of language is haunted by an interior misfortune: the poem of day beginning becomes finally the poem of night and separation, the poet dreaming by the fireside becomes the exhausted traveler who sees only the corpse of the mermaids, until now the companions and guides of his adventure. A desperate solitude invades the space of the dream, which is the space of the poem.

The trees against whose backdrop the poetic drama unfolded shed their leaves in the poet's mouth, which was once the source of brilliant language, and the flower he attempted to bring back in order to prove the marvelous dream withers away as he descends again from the summit. At last, the doors of the dream appear as closed, the voyage of language as useless, and the only possible metamorphosis as one of silence into silence.

## Novelistic Structures

Of narrative assertion and denial, both linguistic and thematic, there are several striking forms. For example, the irrelevance of focus in an entire passage indicated only at its conclusion: "Forests hacked through with a knife, stretches of vines and great trees, prairies, snowy steppes, fights against Indians, stolen sleds, slain deer, you haven't seen the invisible corsair pass by."Or again, the mockingly forgetful tone which cancels out all the preceding statements: "Corsair Sanglot reaches port. The breakwater is of granite, the customs house of while marble. And what silence. What was I talking about? About Corsair Sanglot. He reaches the port, the breakwater is of porphyry and the customs house of molten lava . . . and what silence over that scene." Here, the simplicity of the repeated "silence," which easily outweighs the importance of the "untruth," almost makes us overlook the denial within the paragraph, as if the author really were so engaged in his own lyricism as to merit an excuse for changing unimportant details—a further trick, insulting and successful, since the passage plays on our own lyric sensibility.

Readers will be obliged to feel alienated from a straight narrative line when the story cuts off at the precise point of highest interest. The device is scarcely aimed at a direct communication by the written word. Desnos mocks us, his hero, and himself:

> "Corsair Sanglot undertakes, Corsair Sanglot begins, Corsair
> Sanglot, Corsair, Corsair Sanglot.
> The woman I love, the woman, ah! I was going to write her
> name.
> I was going to write: "I was going to say her name."
> Count, Robert Desnos, count the number of times you have
> used the words "marvelous," "magnificent . . . "[6]

By his circularities, haltings, and change of tone, Desnos stands outside his writing and forces us into the same position. The disengagement is intensified by the author's insistence not just on the dizzying foreground of the text where we are accustomed to concentrate our attention, but on the pre-foreground, so to speak. Our gaze is directed toward the ink on the author's fingers or on the paper, toward the actual pen and the inkstand, so that the impossibility of equating object and expression is greatly aggravated. Desnos effectively communicates to us his own vision of the manuscript as an arid plain, and of books as an actual cemetery of words. Whatever is going on in his mind, it is rarely obvious on the surface of the text, which is all we are given to see.

To some extent, of course, Desnos' attempt to show himself as disengaged from what he writes can be associated with the similar attempt of the "new novelists" in their ironic techniques of interruption, suspension, contradiction, omission, etc. In each case the illusion of literature is to be destroyed both for the author and for the reader—but Desnos seems more deliberately self-conscious in his style ("Count, Robert Desnos, count . . . ") and more elusive. The process can be compared to the logical category called the *self-controverting discourse*, by which the speaker shows, even in making an explicit statement, that he disbelieves what he states or is not primarily interested in it, thus canceling out his first meaning to make way for another meaning.

Among all the other techniques of distancing the reader from the narration, the object from its names, and the scene from the description, the most essential one touches the one thing Desnos takes most seriously: "But all hail to you, whose existence grants a supernatural joy to my days. I love you even just from the sound of your name." We know from exterior evidence whom he is addressing, but since he does not reveal the name on the page itself we are shut out once more; the gap between the written and the audible is already great. When it is emphasized, as it is here, especially in combination with the chasm deliberately provoked between those who do not have privileged knowledge and those who do, the intention of distance is clear.

Furthermore, all the real action and the summits of lyric description seem to take place in the future, or are referred there. Even if we might have hoped to share this future by our enthusiasm for the text, the ground slips out from under us as the narration is once more situated, by a simple tense change, at a permanent remove. We are thus forced to acknowledge that we have been plunged into the realm, not of the real, but of the poetic, or, of the semiotic. Thus our interest in narrative is transferred to that other realm on which the techniques of Desnos seem to insist.

> And the pearl eternally attached to the rudder will be astonished
> that the boat remains eternally immobile under an ocean of oak
> without suspecting the magnificent fate met by its equals on the
> civilized earth, in the towns where the bus boys have sky-colored jackets.
> I shall leave for the coast where no ship ever touches; one will
> arrive with a black flag at its stern. The rocks will make way. I
> shall climb aboard.
> And from then on my friends, from the height of their lookout
> tower, will spy the deeds and gestures of the bands of black
> pennants spread out in the plain, while above them the moon
> will say her prayers. She will count her rosary of stars and
> faraway cathedrals will crumble.

We may prefer to be counted as one of these friends, but we are in any case not to be reassured by the text. *La Liberté ou l'amour!* ends as the sharks are closing in on the boat of Corsair Sanglot, with the inconclusive statement, "It is then that Corsair Sanglot . . . (LA, 118)

Desnos says much later and with some pride that he has learned to write poems whose ends remain as if suspended—but in fact he had already mastered the technique in 1927. In all probability, he never expected us to share with him his brilliant "blind race toward mobile horizons" (LA, 114) and he certainly never intended the horizons to be just the limits of the literary work. None of the surrealists advocated literature as literature, but most demonstrate a faith in the magic of the word even when written and in its evocative power reaching far beyond the horizons of the written. Of all the surrealist poets, and the poets who were at one time surrealists. Desnos seems most often to turn away from his writing and from us. But he was no doubt aware that he would always do so: according to this perspective, perhaps the "mysterious one" of his poems of 1926 and the shadows of 1927 are meant to represent mystery and total darkness only for the readers, the "anonymous mournings" of "Le Poème à Florence" to be griefs unnamed only for us, and the doors of dream never to be open for us at all. The poems are full of closed doors, and the feeling of being shut out pervades everything. "The doors of wonderland are bolted" (DP, 189), says Desnos, predicting future shadows and incommunicability:

> Voici venir les jours où les œuvres sont vaines
> Où nul bientôt ne comprendra ces mots écrits[9]

(DP, p. 188)

> (Behold the approach of days of useless works
> Soon no one will understand these written words)

The evolution of Desnos' writing after the extraordinary poetic novel *La Liberté ou l'amour!* towards a far easier and more "public" kind of verse and the drearily "realistic" and moralizing tone of his later novel, *Le Vin est tiré*, coincides with his departure from surrealism and may be seen to have some relation to his eventual enthusiasm for advertising jingles. Nothing about Desnos seems simple, and nothing seems dull. For example, between the jovial, hard-drinking, infinitely generous, courageous, and obstinate man whose legend has come down to us, and the images of tragedy which abound in his work, devastating its inner reaches, the contrast is extraordinary. This split is undeniably part of his great appeal.

# The Continuity of the Surrealist Adventure

The continuous path of Desnos the surrealist is even clear in the original manuscripts. For example, the minor final changes Desnos made in the early collection of poems called *C'est les bottes de sept lieues cette phrase "Je me vois"* demonstrate the poet's attention to the unbroken line of what are to all appearances his most disconnected and discontinuous poems. Or then, parts of the long and pieced-together epic *The Night of Loveless Nights* cohere, despite the changes in handwriting and form, because of the recurrence of certain obsessive figures, themes, and expressed emotions. Desnos undertook repeatedly his own defense of the continuity of his surrealist spirit beyond the apparent discontinuities of his development, as seen from the outside, and this continuity is supported by internal evidence.

The poems of *C'est les bottes de sept lieues cette phrase "je me vois"* (It's Seven-League Boots, This Sentence "I See Myself"), written in 1926, are linked by the general concern with fate, fear, death: as in the titles "L'Air homicide," "Destinée arbitraire," "Corde," (Homicidal Air, Arbitrary Fate, Cord); in the images of skeletons, eyes ripped out, murder, funerals, coffins, tombs; and in the related theme of voyage stated in the title, for which the most frequent setting is water:[1] "Je vais être noyé!" (I am going to be drowned!)—although the poem quoted, "Corde," would seem to indicate hanging instead. Within each poem, the successive images are linked to each other, so that, for instance, "Destinée arbitraire" moves from the spectacle of the crusades[2] to a closed window through which birds are seen like fish in an aquarium and then like a pretty woman in a store window. The idea of immobility and imprisonment, suggested already in the three closed windows mentioned (including the glass of the aquarium) leads to the figure of a policeman locking handcuffs around the wrists of the poet, statues able to turn away but not to leave their pedestals, and the last immobilized image, that of a beautiful corpse, and the notion of free burial, Suddenly at the end, the poem veers toward the idea of fresh beginnings, when, as an unexpected reversal of the cliché, "I know that my end is near," Desnos writes: "Je sais que mon commencement est proche . . . "[3] (I know my beginning is near . . . ).

The violence of images provides continuity in the long texts, linked by macabre visions and cruelty:

> Un beau corps de femme
> Fait reculer les requins
>
> (A beautiful woman's body
> Makes the sharks turn back)
>> ("Destinée arbitraire")
>
> Avant peu ses deux serres
> M'arracheront les yeux
>
> (Before long her two claws
> will tear out my eyes)
>> ("Porte du second infini")
>
> Ma belle dame mettez vos deux mains
> dans le bec de gaz
>
> (Lovely lady put both your hands
> in the gas burner)
>> ("Que voulez-vous que je vous dise?")
>
> vous êtes perdue si vous ne m'égratignez
> pas un peu
>
> (you are lost if you don't scratch
> me a little)
>> ("Que voulez-vous que je vous dise?")

Le mystérieux concierge enfonce
avec précaution sa clef dans ton œil

(The mysterious concierge carefully
plunges her key in your eye)
   ("Que voulez-vous que je vous dise?")


Et quelque tigre féroce a décalqué
sur ma poitrine le reflet de ses yeux jaunes

(and some savage tiger has transferred to my breast the
reflection of his yellow eyes)
   ("Tes amants et maitresses")

Midi l'heure de l'amour torture délicatement nos oreilles malades.
(Noon the hour of love delicately tortures our sick ears)
   ("Rencontres")


un docteur très savant coud les mains de la prieuse en assurant
qu'elle va dormir.

(a learned doctor sews the hands of the praying woman
together to be sure she'll sleep)
   ("Rencontres")


  In several other cases also, Desnos makes later changes to empha-
size the macabre; for example, in the poem "O Sœurs" and in
*The Night of Loveless Nights*, where a neutral passage, "Toi qui vas
rêvant / Espace ni temps / Et vienne le temps" (You dream along
/ Neither space nor time / And let time come) is dropped for the
gloomier "Cœur qui va rêvant / jusqu'à ce qu'il meure" (Heart that
dreams along / until it dies), and where a "lugubre escalier" becomes

an "escalier ruisselant" (lugubrious staircase ➤ dripping staircase),
an image so strongly implying the image of blood that there is no
need to state it. During the whole period 1924–29, from *Deuil pour
deuil* to "L'Aveugle," a series of images of death, blindness, and fear
is stressed. In spite of the apparently disconnected and lighthearted
nature of his poems: "Mais je suis inventeur d'un téléphone de verre
de Bohème et de tabac anglais (But I'm the inventor of a telephone
of Bohemian glass and English tobacco) the lines joined on to these
are characteristically obsessed: "en relation directe avec la peur!" (in
direct relation to fear!).

*The Night of Loveless Nights*, written in 1928–29 and published in 1930,
is an example of collage in the lyric manner. In spite of its changing tone,
it is poetically unified about the themes of love and dream, of criminals and
prisons, water and bottles, swans, swords, fans, plumes and pens, about
night and dawn, stars and mermaids, phantom ships and phantom heroes,
flowers flourishing and withered. In its final state the poem is composed of
nine or ten different shorter poems—not simply ten different types of verse
forms, but ten different shorter *moments* of writing (judging by the different
handwritings and the colors of ink making up the final collage).[7]

The longest sub-poem, in occasionally stilted alexandrines, sets the text
in a cheerless atmosphere:"Nuit putride et glaciale, épouvantable nuit"
(Putrid and glacial night, appalling night): as it stands, it is divided in three
parts, but it was originally a long poem, as can be judged from the form
and content as well as from the physical appearance of the text, which has
been altered and cut, in order to be re-formed differently. The original
text is first interrupted by a faintly melancholy prose poem on the place of
dream, on the shadows, the solitude, and the immobility characteristic of
the most persistent landscapes of Desnos' surrealist adventure:

> J'habite quand il me plaît un ravin ténébreux . . .
> Le vallon était désert quand j'y vins pour la première fois.
> Nul n'y était venu avant moi. Nul autre que moi ne l'a
> parcouru.

. . .

La saison de l'amour triste et immobile plane en cette solitude.

(DP, p. 220)

(I inhabit when I choose a shadowy ravine . . .
The valley was deserted when I first came there.
No one had come there before me. No other has traversed it.
. . .
The season of sad and immobile love hangs over this solitude.)

Two sub-poems, treating the theme of love with a fair degree of banality, obviously written with great rapidity and facility: "Coucher avec elle" (Sleeping with Her) and "Toujours avoir le plus grand amour pour elle"(Always To Have the Greatest Love for Her) are divided into two fragments each and spliced together, followed by two segments of contrasting alexandrines and then an alternation of the long and short verses of Desnos at his visionary best, written in the style of *Les Ténèbres*:

Blêmes effigies fantômes de marbre dressés dans les palais
    nocturnes
Une lame de parquet craque
Une épée tombe toute seule et se fiche dans le sol
Et je marche sans arrêt à travers une succession
De grandes salles vides dont les parquets cirés ont le reflet de
    l'eau.

(DP, p. 230)

(Pallid effigies marble phantoms risen in the nocturnal palaces
The wooden floor creaks
A sword falls and sticks in the floor
And I walk without stopping through a succession
Of great empty rooms whose polished floors reflect like water.)

A long passage on a macabre hallucination of hands, conveying the rhythm and tone of the most genuine panic reminds us of the "Porte du second infini" found in *C'est les bottes de sept lieues*, a poem on the subject of writing, madness, and fear, dedicated to Antonin Artaud. An obvious breathlessness betrays the genuine emotional center of the poem, which is not only a poem on love, but also on the act of writing itself. The union of these two themes informs the poet's greatest works, and is closely related both to the violent and to the tragic. Doubt and cruelty appear on the surface of the consciousness this time; the threat is still vague but the poet's state of mind is vivid, its expression intensified by the frequent allusion to shadows. The *attente*, the state of waiting often taken as the surrealist equivalent of the state of grace, is more violent than hopeful in this case:

> Les mains sont trompeuses
> Je me souviens encore de mains blanches dans l'obscurité
> étendues sur une table dans l'attente
>
> . . .
>
> Ah! même ma main qui écrit
> Un couteau! une arme! un outil!
> Tout sauf écrire!
> Du sang du sang!
>
>         (*DP*, p. 232)

> (The hands deceive
> I still remember white hands in the darkness
> stretched out on a table waiting
>
> . . .
>
> Ah! even my hand writing
> A knife! a weapon! a tool!
> Anything except writing!
> Blood blood!)

The association often made in *Les Ténèbres* between dream and withered flowers, dry straw, or broken glass pervades the next section of the poem:

Eglantines flétries[7] parmi les herbiers
O feuilles jaunes

. . .

Verre pilé, boiseries pourries, rêves interminables, fleurs flétries

(*DP*, p. 233)

(Sweetbriars withered among the lofts
O yellow leaves

. . .

Shattered glass, rotted wood, interminable dreams, withered flowers)

A mysterious white hand reaching out to his forehead through the darkness poses no threat, and gives no sign of the deception one might connect with the withering of leaves and flowers; rather the hand seems linked to the promise implied in the ensuing image of an invisible bird of paradise, as if the innocence of love were able to create a world beyond shadows and death. But Desnos still consciously inflicts a certain cruelty in this poem. The wings of a bird imprisoned in the room where he lies dreaming pinion his own arm, as the nightmare becomes forever inseparable from the promise of dream. A litany of dawn and night concludes in shriveled thoughts and desires compared to withered fans ("maints éventails flétris") seen falling on the landing of a stair. The image of the stairs is a constant in the poetry of Desnos, particularly in relation to the themes of adventure and dreaming; the landing represents the cessation of reverie; the fall of the heroic flight. It is clear from these remarks that the memory of Mallarmé haunts Desnos' imagination, as is obvious also in his drawings.

Finally, the initial poem starts again with a plea from the poet to himself for silence: "Tais-toi, pose la plume et ferme les oreilles" (*DP*, p. 234) (Be silent, put down your pen and stop your ears). The tone diminishes in volume, the poetic reduction matching the fading of the sky until Desnos at

last invokes, in the final lines, "la sirène et l'étoile à grands cris . . . O Ré-
volte!" (*DP*, p. 235) (the mermaid and the star with loud cries . . . O Re-
volt!). The rebellion against the halt of dream may or may not result in a
renewal of poetry: as is the case in some of the most interesting surrealist
works, neither the reader nor the poet is sure of the "real" ending of the
poem. The spectacle and the drama move away from us, to a less artificial
realm than that of the page.

   In what must be one of the oddest collections of partial poems ever made
into a conglomerate whole, Desnos gives us an autobiography of style and
themes, unevenly interesting, occasionally exaggerated to the point of self-
parody. *The Night of Loveless Nights* would not hold together at all, were it
not for the recurring figures in this landscape: it is a tour de force, an ex-
periment in combinations. Approximately one-fourth of the final poem is on
the aesthetic level of *Les Ténèbres*, and that is the freest part; that he should
have placed it alongside the often badly strained alexandrines is an indica-
tion of his attitude toward poetry as a flexible witness to changing moods.

## Love and Living

   The early Desnos considered himself above all a poet of love and of a
particular love, which formed the subject of all he wrote. "No, love is not
dead," one of the most powerful poems in *A la mystérieuse* ends with these
lines where surrealist pride and personal simplicity meet:

>   . . . moi qui ne suis ni Ronsard ni Baudelaire
>   Moi qui suis Robert Desnos et qui pour t'avoir connue et aimée,
>   Les vaux bien.
>   Moi qui suis Robert Desnos, pour t'aimer
>   Et qui ne veux pas attacher d'autre réputation à ma mémoire sur
>   la terre méprisable.

>   ( . . . I who am neither Ronsard nor Baudelaire

I who am Robert Desnos and who, for having known you and
loved you, am their equal.
I who am Robert Desnos, in order to love you,
Wanting to attach no other reputation to my memory on this
despicable earth.)

What then is the relation between the actual text and the adventure of
dream, the supposedly equivalent of poetry? Do the closed doors in the ear-
ly collection *Les Ténèbres* have a necessary link with the paralyzed landscape
visible in the late collection of *Contrée?* Is the admitted poetic impotence
within the enforced limitations of the latter "real" landscape found after the
early dream has subsided, prefigured in the laments of loneliness and emp-
tiness at the center of the surrealist theater of shadows "the solitary trees
of the theater"? To what extent did Desnos finally discover himself to be a
"free" poet, in spite of the paralyzed and frozen landscape about him?

The statements made by Desnos himself are questions rather than asser-
tions. His style remains one of a chosen ambiguity; his earliest and strongest
works seem to have no exterior conclusion and to suppose no interior clo-
sure. In that they fit our contemporary state of mind. But in the later poems,
the framework is clear, and the landscape limited, while the poetry itself
acquires the formal limitations of rhyme scheme and pattern which might
seem the parallel of that landscape. We might think of the evolution of Paul
Eluard and of Louis Aragon to a more formal and easier, more predictable,
scheme of poetry after their first, difficult and surrealist verse, in the interest
of the majority of readers and partly for political reasons. In fact, Desnos
always wrote alexandrines on the side, for which he was greatly criticized
by Breton. One may see him writing, in these last poems, a pathetic and
fixed end to his own early ambiguities, on which all the force of his surreal-
ist summons seemed to depend.

In a voluntary contrast to his praise of the unknown, of the mysterious and
the tenebrous, his static portraits of mythical personages such as the nymphs
Calixto and Alcestes and his still pictures of a clear and petrified landscape
(such as "Le Coteau," "Le Cimetière," "La Clairière," "La Caverne," "La

Sieste," "La Ville," "La Maison" in *Contrée*) are as shocking to a surrealist-oriented sensibility as is the surrealist attitude to a non-surrealist sensibility. That the subtle critic of the cinema should forsake movement for portraiture and for still life (or more precisely, "nature morte"), is the most difficult of all desertions for the admirers of his early period.

And that he should have taken this step consciously, informing us of it, is the final stumbling block. To experience all the ambiguous potentialities of surrealism at its most mobile and most complex and then to go beyond them to a fixed form is surely as extraordinary as the choice of shipwreck which Desnos made explicitly so many times. But shipwreck is no less logical than navigation, he claims, and perhaps no less adventurous a choice. Desnos is no more trapped in his own shipwreck than his heroine the mermaid is trapped in the sea. On the other side of the poems of obvious adventure, Desnos claims to find another adventure; beyond all the surrealist poetry of freedom, he claims the possible existence of the free poet.

The eventual alienation of Desnos from his reader comes after we have weathered all the early insults and deliberate deceptions. For the heart-break-ing farewell of the poet to the mermaid in "Sirène-Anémone" prefigures an-other and more final one, that of the poet to the reader, a farewell situated within the fragile, appealing, and often tragic temporality of the work:

> Adieu déjà parmi les heures de porcelaine
> (And now farewell among the porcelain hours)

But neither the poet's separation from the mermaid, nor the reader's final exclusion from the imaginative adventure place any limit upon the adventure of the text. In the last message from Desnos in the concentration camp at Theresienstadt to his wife Youki on January 7, 1945, he states with complete conviction that for him, the relation of the poet to poetry is never touched by exterior circumstances, that the faith in poetic adventure can still be completely justified, in the long run and in the smallest detail, in spite of everything else. He sends his friendly greetings "à tous ceux que j'ai admirés," to all those he has admired, and then: "As for the rest, I find a shelter in poetry. It is really 'the horse running on the crests of the mountains' which Rrose Sélavy mentions in one of her poems and which I have found to be justified word for word." ( O, 1279) It is as if, at last, the two terms of freedom and love (*La Liberté ou l'amour!*) had found their resolution—and even, perhaps, their identification—on the summits of the surrealist imagination, where finally no distinction was to be made between mermaid, star, and anemone, between open sea and ice floe, between the mountain, the desert, and the page or the poem.

For in spite of the self-doubting test, the adventure was always to be one of language, with those doubts a source of primary action and continuing complexity. Desnos made, in 1926, a "Confession d'un enfant du siècle," which at once bears perhaps the most telling witness to that active language and makes the most fitting, because most ambiguous, answer to the question of his being remembered: "The only tense of the verb is the present indicative." Of that sentence he might have said, as of his love poetry which finds its source in the same sentiment, that he wanted to be remembered by it only; like a serious gamble on presence.

> un oeil fermé
> une porte fermée
> et pas de clef.
>
> > (Destinée arbitraire)

> (an eye closed
> a door closed
> and no key.)

# NOTES

Some of the translations in this essay differ from those in the chapter of poems; there is room in Desnos' poetry, as in all great poetry, for many interpretations.

1. Georges Neveux, "Robert Desnos," *Confluences*, no. 7 Sept. 1945, p. 680.

2. *Une Vague de rêves*, privately printed, 1924. English translations from Maurice Nadeau, *The History of Surrealism* (Macmillan Co., 1967), pp. 82–83.

3. Ibid.

4. "Le Surréalisme en 1929," *Variété*, June, 1929.

5. Katharine Conley, *Robert Desnos, Surrealism, and the Marvelous of Everyday Life*, p. 6.

6. "Le Paysage" is complemented also by another poem of utopia, "L'Asile," (The Resting Place), where wisdom and action, adventure in the waking and sleeping worlds mingle in the community of men and poets:

Où le sage s'éveille, où le héros s'endort.
Que le rêve de l'un et la réalité
De l'autre soient présents bientôt dans la cite.

(C, p. 57)

(Where the wise man wakes, where the hero sleeps,
Let the dream of one and the other's
Reality be present soon within the city.)

It is in this combination that Desnos finally puts his hope.

7.  Another important example of the same process appears in *LA*, pp. 82–85 where the intensified gaze is concentrated on one object, in this case sponges (an object familiar to the readers of surrealist literature, particularly Aragon's *Le Paysan de Paris*, where the barber's sponge serves as the soft form of coral, as the intermediary between the ocean, privileged place of encounter, and the erotic imaginings of the city dweller). The sudden *ritardando* in rhythm is paralleled by the sudden halting of a second boat (this incident reminiscent both of Breton's image of the locomotive suddenly stopped in the forest and of his wish that all machines might be immobilized by water). Half symbolist and half mocking, the images of the North Pole where the ship is caught in the ice floes and the human pilgrimage ends at a wall of ice are found respectively in Apollinaire's play *Couleur du temps* and Gide's *Le Voyage d'Urien*. The latter, with its extraordinary contradiction of the preceding lyricism, its allusion to the mermaids, to the mirages, and to the "fumes" of the dream, is like Desnos' later references to his own surrealist dreams in the poems of *Contrée*. The *Envoi* begins:

Madame! je vous ai trompée:
nous n'avons pas fait ce voyage.
Nous n'avons pas vu les jardins
ni les flamants roses des plages;

Madam! I deceived you:
we didn't take this trip.
We haven't seen the gardens
Or the pink flamingoes of the beaches

(André Gide, *Romans*, Pléiade ed. [Gallimard, 1958], p. 66.)

In this fashion, Desnos' use of this imagery already calls into play a complex series of allusions, and begins to function as one of his idiosyncratic myths. (One could also compare the tone of certain parts of the Gide sotie with that of *La Liberté ou l'amour!*)

8.  The handwriting changes from upright to slanting, from closely spaced to cramped, with several new beginnings plainly marked. The difference has never been explained, but it is clear that the writing paper is as the handwritings, including grey, blue-green, light blue, pink, and yellowed once-white paper, and either bears the headings of *La Hune* or *Paris-Matinal*, or is unmarked; all these are interspersed, most probably showing the collage-type composition of the famous poem, whose title was originally in English only.

# BIBLIOGRAPHY

# Works by Desnos

Except where indicated, the place of publication is Paris.

*Deuil pour deuil.* Kra, 1924.

*C'est les bottes de sept lieues cette phrase 'Je me vois'.* Galerie Simon, 1926.

*La Liberté ou l'amour!* Kra, 1927.

*Corps et biens.* N.R.F., 1930 (contains most of the poems from 1919 to 1929).

*The Night of Loveless Nights.* Anvers: Privately printed, 1930.

*Les Sans cou.* Privately printed, 1934.

*Fortunes.* Gallimard, 1942 (contains poems written after 1929).

*Le Vin est tiré.* Gallimard, 1943.

*Etat de veille.* Gallimard, 1947.

*Le Bain avec Andromède.* Flore, 1944.

*Contrée.* Robert Godet, 1944 (reprinted with *Calixto*, Gallimard, 1962).

*Trente chante-fables pour les enfants sages.* Librairie Grund, 1944.

*Felix Labisse.* Sequana, Les peintres d'imagination, 1945.

*La Place de l'étoile* (antipoème). Rodez, collection "Humour," 1945 (written in 1927).

*Choix de poemes.* Poèmes  Editions Minuit, 1946.

*Nouvelles inédites. Rue de la Gaité. Voyage en Bourgogne. Précis de cuisine pour les jours heureux.* Les Treize Epis, 1947.

411

*Les Trois Solitaires. Longtemps après hier. Poèmes pour Marie. A la Hollande. Mon tombeau.* Les Treize Epis, 1947.

*Oeuvres posthumes.* Les Treize Epis, 1947.

*Chantefables et chantefleurs.* (ed. Jean-Claude Silbermann). Grund, 1952.

*De l'érotisme considéré dans ses manifestations écrites et du point de vue de l'esprit moderne.* Cercle des Arts, 1953.

[Jehan Sylvius et Pierre de Ruynes.] *La Papesse du diable.* Eric Losfeld, 1966.

*Domaine public.* Gallimard, 1953 (includes *The Night of Loveless Nights* and *Corps et biens* of 1930 and *Fortunes* of 1942, with a selection of other writings).

*Mines de rien.* Broder, 1960.

*Calixto, suivi de Contrée.* Gallimard, 1962.

*La Liberté ou l'amour!* Reprint, with *Deuil pour deuil.* Gallimard, 1962.

*Cinéma,* ed. André Tchernia. Gallimard, 1966.

*Corps et biens.* Gallimard, collection "Poésie," 1968.

*Fortunes.* Gallimard, collection "Poésie," 1969.

*Destinée arbitraire,* ed. M. C. Dumas. Gallimard, collection "Poésie," 1975 (includes a selection of previously published texts and several texts published for the first time: in particular, *Peine perdue* and *Bagatelles,* as well as a group of resistance poems under the title *Ce coeur qui haïssait la guerre*).

*Oeuvres.* (ed. Marie-Claire Dumas. Paris: Editions Gallimard, 1999 (Best critical "complete" works of Robert Desnos)

*Les Rayons et les ombres : Cinéma.* Edition établie et présentée par Marie-Claire Dumas avec la collaboration de Nicole Cervelle-Zonca. Paris: Gallimard, 1992.


See also such journals and pamphlets as *Documents, Les Feuilles libres, Littérature,* and *La Révolution surréaliste,* as well as the newspapers mentioned here to which Desnos was a regular contributor.

## Selected Works by Desnos in English

*Mourning for Mourning* (in*)* *The Automatic Muse: Surrealist Novels* (ed.) Terry Hale & Ian White. (tr.) Terry Hale. London: BCM Atlas Press (Atlas Anti-Classics), 1994, 2007. (www.atlaspress.co.uk)

*Liberty or Love!* (tr.) Terry Hale. London: BCM Atlas Press, 1993, 2007. (www.atlaspress.co.uk)

*Voice of Robert Desnos: Selected Poems.* (tr.) William Kulik. Sheep Meadow Press, 2005.

## Selected Works on Desnos

## Books and prefaces

Berger, Pierre. *Robert Desnos*. Poètes d'aujourd'hui. Seghers, 1949.

Barnett, Marie-Claire, Eric Robertson, and Nigel Saint. *Robert Desnos. Surrealism in the 21$^{st}$ Century* (Modern French Identities) Bern: International Academic Publishers, Peter Lang, 2006. Articles by the editors, and Roger Cardinal, Michael G. Kelly, Katharine Conley, Marie-Claire Dumas, Philippe Met, Andrew Rothwell, Georgiana MM. Colville, Mary Ann Caws, Adelaide Russo, Jonathan Eburne, Renée Rièse Hubert, Elza Adamowicz, Ramona Fotiade, Fern Malkine-Falvey. Contains 20 articles by Desnos, published in *Le Soir* in 1927-8.

Bertelé, René. Prefaces to *Domaine public* and to *Corps et biens*.

Buchole, Rosa. *L'Evolution poétique de Robert Desnos*. Brussels: Palais des Académies, 1956.

Carpentier Alejo. *Tientos y diferéncias*. Montevideo, 1967 (with two so-called "inéditos" on Lautréamont and on the political situation in Cuba previously published in the one issue of the journal *Iman*. 1931).

Caws, Mary Ann. *The Poetry of Dada and Surrealism: Aragon, Breton, Tzara,*

*Eluard, Desnos.* Princeton: Princeton University Press, 1970; reprinted in 1971.

Caws, Mary Ann. *The Surrealist Voice of Robert Desnos.* Amherst: University of Massachusetts, 1977. Includes large selection of translations.

Conley, Katharine & Marie-Claire Dumas. *Robert Desnos pour l'an 2000. Colloque de Cerisy-la-Salle.* Paris: Gallimard, 2000.

Conley, Katharine. *Robert Desnos, Surrealism, and the Marvelous in Everyday Life.* University of Nebraska Press, 2004.

Desanti, Dominique. *Robert Desnos, le roman d'une vie.* Paris: Mercure de France, 1999.

Desnos, Robert, Marie-Claire Dumas, & Roger Dadoun. *L'Herne: Robert Desnos.* Fayard, 1999.

Desnos, Youki. *Les Confidences de Youki.* Fayard, 1957. (1999)

Dumas, Marie-Claire. *Etude de "Corps et biens" de Robert Desnos.* Librairie H. Champion, 1984.

———. *Robert Desnos: Ou, l'exploration des limites.* (Bibliothèque du XXe siècle). Klincksieck, 1980.

———. Poétiques de Robert Desnos: En hommage à a Marie-Claire Dumas: actes de la journee d'etudes journée d'études du 25 Novembre 1995. Contains articles from the *Lettres françaises* and the Swiss journal *Labyrinthe* about the famous « Last poem, » and the fac-simile of articles by Desnos about the Hispanic world.

———, Carmen Vasquez (ed.) *Robert Desnos, le poeté libre.* Indigo/Universite de Picardie Jules Verne, 2007.

Egger, Anne. *Robert Desnos.* Paris : Fayard, 2008.

Ibañez, Iris Acacia. *Apuntaciones estilísticas sobre "Chantefables et Chantefleurs."* La Plata: Centro de Estudios de Estilística Literária, 1964.

Matthews, J. H. *Surrealist Poetry in France.* Syracuse University Press, 1969. journée

———. *Surrealism and the Novel.* University of Michigan Press, 1966.

Murat, Michael. Robert Desnos: *Les Grands jours du poeté.* Paris: Corti, 1988.

# Articles

Mary Ann Caws. "Techniques of Alienation in the Early Novels of Robert Desnos." *Modern Language Quarterly*, vol. 28, no. 4 (December 1967), pp. 473–77.

———. "Robert Desnos and the Flasks of Night." *Yale French Studies*, Intoxication issue, 1974, pp. 108-19.

Marie-Claire Dumas. "Un scénario de Robert Desnos." *Etudes cinématographiques*, nos. 38–39, 1965. (Issues devoted to *Surréalisme et cinema*.)

Tatiana Greene. "Le Merveilleux surréaliste de Robert Desnos." *French Review*, November 1966.

Margit Rowell. "Magnetic Fields: The Poetics." *Joan Miró*. Guggenheim Museum (catalogue), 1972 (especially pp. 55–60, on Desnos).

Jean Tortel. "Robert Desnos aujourd'hui." *Critique*, August-September 1965.

Théodore Fraenkel and Samy Simon. "Biographie de Robert Desnos." *Litterair Paspoort*, Tweede Jaarg., no. 7 (January 1947).

See also the issues of *Signes du temps*, no. 5, 1951, and *Simoun*, nos. 22–23, 1956, Oran, both devoted to Desnos.

*Europe 50*, nos. 517–18 (May, June 1972), has previously unpublished material and a wide range of articles concerning Desnos.

*Le Siècle éclaté: dada, surréalisme et avant-gardes*. Minard, Lettres Modernes, no. 1, articles by Marie-Claire Dumas, Sydney Lévy, Mary Ann Caws on Desnos; no. 2, by Barbara Ann Kwant.

## Official Website for Robert Desnos

www.robertdesnos.asso.fr

Run by the Association des amis de Robert Desnos

## Music/Disque

### CD

*La belle saison est proche...* textes de Robert Desnos, musiques de Wiener, Kosmer, Poulenc, Barraud, Racaille, Boulanger, Spanos, Perrone, & Bouchot. Durée 60' 43 booklet in two languages: Français, Anglais, Maguelone, 2006.

### DVD

*Robert Desnos, Inédits.* Fabrice Maze, including Jean Barral's film *La belle saison est proche.* April, 2008.

# TRANSLATORS

**Mary Ann Caws**: is Distinguished Professor of Comparative Literature, English, and French at the Graduate School of the City University of New York. Her many areas of interest in 20th-century Avant-Garde literature and art include Surrealism, Dada, the poets René Char, André Breton, Robert Desnos, Virginia Woolf and the Bloomsbury Group, and artists including Robert Motherwell, Joseph Cornell, and Pablo Picasso. Author/editor/translator of over 50 books and numerous essays her works include: *The Surrealist Voice of Robert Desnos, Capital of Pain* by Paul Eluard (with Nancy Kline & Patricia Terry), *Mad Love* by André Breton, *Selected Poems of René Char* (with Tina Jolas), *Surprised in Translation, Poems of André Breton* (with Jean-Pierre Cauvin), and many others. She is currently working on (with Nancy Kline): *Furor and Mystery & Other Poems* by René Char for publication by Black Widow Press.

**Terry Hale:** Dr. Hale teaches at the Performance Translation Centre at the University of Hull developing research programs in this neglected field. His books, translations, & essays are numerous and widely acclaimed. They include: *Liberty or Love!* by Robert Desnos, *Four Dada Suicides: Selected Writings of Cravan, Vaché, Rigaut, and Torma, The Automatic Muse: Surrealist Novels by Desnos, Leiris, Peret, and Limbour,* and Huysmans's *The Damned.*

**Martin Sorrell:** is Professor of Literary Translation at the University of Exeter. Dr. Sorrell has published extensively in the field of translation studies. Recent publications include: Verlaine: *Selected Poems,* Rimbaud: *Collected Poems,* and *Claude de Burine: Words Have Frozen Over.*

**Bill Zavatsky:** Poet/writer/translator Bill Zavatsky's works include translations of André Breton's *Earthlight* (with Zack Rogow), *The Poems of A. O. Barnbabooth* (with Ron Padgett, revised edition to be published in 2008 by Black Widow Press), and volumes of his own poems including: *Theory of Rain & Other Poems.* He teaches English at Trinity School in NYC.

**Patricia Terry:** Dr. Terry's recent works include: *Lancelot and the Land of the Distant Isles; Or, The Book of Galehaut Retold* (with Samuel Rosenberg), *Capital of Pain* (with Mary Ann Caws & Nancy Kline), and *Words of Silence.* She is currently working on an augmented/revised edition of her book: *Poems of Jules Laforgue* to be published by Black Widow Press.

**Katharine Conley:** Dr. Conley teaches in the French Dept. at Dartmouth College. Recent works include: *Automatic Women: The Representation of Woman in Surrealism,* and her internationally acclaimed *Robert Desnos, Surrealism, and the Marvelous of Everyday Life.*

**Jonathan Eburne:** Dr. Eburne teaches Comparative Literature and English at Penn. State University. His recent publications include: *Surrealism and the Art of Crime.*

**Timothy Adès:** Teaches at Derby College. His writings include translations from the French, Spanish, German, and Greek. Recent publications include: *How to be a Grandfather* by Victor Hugo, and *Sonnets of the Resistance and Other poems by Jean Cassou, Louis Aragon, & Alistair Eliot.*

**Stephen Romer:** Poet and lecturer at the University of Tours in France. His recent poetry collections include: *Idols, Plato's Ladder,* and *Tribute.* He has translated many French poets including: Philippe Jaccottet, Jean Tardieu, Jacques Dupin, and Paul Valéry. He is also the editor of *20th-Century French Poems.*

**Kenneth Rexroth:** (1905–1982) was a widely acclaimed author, poet, translator, and critical essayist. His extensive translations cover many authors including: Pierre Reverdy, Li Ch'ing Chao, Robert Desnos, and many more.

**Paul Auster:** Poet, editor, translator, screenwriter, and film director. Recent works include: *Travels in the Scriptorium, The Brooklyn Follies, and the Notebooks of Joseph Joubert.*

# TITLES FROM BLACK WIDOW PRESS

**TRANSLATION SERIES**
*Chanson Dada: Selected Poems by Tristan Tzara*
Translated & edited by Lee Harwood

*Approximate Man & Other Writings*, by Tristan Tzara
Translated & edited by Mary Ann Caws

*Poems of André Breton: A Bilingual Anthology*
Translated & edited by Jean-Pierre Cauvin and Mary Ann Caws

*Last Love Poems of Paul Eluard*
Translated with an introduction by Marilyn Kallet

*Capital of Pain,* by Paul Eluard
Translated by Mary Ann Caws, Patricia Terry, and Nancy Kline

*Love, Poetry (L'amour la poésie)*, by Paul Eluard
Translated with an introduction by Stuart Kendall

*The Sea & Other Poems*, by Guillevic
Translated by Patricia Terry with an introduction by Monique Chefdor

*Essential Poems & Writings of Robert Desnos: A Bilingual Anthology*
Edited by Mary Ann Caws

*Essential Poems & Writings of Joyce Mansour: A Bilingual Anthology*
Translated with an introduction by Serge Gavronsky

*Eyeseas (Les Ziaux)* by Raymond Queneau
Translated with an introduction by Daniela Hurezanu & Stephen Kessler
[forthcoming]

*Poems of A. O. Barnabooth* (Valery Larbaud)
Translated with an introduction by Ron Padgett and Bill Zavatsky
[forthcoming]

*Art Poétique* by Guillevic
translated by Maureen Smith
[forthcoming]

## MODERN POETRY SERIES

*An Alchemist With One Eye on Fire*
Clayton Eshleman

*Archaic Design*
Clayton Eshleman

*Backscatter: New and Selected Poems*
John Olson
[forthcoming]

*Crusader-Woman* by Ruxandra Cesereanu
Translated by Adam Sorkin. Introduction by Andrei Codrescu
[forthcoming]

*Grindstone of Rapport: A Clayton Eshleman Reader*
Clayton Eshleman
[forthcoming]


## NEW POETS SERIES

*Signal from Draco: New and Selected Poems*
Mebane Robertson


## LITERARY THEORY/BIOGRAPHY SERIES

*Revolution of the Mind: The Life of André Breton*
(revised and augmented edition)
by Mark Polizzotti
[forthcoming]


# www.blackwidowpress.com

All Black Widow Press titles are printed on acid-free paper and bound into a sewn and glued binding. Manufactured in the United States of America.

www.blackwidowpress.com

This book was set in Simoncini Garamond. The titling font is Aculida, a modernistic typeface used by many of the Dadaists in their typographic artworks.

typeset & designed by Windhaven Press
www.windhaven.com

green
press
INITIATIVE

Black Widow Press is committed to preserving ancient forests and natural resources. We elected to print *Essential Writings Of Robert Desnos* on 50% post consumer recycled paper, processed chlorine free. As a result, for this printing, we have saved:

21 Trees (40' tall and 6-8" diameter)
8,803 Gallons of Wastewater
3,540 Kilowatt Hours of Electricity
970 Pounds of Solid Waste
1,906 Pounds of Greenhouse Gases

Black Widow Press made this paper choice because our printer, Thomson-Shore, Inc., is a member of Green Press Initiative, a nonprofit program dedicated to supporting authors, publishers, and suppliers in their efforts to reduce their use of fiber obtained from endangered forests.

For more information, visit www.greenpressinitiative.org